Acts

Westminster Bible Companion

Series Editors

Patrick D. Miller
David L. Bartlett

Acts

PAUL W. WALASKAY

 Westminster John Knox Press
Louisville, Kentucky

Book design by Publishers' WorkGroup
Cover design by Drew Stevens

First edition
Published by Westminster John Knox Press
Louisville, Kentucky

This book is printed on acid-free paper that meets the American National Standards Institute Z39.48 standard. ∞

PRINTED IN THE UNITED STATES OF AMERICA

98 99 00 01 02 03 04 05 06 07 — 10 9 8 7 6 5 4 3 2 1

Library of Congress Cataloging-in-Publication Data

Walaskay, Paul W., date.
    Acts / Paul W. Walaskay. — 1st ed.
        p.   cm. — (Westminster Bible companion)
    Includes bibliographical references.
    ISBN 0-664-25261-3 (alk. paper)
        1. Bible. N.T. Acts—Commentaries.   I. Title.   II. Series.
BS2625.3.W36   1998
226.6'077—dc21   97-38140

Contents

Part 3. PAUL'S ARREST, TRIAL,
AND JOURNEY TO ROME
Acts 21:17–28:31

10. Paul on Trial (I)   197
Acts 21:17–23:32

11. Paul on Trial (II)   212
Acts 23:33–24:27

12. Paul on Trial (III)   219
Acts 25:1–12

13. Paul on Trial (IV)   222
Acts 25:13–26:32

Series Foreword

This series of study guides to the Bible is offered to the church and more specifically to the laity. In daily devotions, in church school classes, and in listening to the preached word, individual Christians turn to the Bible for a sustaining word, a challenging word, and a sense of direction. The word that scripture brings may be highly personal as one deals with the demands and surprises, the joys and sorrows, of daily life. It also may have broader dimensions as people wrestle with moral and theological issues that involve us all. In every congregation and denomination, controversies arise that send ministry and laity alike back to the Word of God to find direction for dealing with difficult matters that confront us.

A significant number of lay women and men in the church also find themselves called to the service of teaching. Most of the time they will be teaching the Bible. In many churches, the primary sustained attention to the Bible and the discovery of its riches for our lives have come from the ongoing teaching of the Bible by persons who have not engaged in formal theological education. They have been willing, and often eager, to study the Bible in order to help others drink from its living water.

This volume is part of a series of books, the Westminster Bible Companion, intended to help the laity of the church read the Bible more clearly and intelligently. Whether such reading is for personal direction or for the teaching of others, the reader cannot avoid the difficulties of trying to understand these words from long ago. The scriptures are clear and clearly available to everyone as they call us to faith in the God who is revealed in Jesus Christ and as they offer to every human being the word of salvation. No companion volumes are necessary in order to hear such words truly. Yet every reader of scripture who pauses to ponder and think further about any text has questions that are not immediately answerable simply by reading the text of scripture. Such questions may be about historical and geographical details or about words that are obscure or so loaded with meaning that one cannot tell at a glance what is at stake. They may be about the fundamental meaning of a passage or about what connection a particular text might have to our contemporary world. Or a teacher preparing for a church school class may simply want to know: What should I say about this biblical passage when I have to teach it next Sunday? It is our hope that these volumes, written by teachers and pastors with long experience studying and teaching the Bible in the church, will help members of the church who want and need to study the Bible with their questions.

The New Revised Standard Version of the Bible is the basis for the interpretive comments that each author provides. The NRSV text is presented at the beginning of the discussion so that the reader may have at hand in a single volume both the scripture passage and the exposition of its meaning. In some instances, where inclusion of the entire passage is not necessary for understanding either the text or the interpreter's discussion, the presentation of the NRSV text may be abbreviated. Usually, the whole of the biblical text is given.

We hope this series will serve the community of faith, opening the Word of God to all the people, so that they may be sustained and guided by it.

Introduction

THE ACTS OF THE APOSTLES

In the latter part of the first century a Christian man of letters was gracious enough to spend months, perhaps years, of his life gathering written source materials, carefully organizing the transcribed memories of witnesses, and artistically writing an account of the birth of the greatest religious movement in history. Ironically, one may wonder whether he himself fully appreciated the significance of the events which he chronicled. His narrative covers a span of sixty years, from the advent of Jesus in Bethlehem to the arrival of the Christian proclamation about Jesus in Rome.

The author wrote his "book" on papyrus scrolls, the ordinary literary medium of the time. Since his narrative contained so much information about Jesus and the Christian community, he had to use two scrolls, each about thirty-two feet in length. He carefully designed his work so that scroll one covered the life of Jesus of Nazareth—his birth, ministry, arrest, trial, death, resurrection, and ascension. The second scroll narrated the experiences of Jesus' followers as they took their initial steps toward formation of a Christian community. We do not know the title that the author intended for his book. Some have suggested that he might simply have called it "To Theophilus," the apparent patron of the work who is mentioned in the preface (Luke 1:3; Acts 1:1).

These two scrolls were originally meant to be read as a unified work. However, because this narrative circulated as two scrolls (or books), they became separated in the process of incorporation into early collections of Christian writings (what we now call the canon of the New Testament). The first scroll, because of its focus on the life and ministry of Jesus, became one of the cornerstones of the four Gospels—our Gospel According to Luke. The second scroll began to be read separately as a narrative of the accomplishments, or "acts," of Jesus' apostles. By the end of the second

1

century this book became commonly known as The Acts of the Apostles. Furthermore, the form of the book of Acts (as well as other books of the New Testament) soon changed from scroll to codex, the form of publication we normally think of as a "book"—a sheaf of pages bound together on one side.

This is a study of that second book, with full awareness that Acts is not an afterthought or sequel. The Gospel According to Luke and the Acts of the Apostles were intended by the author to be read as one literary work. We are deeply indebted to that first-century Christian who had the foresight to describe the work of God through Jesus and the church. We stand before the author of the Third Gospel and the Acts of the Apostles in grateful awe as fortunate beneficiaries of this man's monumental task.

WHO WROTE THE
ACTS OF THE APOSTLES?

The Acts of the Apostles is different from other books of the New Testament. Most New Testament books were written as gospel or letter. To be sure, Acts contains the same "good news" (which is what "gospel" means) presented in the first four books of the New Testament and it also contains occasional letters (Acts 15:23–29; 23:26–30). Yet the book of Acts is, strictly speaking, neither gospel nor letter. Rather, it is a historical narrative—the first chronicle of the church which surveys events from the time of Jesus' ascension in Jerusalem to Paul's arrival in Rome.

As I mentioned above, by the second century the form of book production shifted from the scroll to the codex. This popular new form greatly facilitated the distribution and collection of early Christian writings (and remember that until Gutenberg's printing press, about 1440, every copy of a book was handwritten—a "manu-script"). Eventually twenty-seven of these books were gathered and arranged into our New Testament. The placement of Acts as the fifth book in the New Testament appears to have been both intentional and strategic. The Acts of the Apostles functions as a bridge between the Gospels and the letters. It completes the Gospel stories about Jesus and serves as an introduction to the letters of his witnesses (Paul, James, Peter, John).

Who wrote the Third Gospel and the Acts of the Apostles? Because the author never tells us his name, discovering his identity is a bit like solving a mystery. By the end of the second century, readers began to gather and assess evidence from the Acts of the Apostles and from the letters of Paul, coming to the conclusion that the author of this narrative was Luke. They noticed that in the last half of the book of Acts, the personal pronouns used in some of the narrative suddenly switch from the *third* person ("*he* went . . . "; "*they* did . . . ") to the *first*-person plural ("*we* came to . . . "). Moreover, these passages occur in narratives that describe travels with Paul, the missionary to the Gentiles. The "we passages" function as a kind of "calling card" to let the reader know that the author was a participant in the story (also see comment on 16:10). Here is a list of those portions of Acts written in the first person:

16:10–17	from Asia to Macedonia
20:5–21:18	from Macedonia to Asia to Palestine
27:1–28:16	from Palestine to Italy

The content of these passages suggests that the author of the Acts of the Apostles was one of Paul's traveling companions.

The early readers of the New Testament then searched through the letters of Paul in order to discover the identity of this traveling companion. Their search brought them to Luke, whom Paul described as a "fellow worker" (Philemon 24) and "beloved physician" (Col. 4:14). At the very end of his ordeals, Paul himself mentions that all of his friends have deserted him—all except Luke (2 Tim. 4:11). These early Christian readers felt that they had solved the mystery of authorship by concluding that Luke, the companion of Paul, wrote the Third Gospel and Acts of the Apostles. For example, at the end of the second century, Irenaeus of Lyons wrote, "Luke the follower of Paul recorded in a book the gospel that was preached by him" (*Against Heresies* 3.1). Luke has become the traditionally acknowledged author of the work which we now call Luke-Acts.

Many modern interpreters have been unwilling to let matters rest with this seemingly obvious solution. Those who challenge the traditional identification of Luke as the author of the Third Gospel and Acts do so for four major reasons:

1. The "we passages" of Acts were drawn from a written source which our author used in compiling his narrative. It looks like our author has woven three sections of someone's travel diary into his story. He chose not to change the first-person language of the diary in order to retain the excitement and life that an eyewitness brings to a story.
2. The author of Acts apparently knew nothing of Paul's letters. He does not refer to them nor does he describe Paul as a letter writer.

3. The author reflects little of Paul's theology. Absent is Paul's strong conviction about freedom from the law and his understanding of God's atoning work for humankind brought about through the death of Jesus.
4. The author ignores significant historical events in the life of the apostle, such as the gathering and presentation of the collection from Gentile churches for the "saints in Jerusalem" (see comments on 21:1–16).

As one might expect, each of these points has been countered by those who support the traditional perspective:

1. The "we passages" may indeed have been drawn from a travel diary—the diary of our author. The language and style of these passages is coherent with much of the rest of Acts. It is not accidental that toward the end of his narrative Luke draws from his personal experiences as an eyewitness—to "events that have been fulfilled among *us*" (Luke 1:1).
2. Just because Luke did not refer to Paul's letters does not mean he did not know of them. An argument from silence is not the strongest of arguments. We shall discover in our study of Acts several instances where Luke's narrative reflects significant themes found in Paul's letters (see comments on 16:19–34 and 20:17–38).
3. There are several points in the book of Acts where the author reveals a deep understanding of Paul's theology. The way our author narrates stories about Paul often reveals that he has sympathetically internalized his hero's message. Moreover, the understanding of the person and work of Jesus reflected in the book of Acts appears to be neither Paul's nor Luke's, but that of the early church—a proper perspective for the author of Acts.
4. Luke may have had his own apologetic, political, or literary reasons for omitting some of the historical events in the life of Paul. Moreover, events like Paul's collection for the church in Jerusalem may have become a faded memory by the time Luke wrote the Acts of the Apostles (faded, but not entirely absent; see 24:17).

On balance, one could conclude that the author of Acts was not a dogged disciple of the apostle Paul, simply reiterating Pauline pronouncements. Rather, he was Paul's sympathetic biographer weaving the apostle's theological concerns into the story of his life. The theological independence which is evident in Luke's writing speaks well of both the apostle and his biographer. Let us leave open for now the issue of whether or not Luke was in fact a travel companion of Paul and the author of the Acts of the Apostles. The reader is invited to come to his or her own conclusion on this matter after careful consideration of those passages which support and those which challenge the traditional understanding of the authorship of Acts. Therefore, without foreclosing discussion about authorship, we will use the traditional designation of "Luke" as the author of the Third Gospel and the Acts of the Apostles.

Finally, let us return to the description of Luke given in Colossians 4:14. "Luke, the beloved physician." This indicates both Luke's profession and Paul's assessment of his care; he was a "*beloved* physician." In 1882, W. K. Hobart (*The Medical Language of St. Luke*) attempted to prove that the two volumes attributed to Luke were indeed written by a physician. According to Hobart, both volumes pay great attention to the healing miracles of Jesus, Peter, and Paul. Furthermore, he suggested that these healing stories contain detailed descriptions and vocabulary that point to a profound knowledge of ancient medical arts. The title "Luke, the beloved physician" appeared to fit the author of these works.

Almost forty years later, however, one of the great American scholars of Lukan literature, Henry J. Cadbury, published his Harvard dissertation, *The Style and Literary Method of Luke*. His careful analysis of Luke's vocabulary indicated that Luke's medical knowledge appears to be no more sophisticated than that of an educated layman. Furthermore, Luke's interest in healing does not exceed that of the other evangelists. It has been quipped that Dr. Cadbury gained his doctorate by depriving Dr. Luke of his.

TO WHOM, WHERE, AND WHEN WAS ACTS WRITTEN?

While Luke's preface clearly indicates that he addressed his writings to Theophilus, it is not at all certain who Theophilus was. Theophilus, a common Greek name that means "lover of God," might have been a Christian (or a non-Christian) benefactor who wished to have further information regarding the founder and followers of this new sect of Judaism. Some have thought of Theophilus as a Roman official who wanted to make a judgment regarding the legal status of Christianity (Is it really part of the ancient and honored Jewish religion?), or who wanted to render a decision about the case against Paul (Acts 21—28).

It has also been suggested that "Theophilus" was not the name of a real person, but stood for certain "lovers of God." Perhaps Luke was addressing a specific group of Christian readers (his own congregation), or he may have written to all who love God and seek deeper truth regarding the Christian message and mission.

It is impossible to tell where Luke did his writing. Since the book of Acts has a special interest in the major cities of the Roman Empire, and since Luke writes in an urbane manner, he may have settled in one of the important urban centers of the empire to do his writing. Perhaps he wrote from Syrian Antioch (the city that seemed to be the hub for Paul's missionary activities) or from Rome (the goal of the book of Acts and the final destination of Paul). There is general agreement that Luke did not do his writing in Palestine, for he seems unfamiliar with the geography of that part of the Roman Empire.

Assigning a date to Luke's work may be a bit easier. In writing his own Gospel, Luke apparently used the Gospel of Mark as one of his sources; he may have had Mark in mind when he wrote that others "have undertaken to set down an orderly account" (Luke 1:1). If this were the case, then copies of Mark's Gospel may have circulated for a few years before eventually falling into Luke's hands. Scholars generally date Mark's Gospel in the latter years of Nero's reign, 66–68 C.E. Furthermore, Luke alludes to the Jewish-Roman War (Luke 13:34; 19:43–44; 21:20), which culminated in the destruction of Jerusalem in 70 C.E. Therefore, it seems unlikely that Luke-Acts was written before the mid-70s. (The reader will note that this study of Acts uses a different set of terms for historical dates. Writers usually break history into B.C. [Before Christ] and A.D. [*Anno Domini*], traditional Christian references. In keeping with the spirit of Luke, who understood Christianity as a branch of Judaism set in a pluralistic and non-Christian context, this book uses the terms B.C.E. [Before the Common Era] and C.E. [Common Era].)

Apparently Luke finished his work before Paul's letters were collected and began to be circulated as a unit among the churches, probably during the last decade of the first century. Luke seems not to have had access to this collection. Therefore, one could assign a date of 75 to 85 C.E. to Luke's literary activity.

LUKE'S LITERARY STYLE

Luke's "Biblical" Greek

As we shall frequently see, Luke's literary style and his theological concerns are linked together. One looks for Luke's theology not only in *what* he says, but also in the *way* he says it.

This observation is sometimes hidden by modern translations, and this is most unfortunate. For example, the New Revised Standard Version is an excellent translation. However, it is so smooth that it often hides Luke's intentional imitation of the Greek translation of the Hebrew Old Testament (known as the Septuagint, translated in the third century B.C.E.). This imitation is especially apparent in the early chapters of both Luke's Gospel and book of Acts. Luke intends for Mary and Elizabeth, Jesus and the disciples to converse in an old-fashioned biblical Greek, the kind of Greek one heard read in synagogues of the dispersion, or diaspora (the word "diaspora" refers to the Jewish community that was scattered outside of Palestine).

Why would Luke do such a thing? Aside from his introductory dedication (Luke 1:1–4, which indicates that Luke was certainly capable of writing in a highly polished style), one could move quite easily and naturally from the pages of the Septuagint to the Gospel of Luke. Just as some folks have their ears "tuned" to the King James Version of the Bible (think about the Twenty-third Psalm), so Jews and Christians of the dispersion heard their Bible in a special way, the Septuagint way, the way the Bible "is supposed to sound." Luke has imitated the "liturgical Greek" of the synagogue as he tells the story of Jesus and the apostles.

While most of Luke's writing is cast in this special biblical style, as he comes nearer to the end of his second volume, Luke's Greek begins to take on the polish of fine courtroom conversation. Nevertheless, even here Luke casts the words of Jesus in "biblical" Greek (Acts 26:14).

Let us return to the question of why Luke would write in such an affected way. For Luke there was *one* story of salvation, which began in the book of Genesis and ends with the preaching of Paul to the Romans. Did Luke intend to write scripture? Probably not. However, he did intend to narrate a historical "account of the events that have been fulfilled among us" as events that fulfill the expectations of the Old Testament in a literary style that immediately reminded the reader or hearer of the Old Testament.

Luke's Parallels and Doublets

A second feature of Luke's style is his peculiar literary architecture. Even the casual reader will notice the parallels between his two volumes:

Gospel of Luke	Acts of the Apostles
birth (of Jesus)	birth (of the church)
mission/ministry (Jesus)	mission/ministry (church)

| trial (Jesus) | trial (Paul) |
| death/resurrection in
    Jerusalem (Jesus) | proclamation in Rome
    about Jesus the Messiah who was
    crucified and raised (Paul) |

The reader will also note that Luke has twice described the ascension of Jesus, in Luke 24:51 and in Acts 1:9.

Likewise, within each volume there are double stories. In his Gospel, Luke offers two images of God—a man looking for his lost sheep, a woman looking for her lost coin (Luke 15). In Acts 9, Peter raises a paralyzed man and a dead woman (stories that have close parallels in the Third Gospel, Luke 5; 8). Acts 3 and 14 contain strikingly similar healing stories. In the first, Peter and John heal a man "lame from birth"; in the second, Paul and Barnabas heal a man "crippled from birth." In Acts 16, Luke narrates contrasting stories about two women—a rich business-woman who became a Christian and a slave girl cleansed of a spirit of divination.

The reader of Acts is encouraged to be on the lookout for twin stories, and to think about why Luke may have put particular stories together. What was Luke's literary purpose in these parallel accounts? And more important, what was his theological motivation? What comparisons and contrasts do you see in them?

THE ACTS OF THE APOSTLES
ON THE STAGE OF HISTORY

Luke's narrative in both his Gospel and Acts takes place amid the cross-currents of Jewish, Greek, and Roman history. A Jewish context is deeply woven into the fabric of his narrative. According to Luke's Gospel, Jesus, when he was eight days old, was circumcised and presented to the Lord in Jerusalem; at twelve he was found in the temple conversing with the teachers there; at thirty, he was baptized by John (whose father was a priest). Shortly afterward, Jesus taught in the synagogues of Galilee. His journey led him to Jerusalem and back to the temple where he challenged the money changers, citing the prophets Isaiah and Jeremiah as warrant for his action. In Acts, Jesus' followers regularly visit the temple for prayers, Paul teaches in synagogues of the diaspora, and, in spite of his adherence to Jewish law, Paul comes into conflict with the Jewish high council (the Sanhedrin) in Jerusalem. Luke offers a brief description of the Sadducees and the Pharisees, and says that some of the latter became Christians—notably

Paul of Tarsus. I noted above Luke's "biblical Greek" which casts his narrative in the rich scriptural idiom of Judaism. And not only was Luke's literary style biblical, he frequently quotes or alludes to the Law, Prophets, and Psalms. Moreover, we encounter in Acts a wide array of representatives of Palestinian and Diaspora Judaism (Jews who lived outside of Palestine and were deeply influenced by the larger Greek culture, e.g., Stephen, Philip, Paul, Lydia, Priscilla, Aquila, and Apollos).

By the time Luke wrote, the western world had been dominated for four centuries by the Greek cultural legacy of Plato, Aristotle, and Alexander the Great. Luke's characters constantly encounter Greek language, philosophy, art, and political ideals. The Roman tribune, Lysias, asks Paul: "Do you know Greek?" Paul not only knew Greek, but he was able to debate with Greek philosophers in Athens (he quotes their poets), he was acclaimed as the god Hermes in Lystra, and he elegantly defended himself (in Greek) before such consummate Hellenists as King Herod Agrippa and his sister Bernice.

While Judea provided the religious milieu and Greece the cultural context, Rome's political, military, and economic network provided the stability so important to the spread of the gospel into Asia and Europe. In his two volumes, Luke mentions four emperors: Augustus (27 B.C.E.–14 C.E.), Tiberius (14–37 C.E.), Claudius (41–54 C.E.), and Nero (54–68 C.E., though he is not mentioned by name). Gallio and Sergius Paulus are identified as proconsuls in senatorial provinces (Achaia and Cyprus respectively). Pilate, Felix, and Festus are procurators in Judea. Roman roads, which were relatively well maintained and protected, assisted Philip, Peter, Paul, Priscilla, and other Christian missionaries in the spread of the Christian gospel. And a rational judicial system offered considerable protection from arbitrary judgments and mob action, especially for Roman citizens like Paul.

In the midst of this complex historical context, Luke has written his chronicle of the church, but it is a chronicle without dates. Historians in antiquity did not have the luxury of our contemporary system of assigning dates (e.g., 1492, 1776, 2000). Those who recorded events often referred to the reigns of monarchs (especially evident in the Old Testament books of 1 and 2 Kings). Isaiah the prophet remembered that his call from God came "in the year that King Uzziah died" (Isa. 6:1). Luke himself sets the beginning of Jesus' ministry "in the fifteenth year of the reign of Emperor Tiberius" (Luke 3:1).

Therefore, any date we assign to an event is derived relatively. A key citation that helps modern historians develop a chronology for events in Acts is found in 18:12: "When Gallio was proconsul of Achaia. . . ." Other ancient sources, including an inscription found at Delphi, place Gallio at Achaia (modern Greece) in 51 C.E. With that historical benchmark, the historian can

Date (C.E.)	Event	Acts
30	Jesus' death, resurrection, and ascension; birth of the church	1
30–35	Mission in Jerusalem	2—6
32	Death of Stephen; mission to Samaria; Paul's call to be a follower of Jesus	7—8 9
35	Conversion of Cornelius; first mission to the Gentiles	10—11
44	**Death of Herod Agrippa**	12
44–48	Paul's first missionary journey	13—14
48	Apostolic Council in Jerusalem	15
48–51	Paul's second missionary journey	16—18
49	**Emperor Claudius' edict expelling Jews from Rome;** Priscilla and Aquila arrive in Corinth from Rome	
51	Paul before **Gallio in Corinth**	18
52–54	Paul's third missionary journey	18—20
54–56	Paul on trial in Jerusalem and Caesarea	21—26
52–55	**Felix, Procurator of Judea**	24
56	**Festus, Procurator of Judea**	25
56–57	Paul's journey to Rome	27
57–59	Paul in Rome	28

Figure 1.
Chronology of Events in the Book of Acts

work backward and forward in assigning approximate dates to events in the book of Acts. The reader may find the chronology in figure 1 helpful. Events listed in boldface can be corroborated in ancient nonbiblical sources, though opinions differ among scholars about specific dates assigned to the procuratorships of Felix and Festus.

LUKE AS HISTORIAN AND THEOLOGIAN

The well-constructed prefaces to both the Third Gospel and the Acts of the Apostles indicate that the author had serious literary intentions. Like other historians in antiquity, Luke offered the reader a lively history by telling stories about women and men who are important in the life of the early church: Zechariah and Elizabeth, Mary and Joseph, Jesus and John the Baptist, Pilate and Herod, Stephen and Philip, Peter and Cornelius, Paul and Lydia, Priscilla and Aquila, Felix and Festus, Agrippa and Bernice. It is through this steady stream of characters that Luke narrates the history of Jesus and his church.

While Luke was concerned about historical context (note the historical references throughout his two volumes, especially Luke 3:1), he was not as concerned as today's historians about historical "objectivity." As we shall see in this study of Acts, there are instances where some of Luke's historical details appear embellished, questionable, or even wrong. But the reader should remember that Luke was writing history in the same manner as other historians of antiquity. Luke wanted to convey, in a thought-provoking and entertaining way, what *really* happened in the early church, even if some of the details are inaccurate. The reader is also encouraged to consider that much of biblical language is marked by hyperbole—wonderful overstatements.

At times this way of writing history means presenting events that go beyond "just the facts," which would be rather boring history. As a historian and theologian, Luke often mixed history and theology. This is not to suggest that he has mixed fact and fantasy. It is to affirm that the history of a people, a nation, a religious community, cannot be understood apart from a consideration of the transcendental forces embedded in that history. Why did the movement come into being? What were its driving forces? What part did God play in the history of the community? How did they know it was God? Why were people attracted to the movement? All these questions, and many more, entered the mind of a historian like Luke who sought to present not only "the facts" but also an interpretation of those facts so that the reader might understand why the Christian community not only survived, but thrived in a sometimes hostile environment. Luke would also want his reader to consider why the Christian movement is the right choice for a person confronted with an array of religious options.

Over the years, scholars have debated whether Luke was a historian or a theologian. I understand him to have been both. The spotlight of Luke's story shines on the heroines and heroes as they come to center stage, but Luke never loses sight of the one around whom the entire narrative revolves. As in the great chronicles of the Old Testament, human history is ultimately God's history. And this gives a different flavor to Luke's history. He does much more than record events like beads on a string. Luke invites the reader to see these events in a much larger context—in light of God's plan for the salvation of humankind. Every life and every death is part of this plan. Nothing has escaped God's notice; everything that happened in the life of Jesus and the early church is part of God's design for nothing less than the redemption of the world. As Paul declared to King Agrippa, "This was not done in a corner" (Acts 26:26).

While Luke reported on events that occurred on the eastern and northern rim of the Mediterranean Sea between 4 B.C.E. and 58 C.E., it is not difficult to discern in Luke-Acts the cosmic dimension of these events. The preface to the Third Gospel indicates that Luke wanted to preserve the tradition "handed on to us by those who from *the beginning* were eyewitnesses and servants of the word" (Luke 1:2). "Beginning" can refer to the beginning of Jesus' lifetime or to the beginning of Jesus' ministry. It can also be interpreted to mean from the beginning of the world; Luke was drawing the reader's attention back to God's initial act of creation. Likewise, in his preface to Acts, Luke suggested that these witnesses will carry on their work "to *the ends* of the earth" (Acts 1:8). This phrase also carries a double interpretation. Since it is linked with places—Jerusalem, Judea, Samaria—it might refer to the limit of the civilized world (both Rome, the center of the empire, and Spain, the western boundary of the known world, are mentioned in ancient literature as the "limit" of the empire). But here, too, Luke may have a cosmic dimension in mind. "The end" in Luke's Greek text is *eschaton*, which in the Bible often refers to the divinely designated conclusion of this age, this world (the theological term "eschatology" means a study of the end times). Luke may have been pointing forward to the final culmination of God's plan for the cosmos when the universe is at last reconciled with God. The sweep of Luke's history is at once particular and cosmic. Between the beginning and the end, between creation and consummation, stands a history of God's redemptive activity through Israel with her law and prophets, and through Jesus and his church.

LUKE'S PURPOSES IN WRITING

While it is impossible to know exactly what was on Luke's mind as he began to write, most scholars agree that the evangelist must have had some purpose for writing. Not everyone agrees on what this purpose was, but several possibilities have been identified.

Educational

Luke's own introduction to the two volumes (Luke 1:1–4) may give us a clue to his intention. "I too decided, after investigating everything carefully from the very first, to write an orderly account for you, most excellent Theophilus, so that you may *know the truth* concerning the things about which you have been *instructed*." It sounds very much as if Luke had a teaching purpose in mind. Perhaps he envisioned that his narrative would be preserved as a body of instruction for catechumens.

The superb quality of Luke's writing, especially obvious in his preface, might suggest that he was intent on reaching the literate and urbane sectors of Roman society. The way in which Luke has set Christianity among the religious and philosophical options of the day suggests that for Luke, Christianity is not simply a provincial sect of Judean Judaism. Rather, it is a world-embracing religion equal to the best thinking and believing of the day. His purpose certainly may have been educational, evangelical, and ecumenical (see comments on Acts 1:1–5).

Theological

There can be no doubt that Luke is concerned to describe the work that God has done in Christ. He might have entitled his two volumes "The Acts of God." From the beginning of his Gospel to the end of his book of Acts, Luke's focus is on the work that God has done through Jesus and his followers. Luke begins with Mary announcing the establishment of God's reign through her yet unborn son and ends with Paul "proclaiming the kingdom of God and teaching about the Lord Jesus Christ" (Luke 1:46–55 . . . Acts 28:31). God's grace and forgiveness toward all humankind is revealed in Christ Jesus and is incarnate in Christ's church, the community of believers.

In the Acts of the Apostles, Luke describes a wonderful new discovery about God and God's relationship with humankind. The God of the Jews is also God of the Gentiles. Jesus' example of care for everyone who came to him served as a model for his apostles who came to understand, as Peter did, that "God shows no partiality" (Acts 10:34). And Paul declared that the "salvation of God has been sent to the Gentiles" (Acts 28:28). The whole cosmic order has been affected by the coming of Christ. In story after story in the Gospel and Acts, Luke proclaims that God makes no distinction between Jew and Gentile, rich and poor, male and female. All are acceptable to God. All are one in Christ. And this, Luke would conclude, was *the* Act of God.

Apologetic

It may have been that Luke was concerned about the relationship between the early Christian community and the Roman Empire. Perhaps Luke intended to present a defense of Christianity, or of Paul, to a Roman official who needed to make a decision concerning the political attitude and legal standing of

Christians. In this case, Luke did his best to show that the church, following the teaching of Paul in Romans 13, does not have a negative attitude toward the state. Paul in particular is a loyal and trustworthy Roman citizen.

It may even be that Luke was attempting to convince fellow believers that, since Jesus' return is delayed, the church needs to come to terms with its ongoing life in the political realm of the Roman Empire and begin to recognize, and take advantage of, the benefits of the *pax Romana*—the great overlay of peace and harmony orchestrated from the imperial office in Rome and maintained in the provinces by the Roman army. Indeed, the Christian mission in Syria, Asia, Africa, Greece, and Italy owes much of its success to the fact that the apostles could travel freely from city to city throughout the empire.

It is also evident that Luke intended to connect the story of Jesus and the early church to the Old Testament tradition. He not only used the Old Testament to interpret the Christ event, but his account of Jesus and the church is itself an interpretation of the Old Testament. By showing that the church has its roots in Israel, perhaps Luke hoped to state quite clearly that the followers of Jesus constituted a sect of Judaism. This served two purposes for Luke. First, it reminded Gentile converts of their debt to the covenants and traditions of Judaism. Second, the Christian community, as a sect of Judaism, could be recognized by the empire as part of an ancient, honorable, and officially protected religion.

Some scholars have thought that Luke intended to "rehabilitate" his hero Paul. It may have been that the apostle to the Gentiles was seen as so anti-law that his entire message was being disregarded. Therefore, Luke takes up the task of portraying Paul as accommodating to the Jewish-Christian leaders in Jerusalem, a portrayal that is probably more accommodating than Paul really was (see comments on Acts 15 and Acts 21).

Conclusion

It is quite likely that Luke had more than one purpose in mind as he "set down an orderly account of the events that have been fulfilled among us." Educational, evangelical, theological, and apologetic concerns—all of these, and more, may have been in the mind of the evangelist as he put pen to papyrus.

A Concluding Observation on Luke's Purpose and the Apparent Anti-Semitisms in Acts

In reading the book of Acts, one has the uncomfortable feeling that Luke has engaged in anti-Semitism in the way he sometimes describes "the Jews." They were "filled with jealousy" (13:45; 17:5), they "opposed and reviled"

Paul (18:5–6), and they constantly stirred up the crowds to take action against Paul (14:19; 17:5; 18:12; 21:27). Moreover, if one compares the arrest and trial of Jesus in Luke's Gospel with an earlier version presented by Mark, one detects a subtle change: Luke shifts responsibility for Jesus' death away from the Romans and onto the Jewish leaders in Jerusalem.

Was part of Luke's purpose to exonerate Christians (and Romans) at the expense of Jews? Was he attempting to shift blame onto the Jews for troubles that seemed to follow in the wake of Christian missionaries?

Scores of examples appear in ancient Greek and Roman literature of clear-cut anti-Semitic sentiment intended to whip up scorn against the Jews. On the one hand, Jews were depicted as a privileged people protected by Roman law—privileges that were highlighted and distorted to provoke non-Jews to become jealous of their Jewish neighbors. On the other hand, Jews (and Christians) were described as a noxious plague infecting the urban lower classes. The anti-Semitism one encounters in Acts does not fit either of these virulent slanders against the Jews.

Some scholars have suggested that the kinds of anti-Semitic statements found in Acts simply reflect the ordinary polemic of the day—a naive, but nonetheless hurtful, anti-Semitism. One way an author distinguished his religion from others was to point out the disparities among them, exaggerating the virtues of his community and the vices of competing religions (or philosophies, political systems, etc.). Luke consistently treats magicians (who are clearly inferior to Christian healers) in this way. But Luke does not seem to convey this kind of naive anti-Semitism. According to Luke, the Christian community (it is probably too early to speak of "Christianity") is a sect of Judaism, and has struggled to find its place within that larger household of faith.

It is the perspective of this study that Luke was groping to try to understand how it was that a good and lawful Jew, Jesus of Nazareth, was executed with the consent of fellow Palestinian Jews. Furthermore, Luke was trying to understand how a pious Pharisaic Jew like Paul could be hounded and persecuted by his fellow Jews, especially fellow diaspora Jews.

Luke, pro-Roman to the core, attempted throughout his writings to distance the Romans from responsibility for the death of Jesus. A convenient rationale for this judicial debacle was to place responsibility squarely on the shoulders of the Jewish leadership in Jerusalem. Even so, Luke tried to soften the blow by suggesting that they "acted in ignorance."

Likewise, over and over again many Jews rejected the gospel preached by Paul and some actively opposed the apostle to the Gentiles. Nevertheless, Paul never quit his missionary program—to the Jews first, then to the Gentiles. He was ever hopeful in reaching out to his Jewish brothers and sisters. Even when the apostle reached his final destination, Rome, the heart of the empire, his mission was to the Jewish community. Luke described the encounter as consistent with other such meetings: "Some were convinced by what he had said, while others refused to believe. So they disagreed with each other" (28:24–25).

Finally, Luke was ambiguous but not antagonistic in his understanding of the relationship between church and synagogue. One has the sense that Luke was struggling to understand what this relationship meant in light of the divine plan. The Christian community was undeniably a sect of Judaism. Christians were enmeshed in the great traditions of Judaism and the Old Testament. But was this community more than a sect of Judaism? If so, in what way? A continuation, surely. An expansion, also to be sure. A replacement, maybe—but then what are we to make of God's people, heirs of the covenants with Abraham, Moses, and David? Are they rejected and replaced? Like Paul, Luke would likely conclude with a resounding, "By no means!" (Rom. 10:1).

So Luke was caught in a bind. He knew that some Jews, including Jewish Christians, occasionally thwarted the efforts of some early Christians, particularly the mission to the Gentiles. He knew that some Jews may have shared responsibility for Jesus' death and that some wanted to ambush and lynch Paul. He also knew that Christians must, for legal, political, and theological reasons, remain in the fold of Judaism. Whatever anti-Semitism we encounter in Acts may be from the voice of a Gentile Christian trying his best to mitigate the pain of being grafted onto "the rich root of the olive tree" (Rom. 11:17)—and trying to make sense of that pain.

THE MESSAGES OF ACTS

God's Continuing Work

In reading the book of Acts (and the Third Gospel), one theme stands above all others. From the beginning of time, God has been continually at work to complete God's own joy. This theme is beautifully illustrated by three of Jesus' parables which are narrated at the midpoint of Luke's Gospel: the parables of the lost sheep, the lost coin, and the lost son (Luke 15).

> The shepherd says, "Rejoice with me, for I have found my sheep that was lost"; and Jesus adds, "Just so, I tell you, there will be more joy in heaven over one sinner who repents than over ninety-nine righteous persons who need no repentance."

The woman says, "Rejoice with me, for I have found the coin that I had lost"; and Jesus adds, "Just so, I tell you, there is joy in the presence of the angels of God over one sinner who repents."

And last of all, the father says, "Let us eat and celebrate; for this son of mine was dead and is alive again; he was lost and is found!"

In the midpoint of Luke's second volume the message of the parables is made clear: The Gentiles who were once far from God and lost have been brought into fellowship with God through the gospel preached by the apostles of Jesus. On their way to Jerusalem, Paul and Barnabas "reported the conversion of the Gentiles, and brought great joy to all the believers" (Acts 15:3).

God desires reconciliation with humanity and has continually worked for this unity by choosing a people, Israel, and giving her the law, prophets, priests, and sages. While these gifts brought a faithful remnant into God's joy, God was not satisfied. Finally, God made reconciliation available to all people through his child Jesus, Israel's Messiah. Anyone who chooses to believe this good news is reconciled with God and experiences a taste of that heavenly celebration—the gift of the Holy Spirit. According to Luke, the vehicle through which God now works to complete God's own joy is the community of Jesus the Messiah.

The Unity of the Church

The joy of God is experienced in the community of those who believe that God has provided for reconciliation through Jesus, God's Messiah. For Luke, divine reconciliation is incarnate in the community of believers, the church. The community stands as an example of unity with God, but there is an inherent problem here. The church is made up of human beings, who, despite their best intentions, do not always act in one accord.

The book of Acts reveals that from the beginning, the church struggled to maintain unity. In spite of Luke's editorial glosses about a church at peace, there is much in his narrative about tensions within the community. The story of Ananias and Sapphira (Acts 5) may be an extreme example, but there were also tensions between "the Hebrews" and "the Hellenists" (Acts 6), Paul and John Mark (Acts 15), Apollos and Priscilla and Aquila (Acts 18), and Paul and James (Acts 15 and 21). Nevertheless, the church of Acts recognized that tensions are inevitable, even desirable because they can lead to intellectual, spiritual, personal, and communal growth. The church—its leaders and laity—talked through their differences and prayed for the Holy Spirit to lead them through the valleys of disagreement. It was crucial to maintain the unity of the church as the incarnation of reconciliation with God.

Christian Unity Embraces Diversity

We have noted that one of the messages of Acts is concern for the unity of the church, and that this unity can be obtained in spite of inevitable tensions that occur among people. It is often the case that these tensions arise from one of the very virtues that the book of Acts promotes: the diversity of the Christian community.

Even a cursory reading of Acts reveals that the church embraced an increasingly diverse population. It began with a group of Galilean Jews led by Jesus of Nazareth. After Jesus' death, the group temporarily took up residence in Jerusalem. Very soon they attracted Jews of Jerusalem and surrounding Judea to their movement. During the Day of Pentecost, the apostles speak of their experience to Jews "from every nation under heaven" (Acts 2). Greek-speaking Jews, also residing in Jerusalem, joined the movement in such numbers that they needed to organize the administration of aid to widows and orphans (Acts 6). One of these Greek-speaking Jews, Philip, led a mission to Samaria and, crossing a racial boundary, brought despised (from a Jewish point of view) Samaritans into the church. Questionable sexuality did not deter Philip from baptizing an Ethiopian eunuch (Acts 8). Finally, Peter was encouraged by a vision from God to bring an unclean (again, from his Jewish perspective) Gentile family into the church (Acts 10). Asians, Greeks, Egyptians, Syrians, Italians, even the "barbarians" of Malta were welcomed into the household of faith. Rich, poor, well, sick, all colors of people without discrimination worked side by side in this new community of faith. Leadership was shared by men and women alike—Priscilla and Aquila, Paul and Lydia, Philip and his four prophet-daughters, Mary and her son John Mark.

One by one the barriers between people fell, without fanfare or pretension. It is true that at many points Luke has idealized life in the church, but he has also given us a vision of life together, free of the indignities we impose, consciously and unconsciously, on those who are not like us. Christian unity embraces diversity. This, for Luke, is the church, the people of God, the incarnation of God's reconciliation.

SOME FEATURES OF THIS BOOK

First, my work relies on the New Revised Standard Version of the Bible (NRSV), published in 1991. There are, of course, shortcomings with all translations of a text:

1. Translations are at the same time interpretations (theological and otherwise).
2. Translations are generally the work of committees, with all the benefits (a group of scholars correcting one another may yield a translation less prone to bias than the work of an individual) and liabilities (a group effort often demands compromise in which some significant insights may be left out) of the committee process.
3. Translation is not an exact science, and word-for-word translations are nearly impossible; at best, one aims at the closest possible approximation in correlating terms of two languages (a formal equivalence translation), or of transmitting the meanings (emotional, political, social, religious) of the text (a dynamic equivalence translation), or some combination of the two approaches.

The NRSV English translation, as good as it is, is not without problems. When important translation problems occur, I note them. Most modern translations include marginal notes that refer the reader to alternative readings of passages in which significant problems confront the translator. It is often worthwhile to consider the alternate reading suggested by the translator.

Second, I occasionally refer to the "ancient reader" and the "modern reader." By "ancient reader" I mean an imaginary first-century reader—one whom Luke had in mind as he wrote his narration. I also recognize that this "reader" would have read Acts aloud in a teaching or liturgical setting. The "ancient reader" also had "ancient hearers." When I address the "modern reader," I mean us. And this leads to a third consideration: worldview.

The worldview of the ancient reader was significantly and irretrievably different from that of the modern reader. The person of the Roman Empire lived in a prescientific, preindustrial, and pretechnological age. This is not to deny that people in antiquity had their own versions of science, industry, and technology. We do know, however, that during the past two centuries (and perhaps beginning with Galileo in the sixteenth

century) human beings have experienced a quantum leap in the way
the world is perceived. To mention a few shifts in perspective, we are no
longer flat-earthers. We no longer think that mother earth is the center
of the universe. We no longer believe that demons are responsible for
illness.

It is virtually impossible even to imagine how a person living in Luke's
time understood the universe, the way it functioned, and a person's place
in it. This leads to a further consideration: What is the relationship between events of the past (near or distant) and the writing of history?

On occasion, I attempt to use Luke's historical framework, augmented
with information from other sources—both ancient and modern—in an
effort to imagine (critically, with an awareness of the limitations of these
sources and the commentator's own imagination) the world of Luke and
the early church. The difficult task of reconstructing events that took place
two thousand years ago may be illustrated by considering efforts to account for the events in Dallas, Texas, in November 1963. Even with all the
tools of modern media, including eyewitnesses and computer analyses,
there is still debate surrounding the assassination of President John F.
Kennedy. Where does the "truth" lie? This question leads us to consider
the relationship between fact and fiction.

I occasionally suggest that Luke has used hyperbole (a common literary
device used to exaggerate or embellish an event) in order to tell a good
story. Part of Luke's purpose as a historian was to make the story of the
early church interesting. He does this through humor, suspense, drama,
exaggeration, and many other devices at the disposal of an effective storyteller. The modern reader can sometimes tell where Luke has gone beyond
the bounds of fact (if there is any such thing). He was not interested in "just
the facts." Nor are we.

And it is here that readers, both ancient and modern, join hearts and
minds in reading the Acts of the Apostles. The wise reader in any age often prefers fact mingled with feeling and this often results in fiction. Because a story is, in part, fictional does not mean that it is not true. As I noted
above, Luke's style of historical narration goes beyond the mere data of
history to tell the reader what *really* happened. A well-told story engages
the reader at the feeling level of events; that "there were tens of thousands
of [Christian] believers . . . among the Jews" (literal translation; Acts 21:20)
is probably an exaggeration based on Luke's enthusiasm for the spread of
the gospel. This enthusiasm for the gospel leads to a truth that runs deeper
than statistical correctness.

THE ACTS OF THE APOSTLES IN THE
LIVES OF CONTEMPORARY CHRISTIANS

The Bible is a collection of literature written over the course of more than a millennium (from about 1000 B.C.E. to about C.E. 100). While the book of Acts was written near the end of this long literary history, it shares a worldview that has much in common with its predecessors. Luke presupposed a three-storied universe (heaven that is the abode of God, earth that is the realm of men and women, and an underworld that is cut off from the upper realms of life and light). He assumed the existence of demons (the cause of illness and disease) and angels (God's heavenly messengers). And he described what it is like to live in a polytheistic world of magic and divination. In short, he had a worldview far different from ours. Our modern minds have a difficult time fully comprehending Luke's narrative. One of the ways to bridge this gap in time is carefully to guide our historical imaginations into Luke's world in order to understand the deeds and messages of his contemporaries. Such a guided journey is one of the functions of this study.

But one must do more than remain in this imaginary world. We must resurface into our own time, bringing with us messages from the first-century church. We will want to examine those messages in light of our own twentieth-century lives—our joys, perplexities, sorrows, challenges, questions, fears, doubts, affirmations, and consternations. I hope that this book will serve a dual function: to make informed comment on the lives of first-century Christians and to encourage you, the reader, to make enlightened commitment with your own life.

I hope that the person who studies the Acts of the Apostles with the aid of this book will come to see Luke's narrative as much more than a chronicle of the early Christian community. Perhaps the reader will come face-to-face with the vital and compassionate faith of those first followers of Jesus of Nazareth, and in so doing will transport that vitality and compassion into our own needy world.

1. The Early Days
Of the Apostolic Church

Acts 1:1–12:25

1. From Jerusalem to the Ends of the Earth
Acts 1:1–26

LUKE'S INTRODUCTION
Acts 1:1–5

> 1:1 **In the first book, Theophilus, I wrote about all that Jesus did and taught from the beginning** 2 **until the day when he was taken up to heaven, after giving instructions through the Holy Spirit to the apostles whom he had chosen.** 3 **After his suffering he presented himself alive to them by many convincing proofs, appearing to them during forty days and speaking about the kingdom of God.** 4 **While staying with them, he ordered them not to leave Jerusalem, but to wait there for the promise of the Father. "This," he said, "is what you have heard from me;** 5 **for John baptized with water, but you will be baptized with the Holy Spirit not many days from now."**

Luke has told us a number of things with his opening sentence. First, this book continues a story. The sentence operates as a hinge that links Luke's two volumes—the Gospel According to Luke and the Acts of the Apostles. Second, in this single sentence Luke summarizes his first volume which was "about all that Jesus did and taught." Third, like other first-century historians, he offers the reader a brief introduction to this volume which will focus on the apostles whom Jesus had chosen. Finally, Luke recalls the name of Theophilus to whom both volumes are dedicated (see the Introduction).

In these verses, Luke vividly sets the scene for his opening chapter by recounting the postresurrection appearances of Jesus to his apostles. A person having just finished Luke's first volume will note something odd about the introduction to volume two. Luke describes the boundaries of his "first book" as beginning with Jesus' ministry and ending with his ascension, "the day when he was taken up to heaven" (Acts 1:1). According to Luke 24:51, Jesus was indeed taken up to heaven, yet in the opening chapter of Acts Jesus is back in Jerusalem with his disciples. The incongruity disappears with a careful reading of the closing verses of Luke's Gospel

(24:44–53) and the opening verses of Acts. Luke has provided the reader with a carefully crafted transition as he moves the reader from book one to book two. It is no accident that the stories of Jesus' last days with his apostles overlap. Luke has carefully developed these transitional sentences which swing the spotlight from Jesus to Jesus' followers.

Luke's note that Jesus "presented himself alive to them by many convincing proofs" recalls the appearances of the resurrected Jesus to his disciples recorded in Luke 24:13–53. A new element in his summary is the important detail that Jesus remained with his disciples for forty days after that first Easter Sunday. "Forty" is a significant number in the Bible, alerting the reader to look for the hand of God in history. During the time of Noah, God caused it to rain forty days and nights. The Israelites were supported by God for forty years in the wilderness of Sinai. David, Israel's ideal king, reigned for forty years.

This concept of sacred time—forty days—is important for understanding the opening sentences of the book of Acts. In the Bible, there are three men who went off by themselves for forty days to discover the will of God. Moses was "with the LORD forty days and forty nights" on Mount Sinai when he received the Ten Commandments (Exod. 34:28). Likewise, the prophet Elijah spent forty days and forty nights on Mount Horeb, "the mount of God," where the word of the Lord came to him in that "still small voice" (1 Kings 19:8–12). Finally, Jesus himself was led by the Spirit of God into the wilderness where he was "tempted by the devil" for forty days (Luke 4:1–2). In this time of testing, Jesus—full of the Holy Spirit—prevailed over the prince of darkness. Two items stand out as intertwined threads in these stories: (1) Moses, Elijah, and Jesus went to a place to be alone to discover the power of God and (2) all three fasted in preparation for their mission to Israel (also see the comments on Moses, Elijah, and Jesus at Acts 1:9–11).

Now Luke presents the Bible reader with a fourth, and last, forty-day period. This time Jesus was not alone and he did not fast—the alternate reading (see marginal note) of the NRSV of Acts 1:4 makes this last point. "While [Jesus was] *eating* with them, he ordered them not to leave Jerusalem." During this sacred time Jesus not only continued to reinforce his teaching about the reign of God—that ultimate sacred time—but he gave his friends a foretaste of that perfect time, which features a divinely catered banquet (Luke 14:15–24), by eating and drinking with them. Finally, Jesus promised his followers not the law of God (brought by Moses), nor even the word of the Lord (brought by Elijah), but the very presence of God—the Holy Spirit.

A MISUNDERSTANDING
Acts 1:6–8

> 1:6 **So when they had come together, they asked him, "Lord, is this the time when you will restore the kingdom to Israel?"** [7] **He replied, "It is not for you to know the times or periods that the Father has set by his own authority.** [8] **But you will receive power when the Holy Spirit has come upon you; and you will be my witnesses in Jerusalem, in all Judea and Samaria, and to the ends of the earth."**

Obedient to the command of Jesus, the apostles remained in Jerusalem, the center of religious and political authority for this small band of Jews. The very first question the apostles put to Jesus is one that deals with religious and political authority: "Lord, is this the time when you will restore the kingdom to Israel?" (v. 6).

The meaning of "kingdom" may escape the casual reader. Twice in her history Israel was a kingdom, first under the dynasty of David (1000–583 B.C.E.), and then under the rule of the Maccabees (165–63 B.C.E.). The first episode of Israel's sovereignty was ended by the Babylonians; the second, by Rome.

During the time of Jesus and his earliest followers, Israel (both the people and their homeland) remained under the rule of Rome. Within Israel there was a wide range of response to this situation:

Cooperation with the "powers that be" (the Sadducees),
Accommodation with the ruling authorities (see Rom. 13:1–7; 1 Peter 2:13–17),
Passive rejection of "Babylon" (a code word for Rome in the book of Revelation),
Active—and sometimes violent—resistance against the Roman government (the Zealot movement).

"Lord, is this the time when you will restore the kingdom to Israel?" Does Luke reveal in this question a basic misunderstanding which the apostles maintained even after Jesus' resurrection? Why did they now ask Jesus about restoring the kingdom to Israel? Were they hoping, now that Jesus had returned to them, that he would lead Israel to sovereignty? Did they expect Jesus to lead them in active resistance against Roman rule? Had they been harboring this hope during Jesus' lifetime, only to articulate it fully at his resurrection?

Jesus responded that such questions about sovereignty are misplaced. He reminded the apostles that God is the source of all sovereignty and

authority. It is precisely this theological notion that guides Luke's interpretation of events in the early church. God is in charge of the work Jesus
has begun.

"Times or periods" refer to a theological and political notion that it is
God who gives sovereignty to each nation in its turn. God establishes a nation's sovereignty at a particular time and for a particular duration. In the
book of Daniel, the beasts described in chapter 7 refer to the successive
rise of empires: Babylonia, Media, Persia, and Greece. The statue in Neb-
uchadnezzar's dream (Daniel 2) contains similar symbolism. In his writings, Josephus, a Jewish historian and a contemporary of Luke, noted that
it was by God's design that sovereignty over the nations had recently
passed to Rome (*Jewish War* 5:367). It is now Rome's "time." God not only
knows the "times or periods" of each reigning people, but God establishes
them "by his own authority" (v. 7).

Behind the apostles' question is a longing in their hearts to be part of
the sovereign political power structure which they hope Jesus will now establish. The reader might recall one of Jesus' statements in Luke's account
of the Last Supper.

> You are those who have stood by me in my trials; and I confer on you, just
> as my Father has conferred on me, a kingdom, so that you may eat and drink
> at my table in my kingdom, and you will sit on thrones judging the twelve
> tribes of Israel. (Luke 22:28–30)

Now the apostles want Jesus to make good on his promise as they indicate their readiness to share in ruling a sovereign Israel. Jesus informs them
that they will indeed receive power, but not the kind they anticipated.

> But *you will receive power* when the Holy Spirit has come upon you; and *you
> will be my witnesses* in Jerusalem, in all Judea and Samaria, and to the ends of
> the earth. (Acts 1:8)

In Jesus' final statement to his apostles he promises that they *will receive
power*—not to rule, but to witness.

THE ASCENSION
Acts 1:9–11

**1:9 When he had said this, as they were watching, he was lifted up, and a
cloud took him out of their sight. [10] While he was going and they were gaz-**

**ing up toward heaven, suddenly two men in white robes stood by them.
11 They said, "Men of Galilee, why do you stand looking up toward heaven?
This Jesus, who has been taken up from you into heaven, will come in the
same way as you saw him go into heaven."**

Luke has now brought the reader to the culmination of Jesus' earthly
ministry. In this passage, the reader is once again struck by an allusion to
Moses and Elijah. While Acts 1:1–5 directed the reader's attention to the
solitary experience of Jesus in the wilderness (Luke 4:1–13), this passage
reminds the reader of the story of Jesus' transfiguration (Luke 9:28–36). In
the story of the transfiguration, Jesus, Peter, James, and John ascended a
mountain to pray. Soon the appearance of Jesus' face changed, "and his
clothes became dazzling white," much like Moses whose face was so bright
with the reflection of God that the people could not look at him. Suddenly,
Jesus' apostles saw two men—Moses and Elijah—talking with Jesus. According to Luke, "they appeared in glory and were speaking of his departure, which he was about to accomplish at Jerusalem" (9:31). Commentators
usually suggest that the discussion is about Jesus' death; however, in light
of the passage in Acts 1:9–11, it could be that the conversation was about
Jesus' ascension. Ancient Jewish readers would have been familiar with stories about the ascension into heaven of *both* Moses and Elijah; Jesus will
shortly follow.

Finally, "a cloud came and overshadowed them; and they were terrified
as they entered the cloud. Then from the cloud came a voice that said,
'This is my Son, my Chosen; listen to him!'" (Luke 9:34–35). The presence of God is an awesome experience.

The parallels between the transfiguration and the ascension are clear.
Jesus and his apostles are again on a mountain, the Mount of Olives (Acts
1:12). From here, Jesus is taken up by a cloud, a symbol of the divine
presence. "*Suddenly two men* [Moses and Elijah?] *in white robes* stood by
them," this time to talk with the apostles. They bring a word of consola-
tion that Jesus will return "in the same way as you saw him go into
heaven" (v. 11).

From here on, the spotlight of Luke's narrative is fully focused on the
followers of Jesus. They will seek to incarnate his life, message, and mission in their new community until his return. Jesus is no longer physically
present. Nevertheless, his followers, then and now, are assured of God's
promise that Jesus will return. In the meantime, under the guidance of the
Holy Spirit, Jesus' followers, then and now, are commissioned to be "witnesses to the ends of the earth." Luke has led his reader through the tran-

sition from his first book to his second, and now he is ready to begin his story of the early church.

THE TWELVE
Acts 1:12–26

> 1:12 **Then they returned to Jerusalem from the mount called Olivet, which is near Jerusalem, a sabbath day's journey away.** [13] **When they had entered the city, they went to the room upstairs where they were staying, Peter, and John, and James, and Andrew, Philip and Thomas, Bartholomew and Matthew, James son of Alphaeus, and Simon the Zealot, and Judas son of James.** [14] **All these were constantly devoting themselves to prayer, together with certain women, including Mary the mother of Jesus, as well as his brothers.**
> [15] **In those days Peter stood up among the believers (together the crowd numbered about one hundred twenty persons) and said,** [16] **"Friends, the scripture had to be fulfilled, which the Holy Spirit through David foretold concerning Judas, who became a guide for those who arrested Jesus—** [17] **for he was numbered among us and was allotted his share in this ministry."**
> [18] **(Now this man acquired a field with the reward of his wickedness; and falling headlong, he burst open in the middle and all his bowels gushed out.** [19] **This became known to all the residents of Jerusalem, so that the field was called in their language Hakeldama, that is, Field of Blood.)** [20] **"For it is written in the book of Psalms,**
> **'Let his homestead become desolate,**
> **and let there be no one to live in it';**
> **and**
> **'Let another take his position of overseer.'**
> [21] **So one of the men who have accompanied us during all the time that the Lord Jesus went in and out among us,** [22] **beginning from the baptism of John until the day when he was taken up from us—one of these must become a witness with us to his resurrection."** [23] **So they proposed two, Joseph called Barsabbas, who was also known as Justus, and Matthias.** [24] **Then they prayed and said, "Lord, you know everyone's heart. Show us which one of these two you have chosen** [25] **to take the place in this ministry and apostleship from which Judas turned aside to go to his own place."** [26] **And they cast lots for them, and the lot fell on Matthias; and he was added to the eleven apostles.**

With these verses Luke has pictured a rapidly growing band of believers who must begin to order their life together. He offers a roll call of the eleven remaining apostles (see a similar list in Luke 6:14–16), a note that women were present, and the observation that members of Jesus' family—his mother and his brothers—were also on hand. According to Luke, this group gathered regularly for prayer in the upper room of a house in Jerusalem.

Like the number forty (see comments on Acts 1:1–5), the number twelve is important in biblical tradition. One recalls especially the twelve tribes of Israel, descendants of the sons of Jacob. Twelve is symbolic of all Israel. The time of David and Solomon was revered as that perfect period in Israel's history when all twelve tribes were united. With the ravages of internal strife and external conquest, Israel became a house divided—and dispersed. All that remained in Luke's time was a collective memory of that perfect time. And imbedded in that memory is a hope that God will perform a miracle—that the twelve tribes will one day be reunited. Ezekiel had a vision of God apportioning once again the land among the twelve tribes (Ezekiel 47–48). And the seer of the book of Revelation envisioned a New Jerusalem with twelve gates, each inscribed with the names of the twelve tribes of Israel. Furthermore, the city would be built on twelve foundations on which the names of the twelve apostles are written (Rev. 21:10–14). The dream of twelve tribes/twelve apostles lives! Eleven simply will not do. Therefore, the first order of business of this community of believers is to select a person to take Judas's place, thus restoring the full complement of the Twelve.

Peter offered a criterion for a successor to Judas. The person must be one who had been with Jesus during the entire time of his earthly ministry, from Jesus' baptism (one cannot press this part of the criterion too hard, since most of Jesus' followers had come to him considerably later than the baptism) until his ascension. Two such men were identified—Barsabbas and Matthias. The latter of the two was chosen by the casting of lots, a custom described in Proverbs:

> The lot is cast into the lap,
>   but the decision is the LORD's alone.
>   (Prov. 16:33)

While exact details about this practice are unknown, apparently the name of each man was inscribed on parchment or on a piece of wood or pottery, placed in a bowl, and shaken until one name fell "into the lap." In this way God's providence invades the human process. The lot fell to Matthias, "and he was added to the eleven apostles." With the election of Matthias, the full complement of the Twelve was restored.

Luke adds his own editorial note on the demise of Judas. According to Luke, Judas died the type of horrendous death reserved for particularly vile people: "falling headlong, he burst open in the middle and all his bowels gushed out" (v. 18). The marginal note in the NRSV suggests that Judas swelled up and burst open. Josephus notes that Herod died in a similar manner (*Jewish Antiquities* 19.8.2; see comments on Acts 12:23) because he put himself in the place of God.

According to Matthew's Gospel, Judas hanged himself (Matt. 27:5). It is impossible to know which version of Judas's death is historically correct. Some creative interpreters try to have it both ways: Judas hanged himself *and* fell to his death as the rope broke! This is the solution taken by Cecil B. De Mille in his classic 1927 film *The King of Kings.* A more cautious approach would suggest that Luke and Matthew are simply heirs of different traditions about the death of Jesus' betrayer.

Finally, it is worth noting that Luke's term for the Twelve is "apostle" rather than "disciple." According to Luke 6:13, Jesus had more than twelve disciples and it is from this larger number that he chose twelve "whom he also named apostles"—representatives appointed to carry out the teacher's mission, which is the meaning of the term "apostle."

In Acts, Luke limits the use of the term "apostle" to the twelve who were closest to Jesus (Acts 14:14 is the single exception where Paul and Barnabas are called "apostles"). The story about the Hebrews and the Hellenists in Acts 6:1–6 makes clear Luke's distinction between apostle and disciple. Here "the twelve" apostles called together "the whole community of the disciples." Furthermore, the apostles have authority to commission disciples for particular works of ministry. I will use the term "apostles" when the context clearly indicates the Twelve.

Luke's history of the church is under way. In this first chapter of Acts, Luke has described the transition from the small band of itinerant followers of Jesus to an established core of twelve apostolic leaders, of which Peter has emerged as spokesman. Moreover, this small band of believers has quickly grown tenfold, fulfilling Jesus' prophetic parable of the pounds (Luke 19:11–27). In chapter 2, Luke will inform the reader that on the Day of Pentecost the church grew a whopping 250 times to over three thousand believers! Luke will also describe another transition as the church expands from a small band of provincial Galilean Jews—the apostles of Jesus—to embrace a large assembly of "Jews from every nation under heaven."

2. Jerusalem: The Birth of the Christian Community
Acts 2:1–5:42

THE GIFT OF THE HOLY SPIRIT
Acts 2:1–13

2:1 **When the day of Pentecost had come, they were all together in one place.** [2] **And suddenly from heaven there came a sound like the rush of a violent wind, and it filled the entire house where they were sitting.** [3] **Divided tongues, as of fire, appeared among them, and a tongue rested on each of them.** [4] **All of them were filled with the Holy Spirit and began to speak in other languages, as the Spirit gave them ability.**

[5] **Now there were devout Jews from every nation under heaven living in Jerusalem.** [6] **And at this sound the crowd gathered and was bewildered, because each one heard them speaking in the native language of each.** [7] **Amazed and astonished, they asked, "Are not all these who are speaking Galileans?** [8] **And how is it that we hear, each of us, in our own native language?** [9] **Parthians, Medes, Elamites, and residents of Mesopotamia, Judea and Cappadocia, Pontus and Asia,** [10] **Phrygia and Pamphylia, Egypt and the parts of Libya belonging to Cyrene, and visitors from Rome, both Jews and proselytes,** [11] **Cretans and Arabs—in our own languages we hear them speaking about God's deeds of power."** [12] **All were amazed and perplexed, saying to one another, "What does this mean?"** [13] **But others sneered and said, "They are filled with new wine."**

Having accomplished the administrative task of replacing Judas with Matthias, the apostles were ready to begin their mission as Jesus' witnesses. Acts 2 stands at the beginning of a cycle of stories (2:1–4:31) that depicts events in the life of the early church during that first Christian Pentecost.

The coming of the Holy Spirit as a fulfillment of Jesus' promise (1:5) is perhaps the most important event in the life of the early church. Luke knew that the significance of this event could not be overstated. It stands as proof to all the world ("Jews from every nation"; 2:5) that God Almighty, the God of the patriarchs and matriarchs of Israel, the God of the kings and prophets of Judah, the one who created all that is, is at work among this small band of people. This same God, who breathed the creative breath of life over the face of the deep, has again breathed the divine breath of creation into these Galilean Jews. This is a major theological theme for Luke (one is tempted to say *the* major theme; see the Introduction). From the first chapter of his first volume (Luke 1:15) to the last chapter of volume two (Acts 28:25) Luke emphasizes the importance of the activity of the Holy Spirit in the life of the emerging church. There can be no doubt that the creation of the church is God's creation. God's Spirit, the Holy Spirit, is its life source foundationally and essentially.

The Day of Pentecost (fifty days after Passover) was also known as the Feast of Weeks, an agricultural festival in which the community celebrated the gathering of the first harvest (wheat) and offered thanks to God for nature's bounty (Exod. 23:14–17; 34:18–24). During the period of early Judaism (300 B.C.E.–100 C.E.) the celebration began to lose its association with agriculture, as attention shifted to concern for preserving the religious heritage of the Hebrew people. By the first century C.E., the Day of Pentecost had become primarily a celebration of God's gift of the law of Moses to Israel.

The fifty-day interval culminating in Pentecost served to remind Luke's first readers of two significant events in the life of Israel and an analogous two events in the life of the earliest Christian community. First, it reminded the reader of the fifty-day interval between Passover in Egypt and the giving of the law at Mount Sinai, two critical events in the life of God's people. Second, the Christian reader would be reminded of the crucifixion of Jesus which occurred at Passover and the gift of the Holy Spirit which occurred fifty days later at Pentecost.

One could expand the analogy between Israel's Pentecost and the Christian interpretation of this festival in two more dimensions. Just as the Jewish community could celebrate both God's gift of harvest and God's gift of Torah, so Luke and his readers could celebrate both the gift of a magnificent harvest ("about three thousand persons"; 2:41) and a divine gift, not of the law of God, but of the Spirit of God.

In the opening lines of this chapter the reader—ancient and modern—hears echoes from the Old Testament.

The creation story of Genesis 1	**Acts**
The "wind from God swept over the face of the waters" to create the world.	"The rush of a violent wind" (2:1) from heaven creates the church.

The tower of Babel in Genesis 11	Acts
"The whole earth had one language" which "the Lord confused."	"Jews from every nation" (2:5) hear the disciples · speaking in their own native language, a reversal of the Babel experience.

Moses receiving the Law in Exodus 20	Acts
Moses received the Law on Mount Sinai amid smoke, thunder, and fire.	The disciples receive the Holy Spirit on Mount Zion amid tongues of fire (2:3).

Luke is never far from his sources, particularly the Old Testament. In telling his story of the church, time and again he draws on the experiences of Israel recorded in scripture to help fill out the theological dimensions of his narrative. Of course it is helpful to remember that for his first readers, the Old Testament *was* their scripture. Luke's own writings—his Gospel and the Acts of the Apostles—did not become authoritative in the church for another fifty years. Luke reminds his Christian readers—then and now—of the rich inheritance we have in the Old Testament.

A rabbinic tradition from Luke's time suggests that when the Law was given by God at Sinai, it was given to all nations in all languages. It is entirely possible that Luke is re-presenting this tradition in light of the Christian experience in Jerusalem on that Day of Pentecost. This time, however, it is the gospel that is being given to "Jews from every nation under heaven . . . in the native language of each" (vv. 5–6).

For centuries Christians have struggled to understand this passage. What exactly was the Pentecost experience? What did it mean? Did the apostles really speak in languages that they did not know? Was this an ecstatic experience (implied by v. 13, "They are filled with new wine")?

Attempts to rationalize this experience have been numerous:

The multitude all spoke Greek and/or Aramaic and could have understood what the apostles were saying.

The apostles included enough idiomatic foreign phrases that people in the crowd could understand their message.

Such close spiritual rapport between the speakers and hearers resulted in a general understanding of what was being said.

Luke (or a predecessor) constructed this compelling story about how the church was launched so quickly and successfully.

It makes little sense to pursue these kinds of rationalizations in light of other New Testament attestations to the experience of glossolalia (speaking in tongues) in the early church (1 Corinthians 12; 14; Acts 10; 19). It is clear that, in the Pauline churches at least, the experience of speaking in tongues did take place. Furthermore, Paul clearly acknowledged that speaking in tongues was (1) a gift from God and (2) an ecstatic experience.

Luke adopts Paul's understanding of this phenomenon and would have no reason to question the Christian Pentecost tradition that was passed on to him. These first Christians received the gift of the Holy Spirit, which was sealed by an outward sign: the ability to speak in other languages "as the Spirit gave them ability." This is the essence of the Pentecostal experience and constitutes the Christian memory about its own beginnings. While Luke has been faithful in reporting this tradition it does not mean that Luke did not add his own coloring to the event. He did. We have already noted that the "violent wind" may have been a detail added to remind the reader of that first magnificent act of creation at the beginning of time recorded in Genesis 1. The second detail, "divided tongues of fire" coming to rest on each apostle, reminds the reader of Jesus' own baptism. In his Gospel, Luke notes that at Jesus' baptism, "the Holy Spirit descended upon him in bodily form like a dove" (Luke 3:22). In comparing Luke's narrative with his source, Mark (1:10), one notes Luke's addition of "in bodily form." Luke has concretized an experience that the other Gospels present metaphorically. Luke, the artist, has added his own details to this event so that, like Salvador Dali's painting of the Last Supper, one can look through the foreground which has been superimposed on a larger landscape. Luke's foreground is the gift of the Holy Spirit (with accompanying tongues of fire, glossolalia, and ecstasy) given to the apostles; concurrently, we look through this event and back in time to see God's gifts to Jesus, to Israel, and to all creation.

PETER'S SERMON
Acts 2:14–42

The Speeches in Acts

In reading through the Acts of the Apostles, one encounters a number of speeches (some of which take the form of a sermon)—maybe as many as twenty-four. Readers have wondered if these speeches are word-for-word transcriptions, or if Luke has condensed the speech, or if he has imaginatively constructed each speech. In the ancient world there were, of course, no tape recorders, though some literate listeners may have taken careful notes of important speeches. Often listeners would form an impression of what was said and record those impressions, including important points of the speech, in order to preserve the essence of the speech for others. A historian, like Luke, may have had access to such written impressions (including his own) and used them to refashion the speeches, maintaining the essence of what was said, using the kind of language that he imagined each speaker used, and constructing a physical setting for each speech.

The speeches in Acts are often a vehicle for Luke to present the collective wisdom of the church regarding its understanding of Jesus and what God has done through him. The early disciples of Jesus must have had many conversations about the meaning of Jesus' life and message, and about how God was active in Jesus Christ. We call this kind of conversation christological—conversation about what God has done in Christ.

Furthermore, Luke has used the technique of placing christological conversations in the mouths of key figures at important times throughout the story. Anyone who watches television soap operas is familiar with this technique. The soaps often present actors talking about the virtues, vices, and relationships of other characters in the story. A partner is always in the conversation, even when the actor is talking with herself. Furthermore, the conversation is scripted (most following a predictable pattern). Likewise, Luke has a conversation partner (really two partners—the audience in the narrative and his imaginary reader). In this passage we are privy to a conversation between Peter and the crowd about Jesus. At the same time, this is a conversation between Luke and his reader (us). And it is a specific kind of conversation—a christological conversation.

Another feature of these speeches also needs to be noted. In the Introduction I noted that Luke occasionally wrote in a "biblical" style of Greek, that is, the vocabulary and syntax would remind the reader of the Greek text of the Old Testament, the Septuagint. For example, when he presents the words of Jesus and his disciples—Jews of Galilee—he has them speak "biblical Greek." They not only speak in a manner one might imagine for Jews living in Palestine, but they speak as Jews living in "biblical times," that is, the kind of Greek spoken in the third century B.C.E. (This is all very amusing, of course, since the real language of Jesus and his apostles was first-century Aramaic!) As the activity recorded in Acts moves from Judea to the wider Greek and Roman world, Luke's stylized language also shifts from provincial Greek reminiscent of the third-century B.C.E. to first-century C.E. Koine (common) Greek—the "official" language of the Roman Empire.

The more important issue for the modern reader of Acts has to do with the substance of these speeches, not their style. Does Luke accurately convey the theological and christological understanding of the speaker? Does he accurately reflect conversation in the early church about God's work in Christ? The short answer is, Yes. As we shall see, the vocabulary of the speeches suggests a very early Jewish-Christian theological context, the same sort of ethos from which Paul also developed his particular Christology. As we encounter each speech we will point out significant early Christian concepts and themes Luke has preserved.

Peter's Sermon

Although Luke has presented a likeness of Peter's sermon, it is not a sermon transcript. Like contemporary sermons, a sermon in the first century was probably much longer than the few paragraphs Luke records. Paul put a person to sleep with one of his (20:7–9)! Therefore, Luke has captured the essence of a typical early Jewish-Christian sermon, condensed it, and styled it as he thought an early Jewish-Christian sermon might sound.

Like many contemporary sermons, Peter's sermon falls into three parts. There is an introductory section that describes the coming of the Holy Spirit as the fulfillment of an oracle given by the prophet Joel. This gift from God is a portent of this world's last days (2:14–21). The middle section is a confession of faith in Jesus as Lord and Messiah (vv. 22–36). The final section is a call to repentance and baptism in the name of Jesus Christ (vv. 37–42).

The Gift of the Holy Spirit as a Sign of the Last Days (Acts 2:14–21)

> 2:14 **But Peter, standing with the eleven, raised his voice and addressed them, "Men of Judea and all who live in Jerusalem, let this be known to you, and listen to what I say.** [15] **Indeed, these are not drunk, as you suppose, for it is only nine o'clock in the morning.** [16] **No, this is what was spoken through the prophet Joel:**
>
>   [17] **'In the last days it will be, God declares,**
>   **that I will pour out my Spirit upon all flesh,**
>   **and your sons and your daughters shall prophesy,**
>   **and your young men shall see visions,**
>   **and your old men shall dream dreams.**
>   [18] **Even upon my slaves, both men and women,**
>   **in those days I will pour out my Spirit;**
>   **and they shall prophesy.**

¹⁹ And I will show portents in the heaven above
and signs on the earth below,
  blood, and fire, and smoky mist.
²⁰ The sun shall be turned to darkness
and the moon to blood,
  before the coming of the Lord's great and glorious day.
²¹ Then everyone who calls on the name of the Lord shall be saved.'

Peter has emerged as spokesman for the apostolic leaders of the church—the Twelve. Luke presents him as an orator who stands, raises his voice, and addresses the crowd: "the men of Judea and all who live in Jerusalem." Peter begins by defending his fellow apostles who have been filled with the gift of the Holy Spirit. Those who received this gift were able to speak in languages other then their own (also known as glossolalia). Some who observed this phenomenon thought that the followers of Jesus were "filled with new wine." The reference to "new wine" might impugn the disciples in two ways. It may simply refer to the state of public drunkenness—being drunk with cheap "new wine." Or, it may be an observation that these are inauthentic prophets who rely on powerful "new wine" for their ecstatic experience, a practice not uncommon in antiquity. Peter seems to be responding to the former concern, though in doing so he takes care of the latter one as well. He quotes Joel, a biblical prophet, to claim that what the onlookers have witnessed is not an inpouring of human spirits, new wine, but an outpouring of God's spirit. God "has poured out this that you both see and hear" (v. 33).

The prophecy Peter quotes is an eschatological one, that is, speculation about the end of the world. Joel is projecting what it will be like "in the last days." Peter identifies what has happened among the disciples as a prophetic sign by citing a text in which God twice declares, "In the last days . . . I will pour out my Spirit."

Peter has chosen this text as a biblical witness to the extraordinary experience occurring in the church. The apostles of Jesus are not drunk; they are filled with God's spirit! That which the crowd sees is evidence that Joel's prophecy about the last days has come to pass. The church lives by and in the Spirit of God—the Holy Spirit.

A Confession of Faith in Jesus as Lord and Messiah (Acts 2:22–36)

2:22 "You that are Israelites, listen to what I have to say: Jesus of Nazareth, a man attested to you by God with deeds of power, wonders, and signs that God did through him among you, as you yourselves know— ²³ this man, handed over to you according to the definite plan and foreknowledge of God, you crucified and killed by the hands of those outside the law. 24 But God raised him up, having freed him from death, because it was impossible for him to be held in its power. 25 For David says concerning him,

> 'I saw the Lord always before me,
> for he is at my right hand so that I will not be shaken;
> 26 therefore my heart was glad, and my tongue rejoiced;
> moreover my flesh will live in hope.
> 27 For you will not abandon my soul to Hades,
> or let your Holy One experience corruption.
> 28 You have made known to me the ways of life;
> you will make me full of gladness with your presence.'

29 "Fellow Israelites, I may say to you confidently of our ancestor David that he both died and was buried, and his tomb is with us to this day. 30 Since he was a prophet, he knew that God had sworn with an oath to him that he would put one of his descendants on his throne. 31 Foreseeing this, David spoke of the resurrection of the Messiah, saying,

> 'He was not abandoned to Hades,
> nor did his flesh experience corruption.'

32 This Jesus God raised up, and of that all of us are witnesses. 33 Being therefore exalted at the right hand of God, and having received from the Father the promise of the Holy Spirit, he has poured out this that you both see and hear. 34 For David did not ascend into the heavens, but he himself says,

> 'The Lord said to my Lord,
> "Sit at my right hand,
> 35 until I make your enemies your footstool."'

36 Therefore let the entire house of Israel know with certainty that God has made him both Lord and Messiah, this Jesus whom you crucified."

With these verses, Luke has presented his readers with one of the earliest Christian confessions of faith. Interspersed in this sermon are citations from the Old Testament which were applied to the life and message of Jesus. This confession is divided into three sections: Jesus the man, Jesus the Messiah, and Jesus as Lord *and* Messiah.

Jesus the Man
from Nazareth (2:22–24)

Part one of the confession begins with a remembrance of who Jesus of Nazareth was, what he did, how he came to be crucified, and how God "raised him up, having freed him from death." A quote from Psalm 16 follows which supports the notion that God has raised Jesus from the realm of the dead: "You will not abandon my soul to Hades." It is important to note that Jesus is clearly described as a human being (twice), this "Jesus of Nazareth." But it is also clear that Peter considered Jesus to be more than an ordinary man. Jesus was "attested . . . by God with deeds of power (literally "powers"), wonders, and signs that God did through him" (v. 22).

Luke used these three attributes—powers, wonders, and signs—to describe the manifestation of God through his messengers, and the reader encounters various combinations of these three words throughout the book of Acts. The reader should also be aware of the trifocal nature of this phrase—past, present, and future. It looks to Israel's *past*, to the time of Moses when God liberated his people with powerful "signs and wonders" (especially prominent in Deuteronomy—4:34; 6:22; 7:19; 26:8; 29:3; 34:11). "Signs and wonders" had become a biblical formula that drew the reader's imagination back to an awesome display of God's power on behalf of God's people during the exodus from Egypt. For Luke, the people of God are beginning a new exodus which will lead them out from the Promised Land and into the wider Hellenistic world (Acts 1:8).

"Powers, signs, and wonders" also draw the reader's attention to Luke's own apostolic age—Luke's *present* time. The phrase had become a standard way of describing life in the early church. It is "proof" of God's work among leaders in the church. Thirty years before Luke wrote Acts, the apostle Paul spoke of himself as one who performed "signs, wonders, and powers" (2 Cor. 12:12; see Rom. 15:19). A phrase near the beginning of the letter to the Hebrews is almost identical to this passage in Acts: "It [the message of salvation] was declared at first through the Lord, and it was attested to us by those who heard him, while God added his testimony by signs and wonders and various miracles [powers]" (Heb. 2:3–4).

Finally, there is a *future* dimension to this phrase. "Powers, signs, and wonders" can be understood eschatologically. Eschatology literally means "a study of the end"; in the biblical context it usually refers to the end of the world as we know it, the end of history. Jews of the first century expected that just prior to the end of time, God would intervene in the course of human history with manifestations of divine power. Healing miracles were a sign that the end was at hand (see Luke 7:18–22; Paul notes that at the end of this age, even Satan will offer his own displays of "power, signs, and *lying* wonders" [2 Thess. 2:9]). It was expected that the one whom God appointed and anointed would manifest God's power. As we shall see in Acts 3, with the advent of the church this power was transferred from Jesus to his disciples.

In spite of these obvious marks of divinity which Jesus possessed, he died a cruel and shameful death. Jesus' death appeared to contradict his life. Therefore, the "scandal" of the cross must be explained. Peter appears to be reciting, in part, a confession of faith carefully crafted in the early church which addressed this crucial issue: "This man, handed over to you according to the definite plan and foreknowledge of God, you crucified and killed by the hands of those outside the law" (v. 23). The death of Jesus, horrible though it was, was part of God's design for salvation. The scandal of the crucifixion, an act of human freedom at its worst, was overcome by God's predetermination. As the ultimate sign that Jesus is indeed the Messiah, "God raised him up, having freed him from death" (v. 24).

Acts 2:23 raises a difficult problem for the reader. Who was responsible for the crucifixion of Jesus? On the one hand, Peter (Luke?) tells us that Jesus was "handed over" to the Jews for crucifixion, a statement confirmed by v. 36, "Jesus whom you crucified." This sounds as if Jesus was put into Jewish hands for execution by the Roman procurator, Pontius Pilate, a detail that squares with Luke's Gospel (Luke 23:25). Yet, Acts 2:23 also indicates that the Romans were actually responsible for Jesus' execution: Jesus was "killed by the hands of those outside the law" (this is supported by Acts 3:13). It is clear from reading Mark, one of Luke's sources, that Jesus was condemned by the Roman procurator and executed by Roman soldiers. But Luke seems to want it both ways.

This portion of Acts forces some difficult questions upon the reader: Are the passages in Acts 2:23 and 2:36 evidence of Lukan anti-Semitism? Or does Luke simply reflect the sentiment of the early church? Or is there a kernel of truth here—were both the Jews of Jerusalem (Luke usually specifies the Sanhedrin) and their Roman overlords responsible for the death of Jesus? These questions cannot be dealt with satisfactorily in this book, though a number of excellent books have been published recently on the death of Jesus. The reader is encouraged to consult these works and to read the Introduction, above, on Luke's purpose and the apparent anti-Semitisms in Acts. Unfortunately, passages like these can be maliciously interpreted, thereby opening the door to anti-Semitism. Yes, some of the Jewish leaders in Jerusalem may have been in league with the Roman procurator out of fear that Jesus was a threat to their positions of power. But to suggest as Peter or Luke does that "the Jews" crucified Jesus is an exaggeration that is not historically accurate.

Jesus the Messiah (2:25–31)

Part two of the confession compares David, the first Messiah, with Jesus the last Messiah. The first Messiah died and was buried; the last Messiah was raised from the dead. In 2:31, as a proof text, Peter cites Psalm 16:10: "He was not abandoned to Hades, nor did his flesh experience corruption." As if to remove any ambiguity, Peter clearly identifies Jesus as "*this Jesus* [whom] God raised up." Later in Acts, we shall see that Paul offers a similar argument (13:26–41).

God Has Made Jesus Both Lord and Messiah (2:32–36)

Part three of the confession declares that those who are witnesses to the resurrection have received the Holy Spirit—"this that you both see and hear." In 2:34 once again Peter has used a Psalm (110:1) to support the notion that Jesus was raised from the dead and ascended into heaven: "The Lord said to my Lord, 'Sit at my right hand . . . '"

The confession of faith concludes with an all-important "Therefore"! Read this passage aloud slowly, and listen to the emphasis placed on each word of this conclusion.

> Therefore let the entire house of Israel know with certainty that God has made him both Lord and Messiah, this Jesus whom you crucified. (Acts 2:36)

The "entire house of Israel" refers to *all* Israel—past, present, and future. It is also clear that Peter wants his hearers to "know *with certainty*" that Jesus is more than an earthly political messiah, that Jesus is greater than David who was remembered as the greatest of Israel's kings. Jesus is God's living Messiah who has transcended time and space through the power of the resurrection.

The terms "Lord" and "Messiah" are particularly weighty in this sentence. Each can be understood in two important ways. "Lord" and "Messiah" possess both political and religious connotations.

The term "Lord" has a wide range of meanings in the New Testament, from polite address which we might render "sir" to a title of honor used by important civic figures. "Lord" is one of the titles used by the Roman emperor in a despotic sense. To say that "Caesar is Lord" is to declare him master over all the Roman realm. And it is in this regard that early Christian teaching about Jesus drew the church into conflict with the Roman authorities. To confess that "Jesus is Lord" is to affirm that Jesus is master over one's life. A Roman patriot might ask, "How can one serve two masters?"

The word "messiah" is derived from a Hebrew word that means "to pour out" and refers to the action of Samuel in pouring oil on David's head: "Then Samuel took the horn of oil, and anointed him . . . ; and the spirit of the LORD came mightily upon David from that day forward" (1 Sam. 16:13). This ritual was used at the coronation of all subsequent kings of Judah, those who have been anointed—Messiahs (also see comments on 3:17–21). To confess that Jesus is Messiah is to acknowledge him as king. A Roman patriot might also say, "We have no king but Caesar!"

It is also important to note that the terms "Lord" and "Messiah" function on a deeper level. The early Christian concept of "Messiah" transcended the confines of earthly politics. It may be that Jesus originally linked the concept of messiahship with suffering, and therefore played out, in his own life and death, the drama of a suffering messiah (there is plenty of evidence in Luke's Gospel that the disciples were confused about Jesus' identity as Messiah *and* suffering servant of God; Luke 9:18–22; 24:25–27, 45–46). Yet, even though Jesus suffered, the early Christian confession claimed that God exalted him as his eternal Messiah (see also 1 Cor. 1:22–24).

This early Christian confession points to another level of understanding of the term "Lord." Jewish readers of the Old Testament were reluctant to utter the divine name "Yahweh"; one would want to be especially careful in using the powerful name of God (remember the Third Commandment about using the name of God in vain; see comments on 3:1–10). Therefore "Lord" was used as a substitute for the divine name. The confession that Jesus is both Lord and Messiah encourages the hearer, especially the Jewish hearer, to connect Jesus with the divine realm. In the same way that Yahweh is Lord over the entire created order, so is Jesus Lord. Paul recites a similar confession in his letter to the Philippians:

> Therefore God also highly exalted him
> and gave him the name
> that is above every name,
> so that at the name of Jesus
> every knee should bend,
> in heaven and on earth and under the earth,
> and every tongue should confess
> that Jesus Christ [Messiah] is Lord,
> to the glory of God the Father.
> (Phil. 2:9–11)

One could come to the conclusion that Peter has de-politicized the Christian understanding of the raised Jesus by declaring that Jesus is a heavenly, not earthly, Lord and Messiah. One might also come to the opposite conclusion, that Peter has raised the political stakes considerably for Christians. According to this confession, Christians owe their ultimate allegiance not to any powerful earthly ruler with pretensions of divinity but to Jesus of Nazareth, a man executed by crucifixion, and yet whom "God has made both Lord and Messiah."

Peter's Call to Repentance and the Response of the Crowd (Acts 2:37–42)

2:37 **Now when they heard this, they were cut to the heart and said to Peter and to the other apostles, "Brothers, what should we do?"** 38 **Peter said to them, "Repent, and be baptized every one of you in the name of Jesus Christ so that your sins may be forgiven; and you will receive the gift of the Holy Spirit.** 39 **For the promise is for you, for your children, and for all who are far away, everyone whom the Lord our God calls to him."** 40 **And he testified with many other arguments and exhorted them, saying, "Save yourselves from this corrupt generation."** 41 **So those who welcomed his message were baptized, and that day about three thousand persons were added.** 42 **They devoted themselves to the apostles' teaching and fellowship, to the breaking of bread and the prayers.**

The people who heard Peter's sermon were deeply affected by the truth he was telling them. The man Jesus was indeed God's anointed, and they had participated—at least as passive observers—in his crucifixion. The Messiah had been crucified! In anguish they cried out to Peter, "Now what should we do?" Peter responded with three imperatives: "Repent . . . , be baptized . . . , and save yourselves from this corrupt generation."

The first imperative, "repent," challenged the people to change their minds about Jesus, to understand that he is indeed the Messiah in spite of the crucifixion. The people were challenged to admit that they were wrong about Jesus. They were asked to look beyond the crucifixion; God had raised Jesus from death to life, and empowered Jesus to sit at the right hand of God. The apostles proclaimed that they were eyewitnesses to the resurrection. "Repent, change your minds about Jesus, come to a new understanding of God's Messiah."

Peter's second imperative was directed to those who do change their minds about Jesus. They were called on to be baptized "so that your sins may be forgiven" (v. 37). The three words—"repent . . . baptize . . . forgiveness"—hark back to the work of John the Baptist. In his Gospel, Luke records that John "went into all the region around the Jordan, proclaiming a baptism of repentance for the forgiveness of sins" (Luke 3:3). When asked if he is the Messiah, John demurs saying, "I baptize you with water; but one who is more powerful than I is coming. . . . He will baptize you with the Holy Spirit and fire" (Luke 3:16). Likewise in the book of Acts, Peter called people to repentance, baptism, and forgiveness. Peter, however, added two new dimensions to John's baptism. First, baptism is done "in the name of Jesus Christ"; those who are baptized are brought under the power and authority of Jesus. Second, baptism brings the gift of the Holy Spirit. The promise of John the Baptist has been fulfilled in the community of Jesus. Peter's hearers were invited to share the gift just given the disciples of Jesus on this first Pentecost of the church.

In the third imperative, Peter exhorted the crowd: "Save yourselves from this corrupt generation" (v. 40). Peter's words would remind his hearers of the biblical notion of a faithful remnant in Israel. In allying themselves with Jesus, these new Christians carry on the tradition of a faithful minority within God's people, designated by God to carry out God's mission in the world.

Luke records that on that birthday of the church, that first Christian Pentecost, "about three thousand persons were added" to the community (v. 41). Peter must have delivered a powerful sermon indeed! For a church to grow from twelve to three thousand in just a few days surely breaks all records for evangelism! It is difficult to know whether or not Luke is exaggerating here. Luke does love to write about multitudes of converts (see especially Acts 21:20 where the Jerusalem elders say of Paul's work, "You see, brother, how many tens of thousands [literal translation] of believers there are among the Jews." And this does not include Gentile believers). These masses streaming into the church are a sure sign that God's blessing is with this movement.

Whether or not Luke is exaggerating the numbers, he is looking back in time some fifty years through somewhat nostalgic eyes to a "golden age" of the church. The description of the church in the next section has a halo glow about it.

LIFE IN THE EARLY CHRISTIAN COMMUNITY
Acts 2:43–47

> 2:43 **Awe came upon everyone, because many wonders and signs were being done by the apostles. 44 All who believed were together and had all things in common; 45 they would sell their possessions and goods and distribute the proceeds to all, as any had need. 46 Day by day, as they spent much time to-**

**gether in the temple, they broke bread at home and ate their food with glad
and generous hearts,** [47] **praising God and having the goodwill of all the people. And day by day the Lord added to their number those who were being
saved.**

In this passage Luke offers the reader a brief description of life in the
infant Christian community. Just as in his Gospel Luke had rendered
Jesus' nativity—with awestruck shepherds and singing angels—in harmonious soft tones, so here he paints a similar picture of the birth of the
church. A romantic glow spreads over the community.

The church was pure and perfect in its infancy. Outsiders stood in awe
because of the many miracles performed by the apostles, and insiders freely
shared their financial resources with one other. Members of the community divided their time between temple piety and household duties. The
reader feels a warm glow coming from the hearths of these house churches
as "they broke bread at home and ate their food with glad and generous
hearts, praising God" (vv. 46–47).

In his Gospel Luke notes that "Jesus increased in wisdom and in
years, and in divine and human favor"; likewise at the end of this "birth
narrative" Luke indicates that the followers of Jesus had "the goodwill of
all the people. And day by day the Lord added to their number those who
were being saved" (v. 47). The church, like her founder, was increasing in
size and favor. But this perfect time, this golden age, was short-lived. Luke,
of course, knew this. Yet he wanted to present a picture of that one-time
experience of perfect harmony in the Christian community. Perhaps he
presented it as a goal for his own church, and it may be a goal for our own
time. There is a longing deep inside each of us for a place of perfect peace
and harmony, where all things—material and spiritual—are shared, and
where we can eat together "with glad and generous hearts." One can almost hear them sing,

> Blest be the tie that binds,
>   Our hearts in Christian love:
> The fellowship of kindred minds
>   Is like to that above.

Luke allows us a fleeting look at a moment in time when that perfect fellowship was fully alive and he holds out the hope that it can happen again.

Luke also reminds us that this was no human undertaking. "Day by day
the Lord added to their number those who were being saved" (v. 47). Luke
realizes that the success of the church (in whatever way one measures

success) was not the doing of Peter, Paul, or any human vessel. It is the Lord's doing.

Luke has looked back fifty years to describe the beginnings of the church. It was, in his mind, a time of excitement, harmony, and growth. The church was ablaze with enthusiasm for a mission to all kinds of people—"Jews from every nation under heaven." At the same time, this polyglot group of believers found ways of living peacefully together, and more than that, they freely shared their individual possessions for the common good. Luke tells us that they devoted themselves to "the apostles' teaching and fellowship, to the breaking of bread and the prayers." And finally, with this spirit of enthusiasm and community came spectacular growth from twelve (plus members of Jesus' family), to 120, to 3,000 in just a matter of days! Remarkable! Perhaps there are some lessons to be learned here about church growth.

PETER AND JOHN HEAL A LAME MAN
Acts 3:1–10

> 3:1 **One day Peter and John were going up to the temple at the hour of prayer, at three o'clock in the afternoon.** [2] **And a man lame from birth was being carried in. People would lay him daily at the gate of the temple called the Beautiful Gate so that he could ask for alms from those entering the temple.** [3] **When he saw Peter and John about to go into the temple, he asked them for alms.** [4] **Peter looked intently at him, as did John, and said, "Look at us."** [5] **And he fixed his attention on them, expecting to receive something from them.** [6] **But Peter said, "I have no silver or gold, but what I have I give you; in the name of Jesus Christ of Nazareth, stand up and walk."** [7] **And he took him by the right hand and raised him up; and immediately his feet and ankles were made strong.** [8] **Jumping up, he stood and began to walk, and he entered the temple with them, walking and leaping and praising God.** [9] **All the people saw him walking and praising God,** [10] **and they recognized him as the one who used to sit and ask for alms at the Beautiful Gate of the temple; and they were filled with wonder and amazement at what had happened to him.**

Toward the end of Acts 2, Luke notes that "many wonders and signs were being done by the apostles." As I suggested above, "signs and wonders" is a standard formula that describes God's extraordinary activity accomplished through human channels (2:22–36). Here in chapter 3, Luke offers an illustration of a specific "wonder"—a man born lame was healed by two of Jesus' apostles.

The reader of Luke's Gospel knows that Luke is fond of reporting the healing miracles of Jesus. He records seventeen healing stories, often with considerable detail (so much so that some readers of his Gospel discern the hand of a physician, "Doctor Luke," behind the literary descriptions; see the Introduction). In narrating the healings performed by Jesus, Luke (like the other Gospel writers) usually follows a set pattern. He begins with (1) a description of the illness, followed by (2) an action of Jesus (by word or touch) that effects a cure, and ends with (3) the response of the healed person and bystanders to the miracle.

While Luke suggests that the apostles also performed miracles during their apprenticeship (Luke 9:6; 10:17), he does not follow the usual pattern in describing a healing miracle. Rather, vague results are mentioned: "They [the twelve] departed and went through the villages, bringing the good news and curing diseases everywhere" (Luke 9:6). "The seventy returned with joy, saying, 'Lord, in your name even the demons submit to us!'" (Luke 10:17).

Finally, in Acts 3, Luke describes in detail a healing miracle performed by an apostle of Jesus. In this scene Luke uses the same narrative formula that he used with Jesus—a description of the man's condition, an action by the apostles (Peter is the main actor while John is mentioned almost as an afterthought), and a description of the response of the healed man and those who knew him. This is a pattern the reader will encounter often in Acts. (A parallel story is recorded in Acts 14 in which Paul heals a man crippled from birth; see also Acts 8:6–7; 9:17–18, 32–35, 36–43; 16:16–18; 20:7–12.)

Peter and John healed the lame man by declaring, "In the name of Jesus Christ of Nazareth, stand up and walk" (3:6). Peter has used the name of Jesus as a source of healing power making it clear from the outset of Acts that "Jesus" is a divine name which can be invoked by those belonging to the community of Jesus (see Acts 19:13–16, and note what happens to nonbelievers who try to invoke the name of Jesus). Later in this chapter Peter declares that Jesus' "name itself has made this man strong" (3:16).

There is tremendous power in the divine name. This is a concept deeply rooted in Hebrew tradition. The Third Commandment states: "You shall not make wrongful use of the name of the LORD your God" (Exod. 20:7; the more familiar version reads, "You shall not take the name of the LORD your God in vain"; RSV). To know the divine name is to be entrusted with the power of that name. Only after Moses learned the name of God, "Yahweh," was he able to use the awesome power of that name to perform mighty "signs and wonders." Power did not reside in the name itself.

Rather, the name represented the power behind it. The Third Commandment implores one to use that name (and its power) with utmost caution. A blessing or curse uttered in the divine name *will* come to pass.

This concept is unlike magical thinking about the power of language—the empowerment of a word. When my daughter was four years old she thought that simply uttering the word "death" would bring it about. For her, there was power in the word itself. Similarly, ancient magic texts suggest that simply using particular words and phrases, including the names "Yahweh" and "Jesus," would cast spells and effect cures. Miracle, however, has to do with God's power and God's sovereignty. The disciples used the name of Jesus with the knowledge that God's power was in that name and that the sovereign will of God would be enacted through that name.

On a more mundane level, the passage reminds the reader that words *do* have power. A word uttered cannot be retrieved. Therefore caution is essential in sensitive situations. But this text is about the miraculous power of words. Peter and the other apostles are Jesus' surrogates with authority to use the divine power that stands behind the name of Jesus.

It is clear that the lame man knew the source of his healing, a source that transcended Peter. "Jumping up, he stood and began to walk, and he entered the temple with them, walking and leaping and *praising God*" (3:8). The lame man wisely recognized that God was the source of his healing.

Luke offers a lively picture of an astonished crowd running to Peter and John. This gathering offered Peter a second opportunity for a sermon about Jesus.

PETER'S SECOND SERMON
Acts 3:11–26

> 3:11 **While he clung to Peter and John, all the people ran together to them in the portico called Solomon's Portico, utterly astonished.** 12 **When Peter saw it, he addressed the people, "You Israelites, why do you wonder at this, or why do you stare at us, as though by our own power or piety we had made him walk?** 13 **The God of Abraham, the God of Isaac, and the God of Jacob, the God of our ancestors has glorified his servant Jesus, whom you handed over and rejected in the presence of Pilate, though he had decided to release him.** 14 **But you rejected the Holy and Righteous One and asked to have a murderer given to you,** 15 **and you killed the Author of life, whom God raised from the dead. To this we are witnesses.** 16 **And by faith in his name, his name itself has made this man strong, whom you see and know; and the faith that**

is through Jesus has given him this perfect health in the presence of all of you.

[17] "And now, friends, I know that you acted in ignorance, as did also your rulers. [18] In this way God fulfilled what he had foretold through all the prophets, that his Messiah would suffer. [19] Repent therefore, and turn to God so that your sins may be wiped out, [20] so that times of refreshing may come from the presence of the Lord, and that he may send the Messiah appointed for you, that is, Jesus, [21] who must remain in heaven until the time of universal restoration that God announced long ago through his holy prophets. [22] Moses said, 'The Lord your God will raise up for you from your own people a prophet like me. You must listen to whatever he tells you. [23] And it will be that everyone who does not listen to that prophet will be utterly rooted out of the people.' [24] And all the prophets, as many as have spoken, from Samuel and those after him, also predicted these days. [25] You are the descendants of the prophets and of the covenant that God gave to your ancestors, saying to Abraham, 'And in your descendants all the families of the earth shall be blessed.' [26] When God raised up his servant, he sent him first to you, to bless you by turning each of you from your wicked ways."

The miraculous healing of the lame man has precipitated Peter's second sermon. Luke's setting for the sermon is Solomon's Portico. Within this magnificent colonnade on the east side of the great court of the temple, Peter and John stand alongside a man flooded with joy and clinging to them both. An excited crowd runs to the trio, "utterly astonished" to see the man upright on his feet, standing with the apostles. Seeing the crowd gathered before him, Peter takes the opportunity to preach another sermon.

Once again, the reader encounters in Peter's sermon an early confessional statement about the person and work of Jesus Christ—a christological confession drawn from the liturgy of the early church. In this sermon Peter securely links Jesus of Nazareth to three major strands of Old Testament tradition: the patriarchs, the kings (especially David), and the prophets (especially Moses).

And as before, Peter's sermon makes three points: (1) Peter argues that Jesus, God's glorified servant-child, was killed by his fellow "Israelites." (2) These Israelites acted in ignorance, unaware that Jesus was more than the servant of God—he was Israel's promised Messiah. (3) Jesus was not only promised by Israel's prophets, he himself was *the* prophet—a prophet like Moses. Jesus is the true child (discussion of this term follows) of Israel's ancestors, prophets, kings, covenants, and God.

Jesus the Servant (3:11–16)

Peter makes clear that it was not his own healing power or piety that restored strength to the man. Rather, the power to heal came from God—the God of Israel's ancestors Abraham, Isaac, and Jacob, and the same God who glorified Jesus. Moreover, while God was the source of healing power, that potential power was made active through faith in the name of Jesus. Though the text does not tell us *whose* faith (the apostles' or the lame man's?) effected the healing, one suspects it was the faith of the apostles who used the name.

Peter uses some interesting christological titles for Jesus in these verses. The titles may be strange to our ears, yet they are among the earliest applied to Jesus of Nazareth. We usually think of Jesus as Son of God, Messiah, Savior. In this passage, Jesus is God's Servant, and he is Holy, Righteous, and Author of Life. Because these christological titles *are* unusual and early, it is worth taking a close look at each one.

Notice that Peter begins and ends his sermon (and remember that the sermon structure may be Luke's) with the statement that Jesus is God's "servant" (vv. 13, 26; according to the marginal note in the NRSV, the term translated as "servant" can also be rendered "child"). Peter may have been attempting to convey an understanding of Jesus drawn from four poems, or songs, found in the writings of the prophet Isaiah (Isa. 42:1–4; 49:1–6; 50:4–11; 52:13–53:12)—the Servant Songs. Peter's statement that God "has glorified his servant Jesus" (Acts 3:13; see also v. 26; 4:25, 27, 30) is probably an allusion to the fourth servant song of Isaiah (Isa. 52:13–53:12; also see Acts 8:26–40). Jesus, like Isaiah's servant of God, did God's will. In spite of this, he was "despised and rejected." According to Isaiah, God's servant was "a man of suffering and acquainted with infirmity, . . . wounded for our transgressions, crushed for our iniquities" (Isa. 53:3, 5). Yet, even though "it was the will of the LORD to crush him with pain," God declares, "The righteous one, my servant, shall make many righteous" (Isa. 53: 10, 11).

Jesus is God's servant. Jesus is also "the Holy and Righteous One . . ., the Author of life, whom God raised from the dead" (Acts 3:14–15). Along with "servant," the terms "Holy" and "Righteous One" are probably the earliest titles the followers of Jesus applied to their master after his death.

As we have seen, Isaiah refers to the servant of God as "the righteous one [who makes] many righteous" (Isa. 53:11). Jesus' followers were convinced that he was legally just or righteous even though he was condemned in a Roman court ("righteous" and "just" are derived from the same Greek word; also see comments on Acts 7:44–53). But more than this, Jesus was judged in the right by God who has exalted him to divine—holy—status (also see John 6:69

where Peter tells Jesus, "We have come to believe and know that you are the Holy One of God"). Jesus is the Servant of God—Holy and Righteous.

The fourth title, "Author of life," is fascinating because of its ironic twist. According to Peter, the "Israelites" had asked for a murderer—a "taker of life"—to be released, and then proceeded to kill the Author of Life. Peter declares, "You [Israelites] killed the Author of life." Luke returns to this theme again and again, protesting too much the culpability of the Jews and downplaying the responsibility of the Romans in the death of Jesus (see comments on 3:11–26; 4:1–12; 5:17–42; 10:34–43; and 13:17–41).

Jesus is God's Servant, Holy, Righteous, and the Author of Life "whom God raised from the dead." Peter puts his finishing touch on this confession of faith: "To this we are witnesses" (v. 15).

Jesus the Messiah (3:17–21)

In his sermon Peter conveys an early Christian understanding of Jesus' identity. Jesus was both God's servant anticipated by Israel's patriarchs (3:13ff.) and he is God's Messiah predicted by Israel's prophets (vv. 18ff.). Building on his sermon of Acts 2, Peter has developed the notion that Jesus the man from Nazareth is also Jesus the Messiah from heaven.

Peter and the early church must have felt compelled to argue theologically and convincingly that Jesus of Nazareth—a good man who suffered and died cruelly and unjustly—was really God's Messiah. First-century Jews had been expecting a messiah, particularly those Jews who felt that they were living in the last days. The word "messiah" is derived from the Hebrew term "to anoint," and it had a specifically religious and political meaning—"to pour oil on the head of a person to be designated as a king in Israel" (see comments on 2:22–36).

In the period between the Old and New Testaments the term "messiah" (translated into Greek as *christos*) began to refer to an ideal future king of Israel. Thus, "Jesus Christ" combines a given name and a title—Jesus the Christ, Jesus the Messiah. In the minds of Peter's hearers, the word "messiah" would have evoked images of a royal figure, a descendant of David, who would lead his people to sovereignty and freedom from Rome's rule.

In verses 17–19, Peter encourages his hearers to reconsider their beliefs and actions. Peter's call to repentance is a call for his hearers to change their minds (which is the meaning of "repent") about Jesus so that their sins against God's Messiah, actions mitigated by ignorance, might be wiped out. Peter has challenged this Jewish audience to revise radically its concept of messiah.

The apostles themselves had to undergo a revision of their understanding of messiah, a revision that Peter attempts to articulate to his audience at the temple. Remember the first question the apostles asked their risen Lord: "Lord, is this the time when *you* will restore the *kingdom* to Israel?" (1:6). An answer to this question is present in 3:21: "Jesus . . . must remain in heaven until the time of universal restoration that God announced long ago through his holy prophets." This Messiah will bring far more than sovereignty to Israel; he will bring "universal restoration." He will bring into existence, as fulfillment of early Christian hope, a creation restored to its original paradiselike state (Rom. 8:19–23; 2 Cor. 5:17; Gal. 6:15; 2 Peter 3:13; Rev. 21:1; also Isa. 65:17).

Peter reflects the early Christian expectation that Jesus' reign will transcend a restored kingdom of Israel. His reign will embrace all the kingdoms of this world. Jesus will reign as king over God's restored creation. Peter's audience might have agreed with this hope. Yes, Israel was expecting a king to come to her rescue. Kings win battles and defeat their enemies; they are strong and they persevere. Kings survive; they do not suffer. But Jesus had suffered at the hands of Rome, and endured an undignified and unkingly death. Yet, Peter announced the amazing paradox that it is precisely this same *Jesus of Nazareth*, who reigns as God's Messiah. Israel was not expecting a suffering messiah. But, says Peter, this should not come as a surprise to anyone who has carefully read the prophets. God foretold these things "through *all* the prophets" (v. 18; also vv. 21, 24).

Jesus the Prophet (3:22–26)

Peter concludes his powerful sermon by placing Jesus squarely in a Jewish context: glorified by the God of the patriarchs—Abraham, Isaac, and Jacob—Jesus is a messiah comparable to the first and greatest of Israel's kings, David. Furthermore, Jesus is a prophet comparable to the first and greatest of Israel's prophets, Moses (v. 22). Quoting Moses, Peter declares,

> The Lord your God will raise up for you from your own people a prophet like me. You *must* listen to whatever he tells you. And it will be that everyone who does not listen to that prophet will be utterly rooted out of the people. (Acts 3:22–23; see Deut. 18:15–16)

According to Jewish tradition, at the end of history God would send his ideal prophet, a "prophet like Moses." Peter has identified Jesus as this eschatological prophet. Again, with a bit of exaggeration Peter suggests that "*all* the prophets, as many as have spoken, from Samuel and those after him, also predicted these days" (v. 24).

Peter's final statement, loaded with double meanings, is clear in its message. "When God raised up [the term can mean "brought into being" or "raised from the dead"] his servant [or "child"], he sent him first to you, to bless you . . . " (v. 26). Out of frail sinful Israel, came a frail obedient servant of God. And out of all this human frailty has come blessing for all the families of the earth, a blessing of cosmic proportions. God sent Jesus "first to you"—to the Jews first, one of Luke's themes. This brutalized and beaten man, Jesus of Nazareth, is in reality God's Servant, Messiah, and Prophet—God's blessing to Israel.

PETER AND JOHN ARE ARRESTED
Acts 4:1–12

4:1 **While Peter and John were speaking to the people, the priests, the captain of the temple, and the Sadducees came to them, 2 much annoyed because they were teaching the people and proclaiming that in Jesus there is the resurrection of the dead. 3 So they arrested them and put them in custody until the next day, for it was already evening. 4 But many of those who heard the word believed; and they numbered about five thousand.**
5 The next day their rulers, elders, and scribes assembled in Jerusalem, 6 with Annas the high priest, Caiaphas, John, and Alexander, and all who were of the high-priestly family. 7 When they had made the prisoners stand in their midst, they inquired, "By what power or by what name did you do this?" 8 Then Peter, filled with the Holy Spirit, said to them, "Rulers of the people and elders, 9 if we are questioned today because of a good deed done to someone who was sick and are asked how this man has been healed, 10 let it be known to all of you, and to all the people of Israel, that this man is standing before you in good health by the name of Jesus Christ of Nazareth, whom you crucified, whom God raised from the dead. 11 This Jesus is
    'the stone that was rejected by you, the builders;
        it has become the cornerstone.'
12 There is salvation in no one else, for there is no other name under heaven given among mortals by which we must be saved."

This scene in Acts is not a surprising one. Since the healing of the lame man and the sermon of Peter took place within the temple precincts, those in charge of temple affairs would naturally be curious. Luke notes that Peter and John were arrested by the priests, the Sadducees, and the officer in charge of the temple police. Since the hour was late, the apostles were held overnight until the Sanhedrin could convene the following morning. Those charged with oversight of religious observance in Jerusalem would be especially anxious about this new sect, for it was growing at a spectacular rate. In a matter of weeks the church had grown from 12 to 120 to 3,000 to 5,000 believers. Truly, something important was happening in this new sect of Judaism and the authorities felt obliged to investigate.

Following the practice of the NRSV translators, I use the words "Sanhedrin" and "council" interchangeably; both words are translations of the Greek word *synedrion*. While this word first occurs in the next section (v. 15), a brief discussion here about the council will help establish the context for this scene and other similar scenes which follow in the book of Acts (5:21ff., the apostles; 6:12ff., Stephen; 22:30ff., Paul; also Luke 22:66ff., Jesus). In Greek literature of the first century, the term "sanhedrin" was used in connection with councils of many types: political, military, trade, and religious. In the New Testament (and other contemporary Jewish literature) "Sanhedrin" came to be identified primarily with the supreme court of chief priests and elders in Jerusalem. In reality, there may have been several "councils" (political, business, and religious) functioning in Jerusalem.

Luke understands the Sanhedrin to be a single high court of Jerusalem's religious and political leaders comprising both Sadducees and Pharisees. This court had judicial responsibility for interpreting and guarding Jewish law and practice, and for disciplining those who did not meet some measure of legal conformance or those who encouraged others to stray from the law (the charge brought against Jesus, Luke 23:5, 14; Stephen, Acts 6:13–14; and Paul, Acts 24:5–6).

Peter and John were arrested and brought before the council for teaching that "in Jesus there is the resurrection of the dead" (v. 2). The charge that the apostles teach about the resurrection would not be pursued very vigorously. To be sure, "the Sadducees say that there is no resurrection" (Acts 23:8; see Luke 20:27), and this group held positions of leadership in the Sanhedrin. However, the Sanhedrin also included Pharisees among its membership. Unlike the Sadducees, they taught that there will be a resurrection of the dead at the end of time. The Pharisaic members of the council would be curious about the teaching of Peter and John, not because they taught about a coming resurrection, but because they proclaimed *"in Jesus," a crucified criminal,* there is resurrection.

Luke offers his own list of those who were members of the council: rulers, elders, and scribes (these terms are ambiguous, and could refer to members who were Sadducees or Pharisees). Luke also includes specific Sadducees: the high priest and all who were in the high-priestly family.

Ultimately the council is not concerned with the apostles' teaching about the resurrection, but "by what power or name" Peter and John healed the lame man. Peter responds to the council that the lame man was healed by means of the name of Jesus Christ of Nazareth. This is followed by two curious statements:

> Jesus . . . , whom *you* crucified,
>   whom *God* raised from the dead.
>   (Acts 4:10)

Luke consistently holds the Sanhedrin responsible for Jesus' death, even though it is clear that Jesus was found guilty of treason (*crimen laesae majestatis*, challenging the sovereignty of the emperor) in a Roman court and crucified by Roman soldiers. A careful reading of Luke's account of the trial of Jesus (Luke 22:54ff.) reveals that Luke appears to have done his best to shift blame for Jesus' death from the Roman provincial government to Jewish leaders in Jerusalem. It may be, as we shall see in later chapters, that for the sake of the peaceful continuance of the church and her mission, Luke was concerned to maintain good relations with Roman civil authorities, and therefore presented the Romans in the best possible light.

As part of his defense (v. 11), Peter adapted a quote from Psalm 118:22, which contains a metaphor drawn from the building trades: "The stone that was rejected by [you,] the builders; it has become the cornerstone." Peter identified Jesus as a stone that might have been rejected as ordinary and useless, but instead was chosen as the cornerstone of God's work toward a redeemed universe (also see Jesus' own use of Psalm 118:22 in his parable of the vineyard; Luke 20:9–18). Note that in this verse, Peter (or Luke) has inserted "*you*"—"the stone that was rejected *by you*"—explicitly identifying those who rejected Jesus (compare with Psalm 118:22, Mark 12:10, Luke 20:17; 1 Peter 2:7).

Peter concluded his speech with a reference to salvation through Jesus. The term "salvation" may encompass both physical healing and spiritual wholeness. The name of Jesus brought salvation in the form of physical healing for the lame man, bringing him into close relationship with the Christian community. The name of Jesus also brings salvation which heals our spiritual natures, bringing us into close relationship with God.

THE COMMUNITY GATHERS AGAIN
TO RECEIVE THE HOLY SPIRIT
Acts 4:13–31

4:13 Now when they saw the boldness of Peter and John and realized that they were uneducated and ordinary men, they were amazed and recognized them as companions of Jesus. [14] When they saw the man who had been cured standing beside them, they had nothing to say in opposition. [15] So they ordered them to leave the council while they discussed the matter with one another. [16] They said, "What will we do with them? For it is obvious to all who live in Jerusalem that a notable sign has been done through them; we cannot deny it. [17] But to keep it from spreading further among the people, let us warn them to speak no more to anyone in this name." [18] So they called them and ordered them not to speak or teach at all in the name of Jesus. [19] But Peter and John answered them, "Whether it is right in God's sight to listen to you rather than to God, you must judge; [20] for we cannot keep from speaking about what we have seen and heard." [21] After threatening them again, they let them go, finding no way to punish them because of the people, for all of them praised God for what had happened. [22] For the man on whom this sign of healing had been performed was more than forty years old.

[23] After they were released, they went to their friends and reported what the chief priests and the elders had said to them. [24] When they heard it, they raised their voices together to God and said, "Sovereign Lord, who made the heaven and the earth, the sea, and everything in them, [25] it is you who said by the Holy Spirit through our ancestor David, your servant:
　　'Why do the Gentiles rage,
　　　　and the peoples imagine vain things?
　[26] The kings of the earth took their stand,
　　　　and the rulers have gathered together
　　　　against the Lord and against his Messiah.'
[27] For in this city, in fact, both Herod and Pontius Pilate, with the Gentiles and the peoples of Israel, gathered together against your holy servant Jesus, whom you anointed, [28] to do whatever your hand and your plan had predestined to take place. [29] And now, Lord, look at their threats, and grant to your servants to speak your word with all boldness, [30] while you stretch out your hand to heal, and signs and wonders are performed through the name of your holy servant Jesus." [31] When they had prayed, the place in which they were gathered together was shaken; and they were all filled with the Holy Spirit and spoke the word of God with boldness.

The council was amazed by the level of conversation conducted by these "uneducated and ordinary men." Perhaps members of the council presumed that ignorant fishermen would always remain so. They seem surprised that laymen could engage religious scholars in a theological conversation at a high level.

It is clear that the disciples of Jesus learned from their master some basic ways of interpreting scripture. The sermons of Peter indicate that the early church had developed its own sophisticated interpretive approach to the law, prophets, and Psalms. Scripture, for the Christian community, is to be read and taught through the experience of Jesus' life, death, and resurrection. These "companions of Jesus" had a good understanding of scriptural content and had developed a convincing method of interpreting it to their hearers. The Sanhedrin, now aware of this principle of interpretation, ordered the apostles not "to speak or teach at all in the name of Jesus" (v. 18).

The council wanted to silence the apostles. Nevertheless, the healed man stood as an undeniable symbol of God's activity through Peter and John—a "sign of healing." One is reminded of the Gospel of John and its understanding of Jesus' miracles as "signs" of God's presence in Jesus' life. In John, Jesus' healing of a man born blind ("signs" John 9:16) leads to a confrontation with the Pharisees, and we are told that, like the healed lame man who was more than forty years old (Acts 4:22), the man who received his sight was a mature adult (John 9:21). Just as Jesus had performed divine signs, so his apostles have performed "a notable sign . . . of healing" (Acts 4:16, 22). God was clearly at work among the apostles.

After Peter and John tell of their experience with the council to the gathered community of Christians, the community enters into prayer. We are most fortunate that Luke has recorded one of the earliest prayers of the church. Notice the repeated christological formula "your holy servant" (see comments on 3:11–16).

Psalm 2:1–2 is quoted in this prayer, then interpreted in the context of recent events in Jerusalem. Herod represents "the kings of the earth," Pilate "the rulers," and the Roman soldiers are "the Gentiles." "The peoples who imagine vain things" are, in this prayer, "the peoples of Israel." The Psalm is clearly applied to Jesus, the Lord's Messiah, and the events surrounding his life. Jesus is the key to interpreting scripture.

In this prayer, the Christian community acknowledges that the actions taken against Jesus by Herod, Pilate, the Gentiles, and Israel were part of God's plan. What appeared to be certain defeat, God has determined will be ultimate victory. This company of believers can take courage, for the "signs and wonders . . . performed through the name of [God's] holy servant Jesus" are tangible evidence that they are part of the divine plan.

At the end of the prayer, the building in which the community gathered was shaken, a sign that their prayer had been heard. This is followed by the coming of the Holy Spirit on the gathered assembly. Perhaps this is to indicate a "second Pentecost" intended for those newly brought into the community. With this literary bracket (Acts 2:4 . . . Acts 4:31), Luke concludes the Pentecostal episode that began in Acts 2. The reader has been led through a series of experiences that clearly prove, from Luke's point of view, God's approval and blessing on this new Jewish messianic movement. The words Luke used to describe the child Jesus—he "grew and became strong, filled with wisdom; and the favor of God was upon him" (Luke 2:40)—might also be applied to the young church. Certainly, the favor of the Lord was upon her. The gift of tongues and the gift of healing were signs that the church was built on the solid foundation of God's grace, with Jesus Christ as her cornerstone. The church was now ready to expand by incorporating into her structure stones of various shapes, sizes, colors, and textures.

THE COMMUNITY SHARES ITS GOODS
Acts 4:32–5:11

4:32 Now the whole group of those who believed were of one heart and soul, and no one claimed private ownership of any possessions, but everything they owned was held in common. 33 With great power the apostles gave their testimony to the resurrection of the Lord Jesus, and great grace was upon them all. 34 There was not a needy person among them, for as many as owned lands or houses sold them and brought the proceeds of what was sold. 35 They laid it at the apostles' feet, and it was distributed to each as any had need. 36 There was a Levite, a native of Cyprus, Joseph, to whom the apostles gave the name Barnabas (which means "son of encouragement"). 37 He sold a field that belonged to him, then brought the money, and laid it at the apostles' feet.

5:1 But a man named Ananias, with the consent of his wife Sapphira, sold a piece of property; 2 with his wife's knowledge, he kept back some of the proceeds, and brought only a part and laid it at the apostles' feet. 3 "Ananias," Peter asked, "why has Satan filled your heart to lie to the Holy Spirit and to keep back part of the proceeds of the land? 4 While it remained unsold, did it not remain your own? And after it was sold, were not the proceeds at your disposal? How is it that you have contrived this deed in your heart? You did not lie to us but to God!" 5 Now when Ananias heard these words, he fell down and died. And great fear seized all who heard of it. 6 The young men came and wrapped up his body, then carried him out and buried him.

7 After an interval of about three hours his wife came in, not knowing what had happened. 8 Peter said to her, "Tell me whether you and your hus-

band sold the land for such and such a price." And she said, "Yes, that was the price." [9] Then Peter said to her, "How is it that you have agreed to put the Spirit of the Lord to the test? Look, the feet of those who have buried your husband are at the door, and they will carry you out." [10] Immediately she fell down at his feet and died. When the young men came in they found her dead, so they carried her out and buried her beside her husband. [11] And great fear seized the whole church and all who heard of these things.

This story is both familiar and difficult. The language of this passage suggests that Luke is nostalgically reflecting on the golden age of the early church in which "there was not a needy person among them." Certainly the principle of community ownership of property and social security of all community members is an important lesson from the past. The story that supports this principle is told in starkly contrasting colors. Barnabas, the symbol of virtue who later becomes a companion of Paul, sold a field and brought the proceeds to the apostles. Ananias and Sapphira, on the other hand, surreptitiously withheld some of the proceeds from a sale of their property. This duplicity cost them their lives.

The example Luke uses to enforce the principle of sharing seems harsh, if not immoral. Peter's treatment of Ananias and Sapphira is severe to say the least. Capital punishment for lying? This dark side of the apostles' "signs and wonders" (also see Acts 13:6ff.) is similar to miracles attributed to Jesus in some of the apocryphal literature. In the *Infancy Gospel of Thomas*, for example, the child Jesus cursed a playmate who inadvertently bumped against him; the careless child immediately died. Even our canonical scriptures contain the story of small boys who jeered Elisha, calling out, "Go away, baldhead!" Elisha responded by cursing them in the name of the Lord. "Then two she-bears came out of the woods and mauled forty-two of the boys" (2 Kings 2:23–24). A more direct Old Testament parallel may be found in Joshua 7, where Achan kept the spoils gained in battle rather than turn them over to the Lord. Unlike Ananias and Sapphira, Achan confessed his sin. Nevertheless, he, along with his entire family, was stoned to death.

Evidently, Luke wished to make the point that lying in the church is tantamount to lying to the Holy Spirit. Perhaps Luke is spinning a vivid yarn in order to impart a moral principle as well as to entertain his reader or hearer. That this is a story somewhat removed from an actual historical context is clear from Peter's question to Sapphira, "Tell me whether you and your husband sold the land for *such and such* a price" (v. 8). It is difficult to imagine that Peter would have actually said those particular indefinite words. Peter then accused Sapphira of conspiracy with Ananias, and with dramatic flair said, "Look, the feet of those who have buried your husband are at the door, and they will carry you out" (v. 9). The reader would not be surprised that "great fear seized the whole church and all who heard of these things" (v. 11).

It is difficult to know what Luke intended by including this tale in his history of the early church. It certainly reveals a downside to the golden age of early Christianity. Perhaps Luke meant to address what he perceived as a relaxation of ethics in his own church. If this is the case, then the story of Ananias and Sapphira was a moral tale that ends with "see what happens!" Or perhaps Luke intended to link the rapid growth of the church to the church's radical obedience to apostolic leadership. While it is impossible to know with certainty why Luke included this difficult story (shock value, moral emphasis, entertainment, to accentuate apostolic authority, or some combination of these), the fact that the story *is* in Acts forces the reader to consider seriously the content and thrust of the story.

The tale of Ananias and Sapphira may fit our own times (just as Luke recorded it for the benefit of his church). There is renewed debate in the United States and in many European nations about a nation's obligations for the health and welfare of its own poor, many of whom are children and the elderly. This story reminds us that all that we have—individually and nationally—belongs to God. It is by God's grace that most people who read this book have resources sufficient for the necessities of life and more. The story should remind the reader that his or her "gift" to church, school, and charity already belongs to God. God claims it all and God's grace gives us an abundant allowance; even those who tithe keep 90 percent. Yes, most of us work by "the sweat of our brow"—the hot sweat of physical labor or the cold sweat of anxiety keeping an enterprise viable. And many of us mistakenly assume that the paycheck is compensation *to us* for our labors. Rather, we are being compensated for God's gracious gifts of life, energy, strength, intellect, creativity, and talent. That paycheck is God's. We take out our living allowance, which is usually quite generous, and share (not "give") the rest with those in need. Lying about the source of our resources is self-deceit and arrogance, and it puts "the Spirit of the Lord to the test" (v. 9). As the offertory prayer reads:

> All things come of Thee, O Lord;
> and of Thine own have we given Thee.

The story of Ananias and Sapphira is a tale for our own time, and we dismiss it as an absurd curiosity to our individual and national peril.

LUKE'S EDITORIAL COMMENT
ABOUT THE EARLY CHURCH
Acts 5:12–16

5:12 **Now many signs and wonders were done among the people through the apostles. And they were all together in Solomon's Portico. 13 None of the rest dared to join them, but the people held them in high esteem. 14 Yet more than ever believers were added to the Lord, great numbers of both men and women, 15 so that they even carried out the sick into the streets, and laid them on cots and mats, in order that Peter's shadow might fall on some of them as they came by. 16 A great number of people would also gather from the towns around Jerusalem, bringing the sick and those tormented by unclean spirits, and they were all cured.**

Luke notes that the apostles continued to gather at the temple (on Solomon's Portico, see comment on 3:11). While passersby were wary of this group, they nevertheless held the apostles "in high esteem," and many brave souls became believers.

Luke conveys the notion that the popularity of the apostolic church was due primarily to the healing power—"the signs and wonders"—of this group. The very shadow of Peter possesses healing power. It may be that Luke has slipped into a popular pagan concept that identified a particularly powerful person as a "divine-man." Has Luke inadvertently drifted from miracle to magic? Peter had earlier argued strenuously that healing did *not* come through his own power or piety, but by the name of Jesus (3:12, 16). In this passage, however, Luke suggests that Peter himself, even his shadow, was the vehicle of healing. This momentary lapse may indicate Luke's attempt to make a connection with some of his readers who are outside the mainstream of early Judaism and Christianity—Gentiles who needed a display of miracles as an inducement to become believers (see 13:12).

THE APOSTLES ARE AGAIN
BROUGHT BEFORE THE SANHEDRIN
Acts 5:17–42

5:17 **Then the high priest took action; he and all who were with him (that is, the sect of the Sadducees), being filled with jealousy, 18 arrested the apostles and put them in the public prison. 19 But during the night an angel of the Lord opened the prison doors, brought them out, and said, 20 "Go, stand in the temple and tell the people the whole message about this life." 21 When they heard this, they entered the temple at daybreak and went on with their teaching.**

When the high priest and those with him arrived, they called together the council and the whole body of the elders of Israel, and sent to the prison to have them brought. [22] But when the temple police went there, they did not find them in the prison; so they returned and reported, [23] "We found the prison securely locked and the guards standing at the doors, but when we opened them, we found no one inside." [24] Now when the captain of the temple and the chief priests heard these words, they were perplexed about them, wondering what might be going on. [25] Then someone arrived and announced, "Look, the men whom you put in prison are standing in the temple and teaching the people!" [26] Then the captain went with the temple police and brought them, but without violence, for they were afraid of being stoned by the people.

[27] When they had brought them, they had them stand before the council. The high priest questioned them, [28] saying, "We gave you strict orders not to teach in this name, yet here you have filled Jerusalem with your teaching and you are determined to bring this man's blood on us." [29] But Peter and the apostles answered, "We must obey God rather than any human authority. [30] The God of our ancestors raised up Jesus, whom you had killed by hanging him on a tree. [31] God exalted him at his right hand as Leader and Savior that he might give repentance to Israel and forgiveness of sins. [32] And we are witnesses to these things, and so is the Holy Spirit whom God has given to those who obey him."

[33] When they heard this, they were enraged and wanted to kill them. [34] But a Pharisee in the council named Gamaliel, a teacher of the law, respected by all the people, stood up and ordered the men to be put outside for a short time. [35] Then he said to them, "Fellow Israelites, consider carefully what you propose to do to these men. [36] For some time ago Theudas rose up, claiming to be somebody, and a number of men, about four hundred, joined him; but he was killed, and all who followed him were dispersed and disappeared. [37] After him Judas the Galilean rose up at the time of the census and got people to follow him; he also perished, and all who followed him were scattered. [38] So in the present case, I tell you, keep away from these men and let them alone; because if this plan or this undertaking is of human origin, it will fail; [39] but if it is of God, you will not be able to overthrow them—in that case you may even be found fighting against God!"

They were convinced by him, [40] and when they had called in the apostles, they had them flogged. Then they ordered them not to speak in the name of Jesus, and let them go. [41] As they left the council, they rejoiced that they were considered worthy to suffer dishonor for the sake of the name. [42] And every day in the temple and at home they did not cease to teach and proclaim Jesus as the Messiah.

The reader is told that the apostles were again arrested by the high-priestly group—the Sadducees. This time "the apostles" (how many? all?)

were put in prison for the night until a hearing could be held the next morning. In Luke's narration the apostles were miraculously released during the night by an "angel of the Lord." To suggest, as does one commentator, that it was a sympathetic guard who became "an angel of the Lord" to the apostles is an unnecessary rationalization of Luke's story.

The phrase "angel of the Lord" is used dozens of times in the Old Testament and refers to the typical agent of God's miraculous intervention. In Acts, Luke continues this traditional way of describing God's activity on behalf of believers (see Acts 8:26; 12:7, 23). The miraculous release of the apostles is the first of three such occurrences in Acts (Peter, Acts 12; Paul, Acts 16). Once released, the apostles immediately return to the temple precincts to continue their teaching. The angel has instructed them to "tell the people the whole message about this life" (v. 20). Though the phrase sounds strange, it is probably the case that "this life" also means life-giving "salvation" (see 13:26). The apostolic message is about "life"— "salvation"—which Jesus brings to the believer.

The next morning the temple police were ordered to retrieve the apostles from prison. To their amazement, the prison was empty and the police report their discovery to perplexed chief priests. Soon someone rushed in to report that the apostles were at it again! There they were, still teaching in the temple! And once again, the apostles were rounded up and brought before the council to explain why they persisted in disobeying the council's orders not to teach about Jesus (see 4:18). The burning issue for the council was now both the content of the apostles' message and their unwillingness to submit to the council's authority.

The apostles have "filled Jerusalem" with their teaching; it is the talk of the town. Moreover, there is a threat that such teaching may be politically destabilizing. The apostles seem "determined to bring this man's blood on us" (an echo of Matthew 27:24–25). It is clear from the speech of Gamaliel which follows (Acts 5:35–39) that the council was afraid that the apostles might incite the people to rebel either against the aristocratic Sadducees (whose religious and political authority was granted by Rome) or against the Roman authorities themselves.

Peter (Luke adds "and the apostles," though it is clear throughout the first five chapters of Acts that Peter leads and speaks for the Christian community) puts the question of authority to rest, at least as far as the followers of Jesus are concerned: "We must obey God rather than *any* human authority."

For Peter, and for Luke, all the Jerusalem authorities—Jewish and Gentile—share responsibility for Jesus' death, "whom you had killed by hanging him on a tree" (v. 30). In spite of this ignominious death, God "exalted him at his right hand as Leader and Savior" (v. 31). Therefore, the Christian community must declare its obedience to God's authority, and not to any human authority, especially a human authority which, because of ignorance (3:17), killed God's Messiah.

The heart of this little speech by Peter (vv. 30–31) contains the kernel of a significant theological problem that needed to be clearly and competently addressed by this primitive Christian community. The problem has already been broached and, as in this passage, glossed over by Luke. One might wonder if Luke was really aware of the significance of the problem.

The problem is contained in the phrase "hanging him on a tree" (v. 30). This refers, of course, to the crucifixion of Jesus and the phrase is drawn from the book of Deuteronomy: "When someone is convicted of a crime punishable by death and is executed, and you hang him on a tree, his corpse must not remain all night upon the tree; you shall bury him that same day, for anyone hung on a tree is under God's curse" (Deut. 21:22–23). The problem: Can a crucified man—a man under God's curse—be God's Messiah? We touched on this question above (Acts 3:11–26), but the issue presses even harder here. Can a man whose death is a sign of God's curse, actually be exalted by God as "Leader and Savior"? The religious leaders of Jerusalem would respond, "Absolutely not!" Yet, Christians came to believe that this is precisely the situation as God has willed it. God has done the incomprehensible, the impossible! God has blessed (exalted) a man who was under God's own curse. As paradoxical as this may be, the apostles declare, "We are witnesses to these things, and so is the Holy Spirit" (5:32).

Of course members of the Sanhedrin are "enraged" when they hear with even more clarity the theological message that Jesus' followers are proclaiming. Not only do they make the inflammatory accusation that the Sanhedrin was responsible for the death of Jesus, but they declare that this executed criminal is God's Messiah! This is blasphemous! A man under God's curse cannot possibly be God's blessed Messiah! Utter nonsense, theologically illogical, and politically dangerous! "They were enraged and wanted to put [the apostles] to death." And we are not surprised.

But a single voice rises above the angry din, the voice of a rabbi— "Gamaliel, a teacher of the law, respected by all the people" (v. 34). The voice of this teacher is a minority one, to be sure; and he is a Pharisee. Yet it is a voice that will be listened to carefully, and in the end heeded, because it belongs to the most distinguished scholar of the day. The voice belongs to the grandson of Hillel, founder of the liberal school of the Pharisaic party.

It is impossible to know how Luke came to know the content of this speech spoken in a closed meeting. Perhaps Gamaliel passed on an account of this speech to his student, Paul of Tarsus, who relayed it to Luke.

Gamaliel first asks members of the council to "consider carefully" any action they might take against the apostles. Still thinking politically, Gamaliel recounts the activities of two recent notorious revolutionaries, Theudas and Judas. This may have been good internal politics on the part of Gamaliel, for the majority party, the Sadducees, would have been quite concerned to maintain their political standing with the Romans. Revolutionaries like Theudas and Judas threatened this accommodation between the Sadducees and the Roman government.

It is curious to note that Gamaliel (Luke?) has the historical order of these two men reversed. Judas the Galilean led a tax revolt against the Romans in 6 C.E. following the census which Rome imposed on the people of Judea (see Luke 2 for the response of Mary and Joseph to the census). Forty years later (according to Josephus, *Jewish Antiquities* 20.97ff.), Theudas prompted a band of men to repeat Joshua's miracle of dividing the Jordan River and walking across the dry river bottom. Before he could carry out this miracle, however, a Roman squadron routed the rebels and decapitated Theudas in 44 C.E., fourteen years *after* Gamaliel was addressing the council! So we have two historical problems to consider. Not only is the historical order of Judas and Theudas reversed, but Gamaliel reports an event long before it occurred. It may be that (1) Gamaliel knows of a revolutionary named Theudas who was alive before 6 C.E. (about whom we have no corroborating evidence), (2) Gamaliel is simply wrong in his facts, (3) Luke may have a faulty transcript of Gamaliel's speech before him, or (4) Luke may have invented this portion of Gamaliel's speech and mixed up the history (though Luke is otherwise a rather careful historian).

Judas and Theudas are remembered as political figures who intended rebellion against Roman rule in Palestine, and the apostles are placed in this context. Perhaps Gamaliel wisely saw that the real concern of the Sanhedrin was not religious but political. Nevertheless, the great rabbi closes his speech with a theological statement: "If this plan or this undertaking is of human origin, it will fail; but if it is of God, you will not be able to overthrow them— in that case you may even be found fighting against God!" (vv. 38–39).

Even though the Sanhedrin was convinced by Gamaliel's argument, the apostles are still flogged as troublemakers. The apostles are also ordered not to speak in the name of Jesus.

This was the first clear-cut case of Christian civil disobedience. The apostles ignored the order of the council and "every day in the temple and at home they did not cease to teach and proclaim Jesus as the Messiah" (v. 42).

3. Jerusalem and Samaria: The Church Reaches Out to Hellenistic Jews and to Samaritans
Acts 6:1–8:40

THE ELECTION OF THE SEVEN
Acts 6:1–7

6:1 **Now during those days, when the disciples were increasing in number, the Hellenists complained against the Hebrews because their widows were being neglected in the daily distribution of food. ² And the twelve called together the whole community of the disciples and said, "It is not right that we should neglect the word of God in order to wait on tables. ³ Therefore, friends, select from among yourselves seven men of good standing, full of the Spirit and of wisdom, whom we may appoint to this task, ⁴ while we, for our part, will devote ourselves to prayer and to serving the word." ⁵ What they said pleased the whole community, and they chose Stephen, a man full of faith and the Holy Spirit, together with Philip, Prochorus, Nicanor, Timon, Parmenas, and Nicolaus, a proselyte of Antioch. ⁶ They had these men stand before the apostles, who prayed and laid their hands on them.**

⁷ The word of God continued to spread; the number of the disciples increased greatly in Jerusalem, and a great many of the priests became obedient to the faith.

"Now during those days" alerts the reader to a shift in Luke's narrative (see 1:15; 11:27). With chapter 6, Luke describes a Christian community that is becoming more complex. We now see clearly the distinction Luke makes between "apostles" and "disciples." In order to settle the first dispute in the church, "the twelve [apostles] called together the whole community of the disciples" (v. 2). The "Hebrews" of this community were Aramaic-speaking Jews (like the apostles) who had grown up in Palestine, while the "Hellenists" were Greek-speaking Jews who had either moved to Jerusalem or were visiting the Holy City from the diaspora ("diaspora" refers to Jewish communities outside of Palestine. The reader will also encounter the term "Hellenistic," which means "Greeklike." With the zeal of a missionary for Greek culture, Alexander the Great [356–323 B.C.E.] intended to Hellenize the lands around the Mediterranean Sea which he conquered. That Hellenization process even included the New Testament which was originally written in Greek).

It has been suggested that many pious Jews from the diaspora settled in Jerusalem in their later years. As the men died off, the number of widows grew and became dependent on public charity. From its beginning at Pentecost, the church saw herself as a mission reaching beyond local Aramaic-speaking Jews to Jews of the diaspora living in Jerusalem ("Jews from every nation under heaven"; 2:5). The Greek-speaking widows who had been drawn into the Christian community were in need and apparently were being neglected by the Aramaic-speaking "Hebrew" members of the church.

It is worth noting that blame for this neglect is not assigned. Rather, a solution is proposed. It is implied that the Twelve are responsible for charitable distribution of food. So that they might continue to lead the community through prayer, preaching, and teaching, the Twelve propose that seven Greek-speaking Christians be chosen to take over this responsibility.

I have already discussed the significance of "the twelve" apostles—those Aramaic-speaking, Galilean Jews who were the first followers of Jesus (see comments on 1:1–5). In the early Christian community, a second group was formed—"the seven." In biblical texts numbers often have symbolic meaning. If "the twelve" alludes to the twelve tribes of Israel, "the seven" might remind the reader of the seven days of creation, and therefore all the nations of the world. (Compare the geographic contexts of the two stories about Jesus feeding the multitude: Mark 6:30–45, "twelve baskets" of bread are retrieved; Mark 7:31; 8:1–10, "seven baskets." Also note Jesus' question in Mark 8:19–21.)

It has been suggested that "the seven" may have been modeled on the town councils established in local Jewish communities, sometimes known as "The Seven of the Town." "The seven" in this passage appear to represent the dispersion of Judaism throughout the world. They may also foreshadow the spread of Christianity to lands outside of Palestine.

All seven men have Greek names and one is identified specifically as a proselyte, that is, a Gentile convert to Judaism. The seven stood before the apostles who prayed and laid hands on them. This ritual was borrowed from Judaism and implies the passing on of power through the physical contact of one person with another, in this case from "the twelve" to "the seven" (see also 1 Tim. 4:14; 2 Tim. 1:6). While this looks like the first instance of ordination in the church, it is not likely that this "ordination" was to an office such as elder or deacon. There is no evidence of an established set of church offices at this early stage in the life of the Christian community. Rather, these men are designated simply as "the seven," leaders of the Greek-speaking Jewish-Christian branch of the church.

Luke closes this scene with an editorial comment, noting that the increasing number of disciples also included a great number of priests. It has been estimated that at this time there were about eight thousand priests who served the temple one or two months each year (recall the story of Zechariah, the father of John the Baptist, who served his term each year; Luke 1:5ff.). Because this was part-time employment, they were obliged to maintain a trade for their livelihood. If, as it has been suggested, these priests were socially, economically, and perhaps even religiously distanced from the office of the high priesthood, then it is not surprising that many disaffected priests became members of the Christian sect of Judaism. This new sect, after all, tended toward a more egalitarian form of fellowship, asking its members to be "obedient to the faith" rather than to a hierarchy. Perhaps Luke is also attempting to make the point that the church was not outside the mainstream of Judaism. Priests, a fairly conservative element in first-century Judaism, were attracted to the Christian sect.

STEPHEN IS ARRESTED
Acts 6:8–15

> 6:8 **Stephen, full of grace and power, did great wonders and signs among the people.** [9] **Then some of those who belonged to the synagogue of the Freedmen (as it was called), Cyrenians, Alexandrians, others of those from Cilicia and Asia, stood up and argued with Stephen.** [10] **But they could not withstand the wisdom and the Spirit with which he spoke.** [11] **Then they secretly instigated some men to say, "We have heard him speak blasphemous words against Moses and God."** [12] **They stirred up all the people as well as the elders and the scribes; then they suddenly confronted him, seized him, and brought him before the council.** [13] **They set up false witnesses who said, "This man never stops saying things against this holy place and the law;** [14] **for we have heard him say that this Jesus of Nazareth will destroy this place and will change the customs that Moses handed on to us."** [15] **And all who sat in the council looked intently at him, and they saw that his face was like the face of an angel.**

Stephen, a Hellenistic Jewish Christian and one of the Seven, is presented as a true hero in the history of the early church. Luke piles up superlatives in describing him: full of grace and power, a worker of great wonders and signs, possessing wisdom and the Spirit. Finally, Stephen, the first Christian martyr, has a "face . . . like the face of an angel" (v. 15).

The reader can assume that the argument between Stephen and his accusers had something to do with Jewish law. The argument became so heated that Stephen was accused of blasphemy against Moses (the Law) and God. His accusers are identified as (1) a Jerusalem synagogue ("the synagogue of the Freedmen"—perhaps descendants of Jews taken captive by Pompey in 63 B.C.E. and later released), (2) Jews from Cyrene and Alexandria (along the south coast of the Mediterranean Sea), and (3) Jews from Cilicia and Asia (along the north coast of the Mediterranean Sea). With the possible exception of the first group, Stephen's opponents are fellow Hellenistic Jews from the diaspora.

The argument turned to anger, and a conspiracy was formed to do away with Stephen. Like the Aramaic-speaking Jewish Christians before him (Peter and John), Stephen was brought before the council where he was accused of "saying things against this holy place [the temple] and the law." The next phrase is an elaboration of this accusation: "We have heard him say that this Jesus of Nazareth will destroy this place and will change the customs that Moses handed on to us" (v. 14).

The first part of this charge, that Jesus will destroy the temple, had been used in Jesus' own trial. According to Mark and Matthew false witnesses testified that Jesus said, "I will destroy this temple" (Mark 14:58; Matt. 26:61). The modern reader might compare the trial of Jesus in Luke with Mark's account, remembering that Luke used Mark as one of his sources. Luke omits Mark's mention of false witnesses and the alleged threat to the temple, shifting these items to Stephen's trial. Perhaps one of Luke's reasons for doing this was to eliminate any semblance of legitimacy in the council's discussion with Jesus; no witnesses are to be found, not even false ones.

The Gospels record that Jesus did, in fact, speak of the destruction of the temple. In Mark 13:2 Jesus predicts, "Do you see these great buildings? Not one stone will be left here upon another; all will be thrown down" (see also Luke 21:5–6). John records a more specific reference to the temple. After cleansing the temple of money changers, the Jews ask for a sign that would legitimatize this action. Jesus responds, "Destroy this temple, and in three days I will raise it up" (John 2:19). The first half of Jesus' prediction was fulfilled in 70 C.E. when the Roman army stormed Jerusalem and razed the temple.

Luke, however, never directly ties the charge of threatening the temple to Jesus during Jesus' lifetime. The statement about destroying and rebuilding the temple in three days, which occurs in all three other Gospels, is absent from Luke's Gospel (Matt. 26:61; Mark 14:58; John 2:19). Rather, Luke reserves this prediction for Acts, and places it in the context of Stephen's "trial." In this account, "false witnesses" charge Stephen with saying that Jesus will destroy the temple. It may be that Luke, writing after the destruction of the temple in 70 C.E., wishes to deny as much as possible any Christian responsibility for this event, even to omit such a prediction made by Jesus. Therefore, Luke notes that "false witnesses" testify that Stephen talked about the destruction of the temple (see Mark 14:56 where "false witnesses" similarly accused Jesus). This was apparently a highly charged issue that must be addressed by both Stephen and Luke. The speech that follows will focus on the temple, though in a strangely circuitous way. In the end, Stephen will declare that the temple is an irrelevant piece of property, for "the Most High does not dwell in houses made with human hands" (Acts 7:48).

STEPHEN'S DEFENSE
Acts 7:1–53

Stephen's Account of Israel's History
(Acts 7:1–43)

7:1 **Then the high priest asked him, "Are these things so?" 2 And Stephen replied:**

"Brothers and fathers, listen to me. The God of glory appeared to our ancestor Abraham when he was in Mesopotamia, before he lived in Haran, 3 and said to him, 'Leave your country and your relatives and go to the land that I will show you.' 4 Then he left the country of the Chaldeans and settled in Haran. After his father died, God had him move from there to this country in which you are now living. 5 He did not give him any of it as a heritage, not even a foot's length, but promised to give it to him as his possession and to his descendants after him, even though he had no child. 6 And God spoke in these terms, that his descendants would be resident aliens in a country belonging to others, who would enslave them and mistreat them during four hundred years. 7 'But I will judge the nation that they serve,' said God, 'and after that they shall come out and worship me in this place.' 8 Then he gave him the covenant of circumcision. And so Abraham became the father of Isaac and circumcised him on the eighth day; and Isaac became the father of Jacob, and Jacob of the twelve patriarchs.

9 "The patriarchs, jealous of Joseph, sold him into Egypt; but God was with him, 10 and rescued him from all his afflictions, and enabled him to win favor and to show wisdom when he stood before Pharaoh, king of Egypt, who

appointed him ruler over Egypt and over all his household. [11] Now there came a famine throughout Egypt and Canaan, and great suffering, and our ancestors could find no food. [12] But when Jacob heard that there was grain in Egypt, he sent our ancestors there on their first visit. [13] On the second visit Joseph made himself known to his brothers, and Joseph's family became known to Pharaoh. [14] Then Joseph sent and invited his father Jacob and all his relatives to come to him, seventy-five in all; [15] so Jacob went down to Egypt. He himself died there as well as our ancestors, [16] and their bodies were brought back to Shechem and laid in the tomb that Abraham had bought for a sum of silver from the sons of Hamor in Shechem.

[17] "But as the time drew near for the fulfillment of the promise that God had made to Abraham, our people in Egypt increased and multiplied [18] until another king who had not known Joseph ruled over Egypt. [19] He dealt craftily with our race and forced our ancestors to abandon their infants so that they would die. [20] At this time Moses was born, and he was beautiful before God. For three months he was brought up in his father's house; [21] and when he was abandoned, Pharaoh's daughter adopted him and brought him up as her own son. [22] So Moses was instructed in all the wisdom of the Egyptians and was powerful in his words and deeds.

[23] "When he was forty years old, it came into his heart to visit his relatives, the Israelites. [24] When he saw one of them being wronged, he defended the oppressed man and avenged him by striking down the Egyptian. [25] He supposed that his kinsfolk would understand that God through him was rescuing them, but they did not understand. [26] The next day he came to some of them as they were quarreling and tried to reconcile them, saying, 'Men, you are brothers; why do you wrong each other?' [27] But the man who was wronging his neighbor pushed Moses aside, saying, 'Who made you a ruler and a judge over us? [28] Do you want to kill me as you killed the Egyptian yesterday?' [29] When he heard this, Moses fled and became a resident alien in the land of Midian. There he became the father of two sons.

[30] "Now when forty years had passed, an angel appeared to him in the wilderness of Mount Sinai, in the flame of a burning bush. [31] When Moses saw it, he was amazed at the sight; and as he approached to look, there came the voice of the Lord: [32] 'I am the God of your ancestors, the God of Abraham, Isaac, and Jacob.' Moses began to tremble and did not dare to look. [33] Then the Lord said to him, 'Take off the sandals from your feet, for the place where you are standing is holy ground. [34] I have surely seen the mistreatment of my people who are in Egypt and have heard their groaning, and I have come down to rescue them. Come now, I will send you to Egypt.'

[35] "It was this Moses whom they rejected when they said, 'Who made you a ruler and a judge?' and whom God now sent as both ruler and liberator through the angel who appeared to him in the bush. [36] He led them out,

having performed wonders and signs in Egypt, at the Red Sea, and in the wilderness for forty years. [37] This is the Moses who said to the Israelites, 'God will raise up a prophet for you from your own people as he raised me up.' [38] He is the one who was in the congregation in the wilderness with the angel who spoke to him at Mount Sinai, and with our ancestors; and he received living oracles to give to us. [39] Our ancestors were unwilling to obey him; instead, they pushed him aside, and in their hearts they turned back to Egypt, [40] saying to Aaron, 'Make gods for us who will lead the way for us; as for this Moses who led us out from the land of Egypt, we do not know what has happened to him.' [41] At that time they made a calf, offered a sacrifice to the idol, and reveled in the works of their hands. [42] But God turned away from them and handed them over to worship the host of heaven, as it is written in the book of the prophets:

'Did you offer to me slain victims and sacrifices
    forty years in the wilderness, O house of Israel?
[43] No; you took along the tent of Moloch,
    and the star of your god Rephan,
        the images that you made to worship;
so I will remove you beyond Babylon.'

This is the longest, and one of the strangest, speeches in the book of Acts (it continues into verses 44–53). So far, Stephen has not presented a very good defense. He has not directly addressed the two charges brought against him: threatening the destruction of the temple and changing the customs of Moses. Rather than a legal defense, one reads in these verses a biblical-historical narrative tinged with Pharisaic coloring (we shall return to the Pharisaic nature of this speech).

It has been suggested that this speech is a product of Luke himself. It is doubtful that Stephen would have offered this account of Israel's history for the council's edification. They, of all people, would know the story. Nevertheless, Stephen (Luke) has given us the most comprehensive history of Israel recorded in the New Testament, with at least thirty citations from the Old Testament. Certainly, all of the big names of Israel's history are mentioned:

Patriarchs:
    Abraham, Isaac, Jacob, Joseph
Leaders of the exodus:
    Moses, Aaron, Joshua
Israel's first great kings:
    David, Solomon

Luke probably used this setting as an opportunity to educate his readers, many of whom would have been non-Jews, by including a brief history of Israel in his narrative. This is a stylized speech that looks well-honed and appears to draw on standard themes that narrate Israel's history. Perhaps Luke constructed this historical account from a collection of materials used for educational purposes in the early church.

This account includes both positive and negative aspects of Hebrew history. Joseph was the last of the great patriarchs, yet his own brothers betrayed him and sold him into slavery. Moses was Israel's liberator, yet he was also a murderer. Moses led Israel out from bondage with mighty "signs and wonders" and he received God's law in the wilderness, yet the people rejected him.

It is this bimodal aspect of Israel's history that Luke, through Stephen, is reflecting upon. The Christian sect has experienced both acceptance (by the people, 5:13, 26; by the priests, 6:7; by the Pharisees, 15:5 and 23:9) and rejection (primarily by the Sadducees).

There are some details in this passage that indicate a connection with Pharisaic Judaism. Stephen states that Moses was "the one who was in the congregation in the wilderness with the angel who spoke to him at Mount Sinai . . . ; and he received living oracles to give to us" (v. 38). According to Pharisaic tradition, it was an angel of the Lord who actually transmitted the law of God to Moses, thus preserving God's transcendence (see v. 53; also Gal. 3:19; Heb. 2:2). Moreover, according to the Pharisees, Moses received not only the written code but also the oral law ("living oracles"). We are not specifically told that Stephen was a Pharisee; perhaps this historical recitation was designed to convince Stephen's hearers of his theological orthodoxy.

One might see in these verses a rather roundabout, and dangerous, defense for "changing the customs of Moses." Stephen's rhetorical approach appears to be counteraccusatory, and it proves to be counterproductive. According to Stephen, those who had received the law did not keep it. The wandering Israelites exchanged the "living oracles" of God for a dead animal sacrificed to a golden calf. Stephen might have extrapolated from this argument the premise that Christians have recovered a sense of God's living oracles through their new christological interpretation of scripture. They live by God's law understood in light of the believer's experience of the life and message of Jesus. Christians, Stephen argued, had not changed the "customs of Moses." Rather, rejection of Moses lies deeply embedded in Israel's own history, rejection that continues in those who hear Stephen's speech. Perhaps Stephen's recitation of Israel's history bears witness to the contemporary adage that those who forget their past are condemned to repeat it. His speech suggests how essential it is to engage the educational process of information and formation for each generation of Christians.

In 7:44–53 Stephen defends, though somewhat weakly, the second charge against him: insufficient reverence for the temple.

God Does Not Dwell in Houses
Made with Human Hands (Acts 7:44–53)

> 7:44 "Our ancestors had the tent of testimony in the wilderness, as God directed when he spoke to Moses, ordering him to make it according to the pattern he had seen. 45 Our ancestors in turn brought it in with Joshua when they dispossessed the nations that God drove out before our ancestors. And it was there until the time of David, 46 who found favor with God and asked that he might find a dwelling place for the house of Jacob. 47 But it was Solomon who built a house for him. 48 Yet the Most High does not dwell in houses made with human hands; as the prophet says,
>
> 49 'Heaven is my throne,
>   and the earth is my footstool.
> What kind of house will you build for me, says the Lord,
>   or what is the place of my rest?
> 50 Did not my hand make all these things?'
> 51 "You stiff-necked people, uncircumcised in heart and ears, you are forever opposing the Holy Spirit, just as your ancestors used to do. 52 Which of the prophets did your ancestors not persecute? They killed those who foretold the coming of the Righteous One, and now you have become his betrayers and murderers. 53 You are the ones that received the law as ordained by angels, and yet you have not kept it."

Apparently Stephen's defense was not intended to placate his accusers, and it is clear that he will succeed. Stephen seems to go out of his way to offend them, as he finally gets around to the charge of speaking against the temple. The pattern given to Moses was for a portable tent, not a permanent building. The "pattern" reminds the modern reader of the letter to the Hebrews, which likewise argues that the pattern Moses received for "the tent of the Lord" was "a sketch and shadow of the heavenly one" (Heb. 8:1–5; see Exod. 25:40). Both Hebrews and the book of Acts raise an ancient argument that has roots in the Old Testament itself. What sort of center for worship, if any, does God desire (see 2 Sam. 7:1–7)? Does the temple building, in fact, symbolize a drift away from true worship of God, a drift toward focus on the cultus and its trappings rather than upon God (see Jeremiah's temple sermon, Jeremiah 7:1–15; also see Micah 6:6–8).

Stephen recounts that even the most virtuous of Israel's kings, David, did not build a house for God (the NRSV marginal note may be the better reading here: "a dwelling place for *the God of* Jacob"; v. 46). It was left to the great architect of Jerusalem, King Solomon, to construct a house for God. "Yet," says Stephen, "the Most High [e.g., the God who transcends all mortals and their institutions] does not dwell in houses made with human hands." To support this point, in v. 49 Stephen quotes Isaiah 66:1:

> Heaven is my throne,
>> and the earth is my footstool.
> What kind of house will you build [could you build] for me,
>> says the Lord . . . ?

Stephen's final blast is also reminiscent of the Old Testament prophets. He calls the council "stiff-necked" (Exod. 33:3, 5), and uncircumcised in heart and ears (Jer. 6:10; 9:26). Here Stephen links the council with their ancestors who also opposed the Holy Spirit (e.g., the spirit of prophecy). His comment, "Which of the prophets did your ancestors not persecute?" is an echo of Jesus' statement to the scribes and Pharisees: "Thus you testify against yourselves that you are descendants of those who murdered the prophets. Fill up, then, the measure of your ancestors" (Matt. 23:31–32; also Luke 11:47–48).

The prophets "foretold the coming of the Righteous One." Righteous One may be one of the earliest titles used of Jesus (see comments on 3:11–16; also see 22:14). It indicates not only Jesus' right relationship with God but also Jesus' legal innocence. He was so obviously unjustly condemned and executed that even the Roman centurion at the cross declared, "Certainly this man was *innocent*"—the same Greek word translated as "righteous" (Luke 23:47; note how Luke revised his Markan source = "Truly this man was *the Son of God!*" [Mark 15:39, RSV]; Luke has turned a christological confession into a judicial pronouncement).

Perhaps Stephen or Luke was reflecting an early piece of Christian tradition that understood Jesus' relationship with God not in terms of sonship, but in terms of innocence (see also Matt. 27:19). The one found guilty in a human court was declared innocent by God's court. This fits well with one of Luke's themes: the messianic age brings surprising reversals of fortune (Luke 1:46–55; 6:20–26).

Stephen accused the council of betraying and killing the "Righteous/Innocent One." In doing this, these religious leaders have broken the very law they claim to preserve and protect. "You are the ones that received the law as ordained by angels, and yet you have not kept it" (v. 53). It is *they*, the religious elite, who have "changed the customs of Moses."

It will not be difficult for the reader to guess the outcome of this confrontation.

STEPHEN, THE FIRST CHRISTIAN MARTYR
Acts 7:54–8:1a

> 7:54 **When they heard these things, they became enraged and ground their teeth at Stephen.** [55] **But filled with the Holy Spirit, he gazed into heaven and saw the glory of God and Jesus standing at the right hand of God.** [56] **"Look,"** **he said, "I see the heavens opened and the Son of Man standing at the right hand of God!"** [57] **But they covered their ears, and with a loud shout all rushed together against him.** [58] **Then they dragged him out of the city and began to stone him; and the witnesses laid their coats at the feet of a young man named Saul.** [59] **While they were stoning Stephen, he prayed, "Lord Jesus, receive my spirit."** [60] **Then he knelt down and cried out in a loud voice, "Lord, do not hold this sin against them." When he had said this, he died.** [8:1a] **And Saul approved of their killing him.**

The dispute between Stephen and the Sanhedrin quickly reached the boiling point. The council was thoroughly enraged when Stephen described a theophany he was experiencing. In his vision of heaven, Stephen saw the "Son of Man" standing next to God. The term "Son of Man" is used often of Jesus in the Gospels. Yet, surprisingly, outside the Gospels it occurs only here and in Revelation 1:13. Stephen's statement, "I see . . . the Son of Man standing at the right hand of God," reflects Jesus' own words, also spoken before the Sanhedrin: "From now on the Son of Man will be seated at the right hand of the power of God" (Luke 22:69). It has been suggested that in Stephen's theophany, Jesus is standing either to welcome Stephen to heaven, or he is standing (as a judge stood in antiquity to render a verdict) to pronounce Stephen innocent and the Sanhedrin guilty of yet another murder of an innocent man.

Stephen was dragged out of the city and stoned to death. Mention of "the witnesses" indicates that the Sanhedrin made a judgment and reached a verdict, though the text of Acts reads more like a mob action and impassioned lynching. According to Jewish law, the witnesses were part of the official execution procedure. The first witness pushed the condemned person down from the place of execution (a drop of about twelve feet). If the victim survived the fall, a second witness dropped a large boulder that was intended to crush the victim's chest.

Luke uses this scene to introduce a person who will become a major figure in his narrative. Saul of Tarsus, Gamaliel's precocious rabbinical student, suddenly pops into view. Unlike the earlier confrontation between the apostles and the council in which Gamaliel's tempering presence mitigated a potentially violent situation, here the reader meets Gamaliel's far less tolerant student who "approved of . . . killing" Stephen (8:1a).

Stephen's last words echo those of his master: "Lord, do not hold this sin against them" (note that Jesus' cry from the cross, "Father, forgive them . . . ," is found only in Luke 23.34). The parallel between the death of Stephen and the death of Jesus is clear, and these biblical accounts become the literary paradigm for future stories about Christian martyrs.

Stephen was a Greek-speaking Jew, perhaps a Pharisee, who began to see problems with legalistic religion, and he was finally victim of a legal system that has the shortcoming of all legal systems: it cannot guarantee that passion will be displaced by reasoned discourse. It cannot guarantee that innocent people will not become victims of a system that intends to protect the innocent. It is ironic that at the end of this scene we meet another Greek-speaking Jew, a Pharisee named Saul, who will also begin to see some real problems with the legal system of which he is a master.

THE CHRISTIAN COMMUNITY IS PERSECUTED
Acts 8:1b–3

8:1b **That day a severe persecution began against the church in Jerusalem, and all except the apostles were scattered throughout the countryside of Judea and Samaria.** [2] **Devout men buried Stephen and made loud lamentation over him.** [3] **But Saul was ravaging the church by entering house after house; dragging off both men and women, he committed them to prison.**

The peace that the church enjoyed during its early days is suddenly shattered. Like Thomas Cole's allegorical painting *Voyage of Life* (which in four panels portrays the stages of human life from birth to the ravages of old age), so Luke's portrait of the infant church begins to show the shades and shadows of aging in an unappreciative world.

According to Luke, all the believers left Jerusalem except for the Twelve. This seems a bit odd. Ordinarily, troublesome organizations were decapitated by capturing and killing the leadership.

Saul took personal responsibility to uproot and destroy this noxious sect (the first-time reader of Acts would still be unaware of the full importance of this person; later in Acts Luke tells the reader that Saul's Roman name is Paul). The angry attitude of Paul toward the Christian sect of Judaism squares with the apostle's own memory of his pre-Christian zeal. This highly educated scripture scholar was infamous for his violent attacks on the Christian community. His reputation even reached people in the hinterlands of Galatia. In his letter to the Galatians, Paul recounts, "You have heard, no doubt, of my earlier life in Judaism. I was violently persecuting the church of God and was trying to destroy it" (Gal. 1:13).

A contemporary reader might conclude that Paul's anger with the new sect of Judaism was overdetermined. His extreme reaction seems to indicate that he was so threatened by these messianists that his rage against the sect exceeded the limits of reason. Perhaps their teaching about God's saving grace through Jesus the Messiah held a kernel of truth that threatened to destroy Paul's carefully constructed religious world. His teacher, the even-tempered Gamaliel, may have been embarrassed by the actions of his rash disciple. But then, this was not the first time—nor would it be the last—that zealous students have embarrassed their teachers.

PHILIP BRINGS THE GOSPEL TO SAMARIA
Acts 8:4–8

> 8:4 **Now those who were scattered went from place to place, proclaiming the word. 5 Philip went down to the city of Samaria and proclaimed the Messiah to them. 6 The crowds with one accord listened eagerly to what was said by Philip, hearing and seeing the signs that he did, 7 for unclean spirits, crying with loud shrieks, came out of many who were possessed; and many others who were paralyzed or lame were cured. 8 So there was great joy in that city.**

Luke understands that it is because of persecution that Christianity began to spread beyond Jerusalem. The reader can begin to see the formation of concentric circles of believers. The twelve apostles residing in Jerusalem are at the core of the Christian community (remaining there even during the storm of persecution), Aramaic-speaking Jewish Christians populate the next circle, and beyond them are Greek-speaking Jewish Christians (drawn from the diaspora with the Seven as leaders). Now the church is reaching further from its core, to the residents of a city in Samaria, a reach that is more than spatial; it is a reach that crosses the boundaries of religion and race.

While our English text reads "the city of Samaria" (v. 5), the NRSV marginal note offers "a city," an alternative reading worth considering.

Samaria, during the New Testament period, was a region between Galilee to the north and Judea to the south. This region certainly had more than one city, and the city known as Samaria in the Old Testament is, during Luke's time, a Greek city known as Sebaste. It is clear that Philip is encountering the people of the *region* of Samaria—the Samaritans, who were historically related to Jews, but despised by them.

A graphic and very negative description of Samaritans is found in 2 Kings 17:24–34. In 721 B.C.E. the kingdom of Israel was defeated by the Assyrians and much of the population was deported to the east (in 922 B.C.E. the kingdom of David and Solomon was divided into a northern kingdom [Israel] and a southern kingdom [Judah]. It is the area of the Northern Kingdom that was later populated by people who were called "Samaritans"). Moreover, the Assyrian king, Sargon II, transported other peoples whom he defeated into the territory of Israel. Eventually, inter-marriages took place between these foreigners and the Israelites who were left in the land resulting in a mixed race of people who came to be known as "Samaritans." The title usually given to the parable of Jesus in Luke 10, "The Good Samaritan," would have been an oxymoron to Jesus' Jewish hearers. There was no such thing as a *good* Samaritan!

The discussion between Jesus and the Samaritan woman in John's Gospel echoes the debate between Jewish and Samaritan religious leaders (John 4). The Samaritan woman declared, "Our ancestors worshiped on this mountain [Mount Gerizim in Samaria], but you [plural, indicating "you Jews"] say that the place where people must worship is in Jerusalem." Jesus' reply hints at the superiority felt by most Jews: "You [plural, "Samaritans"] worship what you do not know; we [Jews] worship what we know, for salvation is from the Jews." Fortunately, Jesus went beyond affirming Jerusalem's party line: "But the hour is coming, and is now here, when the true worshipers will worship the Father in spirit and truth." God will no longer be worshiped "on this mountain nor in Jerusalem."

For Luke, that hour of true worship is now present in the ministry of Philip to the Samaritans. As a result of Philip's preaching "the good news about the kingdom of God and the name of Jesus Christ," many Samaritans "were baptized, both men and women" (Acts 8:12). Philip has broken through two important barriers: religion and race. God loves even the Samaritans, and they are welcome to join this new inclusive Jewish sect, the community of the Messiah. In spite of Jesus' commission to be his witness in Samaria (1:8), such a breakthrough apparently raised eyebrows among the Jewish-Christian leaders in Jerusalem. As we shall see (8:14), Peter and John were sent to Samaria to look into this matter.

SIMON THE MAGICIAN
ENCOUNTERS APOSTOLIC AUTHORITY
Acts 8:9–25

8:9 Now a certain man named Simon had previously practiced magic in the city and amazed the people of Samaria, saying that he was someone great. 10 All of them, from the least to the greatest, listened to him eagerly, saying, "This man is the power of God that is called Great." 11 And they listened eagerly to him because for a long time he had amazed them with his magic. 12 But when they believed Philip, who was proclaiming the good news about the kingdom of God and the name of Jesus Christ, they were baptized, both men and women. 13 Even Simon himself believed. After being baptized, he stayed constantly with Philip and was amazed when he saw the signs and great miracles that took place.

14 Now when the apostles at Jerusalem heard that Samaria had accepted the word of God, they sent Peter and John to them. 15 The two went down and prayed for them that they might receive the Holy Spirit 16 (for as yet the Spirit had not come upon any of them; they had only been baptized in the name of the Lord Jesus). 17 Then Peter and John laid their hands on them, and they received the Holy Spirit. 18 Now when Simon saw that the Spirit was given through the laying on of the apostles' hands, he offered them money, 19 saying, "Give me also this power so that anyone on whom I lay my hands may receive the Holy Spirit." 20 But Peter said to him, "May your silver perish with you, because you thought you could obtain God's gift with money! 21 You have no part or share in this, for your heart is not right before God. 22 Repent therefore of this wickedness of yours, and pray to the Lord that, if possible, the intent of your heart may be forgiven you. 23 For I see that you are in the gall of bitterness and the chains of wickedness." 24 Simon answered, "Pray for me to the Lord, that nothing of what you have said may happen to me."

25 Now after Peter and John had testified and spoken the word of the Lord, they returned to Jerusalem, proclaiming the good news to many villages of the Samaritans.

Two authorities confront each other in this passage. On one side we meet Simon, a magician revered by the people of Samaria as "great" (he is remembered in later Christian literature by the name Simon Magus). According to the Samaritans, Simon not only has the power of God, he "*is* the power of God that is called Great" (*megas;* v. 10). Philip, however, appeared on the scene performing his own impressive "signs and great miracles" (v. 13). According to Luke, "even Simon believed."

When Peter and John arrived from Jerusalem they brought with them the true power of God which surpasses all magic. Moreover, by the laying on of hands, they were able to convey to others the source of this great power—the Spirit of God, the Holy Spirit.

It is interesting to note how the substance of this story shifts from a tale of competing wonders (Philip's miracles and Simon's magic) to a consideration of the source of miraculous power, the Holy Spirit. One has the impression (v. 13) that Simon hung around Philip in order to learn a few new tricks of the trade. But once Simon encountered the "real authorities" from Jerusalem, his interest in Philip faded.

Having seen Peter and John convey the Holy Spirit through the laying on of hands, Simon attempted to purchase the power to do likewise. Simon's encounter with Peter certainly gives perspective to Simon's own "divinity." He was scolded by Peter and told, "Repent . . . , and pray to the Lord that . . . the intent of your heart may be forgiven you" (v. 22). One might safely speculate that Peter clearly understood the motive behind Simon's request. His "intent" was to profit from the ability to convey the Holy Spirit to others. The entrepreneurial Simon could in turn sell the healing effects of the Spirit, or, for a price, he could lay *his* hands on others and grant them the power of the Spirit. He could develop his own cultic following and profit financially at the same time, confirming the myth that he is indeed "the power of God that is called Great."

A number of early Christian fictional accounts elaborated on this intriguing person. According to one of these stories, a cult formed around Simon in which priests of the cult lived exceedingly luxurious and licentious lives, devoting themselves to the study and practice of magic. The medieval term "simony," derived from the name Simon, refers to the buying and selling of church offices (a bishopric might be offered for sale to the highest bidder), just as Simon had tried to purchase the power of the Holy Spirit from Peter.

The reader is left up in the air about Simon's ultimate fate. His final appeal to Peter, however, clearly belies his divinity. He begs of Peter, "Pray for me to the Lord, that nothing of what you have said may happen to me" (v. 24). Simon Magus has been reduced to a frightened little "god"!

This story also offers Luke an opportunity to enter into a discussion of the distinction between water baptism and baptism in the Holy Spirit. Philip had baptized believing Samaritans "in the name of the Lord Jesus." Apparently water baptism was an insufficient mark of Christian identification. This rite was taken over by the early church from John the Baptist who had baptized Jesus. According to the Gospel of John, Jesus himself did not baptize, though his disciples did baptize new followers. It would appear that the apostles maintained this rite of initiation, a symbol of repentance, making it an important aspect of Christian life. But with the experience of Pentecost, a second baptism—in the Holy Spirit—appears to supersede water baptism in importance.

Throughout Acts, Luke narrates instances of these two baptisms: baptism in the name of Jesus through water and baptism in the Holy Spirit through the laying on of hands. Moreover, in the earliest days of the church, water baptism seems to have been given by most church leaders; baptism in the Holy Spirit, on the other hand, was conveyed only by the apostles. Soon, others as well have the authority to lay on hands and convey the Holy Spirit (Acts 9:17, Ananias on Saul, and 19:1–6, Paul on Ephesian Christians). Acts 19:1–6 illustrates the practice that eventually emerged in the early church. The Ephesians confess that they were baptized "into John's baptism," whereupon Paul baptizes them in "the name of the Lord Jesus. When Paul had laid his hands on them, the Holy Spirit came upon them" (19:5–6).

Luke looks back on a time when both baptisms existed side by side. By Luke's own time, the two baptisms were probably conflated; water baptism also brought with it conferral of the Holy Spirit. In the early chapters of Acts, we may be witness to a time when the church struggled to maintain the independence of these two rites.

Peter and John, having concluded their business in this Samaritan city, proclaim the good news to other villages of Samaria along their journey back to Jerusalem. Jerusalem—Judea—Samaria. The mission is well under way. Now, the "ends of the earth"—the lands of the Gentiles—lay before the witnesses of Jesus.

PHILIP BRINGS THE GOSPEL
TO AN ETHIOPIAN
Acts 8:26–40

8:26 **Then an angel of the Lord said to Philip, "Get up and go toward the south to the road that goes down from Jerusalem to Gaza." (This is a wilderness road.)** [27] **So he got up and went. Now there was an Ethiopian eunuch, a court official of the Candace, queen of the Ethiopians, in charge of her entire treasury. He had come to Jerusalem to worship** [28] **and was returning home; seated in his chariot, he was reading the prophet Isaiah.** [29] **Then the Spirit said to Philip, "Go over to this chariot and join it."** [30] **So Philip ran up to it and heard him reading the prophet Isaiah. He asked, "Do you understand what you are reading?"** [31] **He replied, "How can I, unless someone**

guides me?" And he invited Philip to get in and sit beside him. [32] Now the passage of the scripture that he was reading was this:
"Like a sheep he was led to the slaughter,
and like a lamb silent before its shearer,
so he does not open his mouth.
[33] In his humiliation justice was denied him.
Who can describe his generation?
For his life is taken away from the earth."
[34] The eunuch asked Philip, "About whom, may I ask you, does the prophet say this, about himself or about someone else?" [35] Then Philip began to speak, and starting with this scripture, he proclaimed to him the good news about Jesus. [36] As they were going along the road, they came to some water; and the eunuch said, "Look, here is water! What is to prevent me from being baptized?" [38] He commanded the chariot to stop, and both of them, Philip and the eunuch, went down into the water, and Philip baptized him. [39] When they came up out of the water, the Spirit of the Lord snatched Philip away; the eunuch saw him no more, and went on his way rejoicing. [40] But Philip found himself at Azotus, and as he was passing through the region, he proclaimed the good news to all the towns until he came to Caesarea.

In fine Old Testament fashion, an angel of the Lord came to Philip with traveling orders. So as Philip walked along a deserted road between Jerusalem and Gaza he encountered an Ethiopian riding in a carriage. The story is familiar: Philip heard the Ethiopian reading from the book of Isaiah and asked if the Ethiopian understood the passage. The Ethiopian, not at all offended by the question, appealed for guidance and invited Philip to join him in the carriage.

The Ethiopian had been reading from the prophet Isaiah. Readers of the Bible have long noted that toward the end of Isaiah there are four poems that describe the servant of God: the Servant Songs (Isa. 42:1–4; 49:1–6; 50:4–11; 52:13–53:12; see comments on Acts 3:11–16). The identity of this "servant of God" has been somewhat of a mystery, though Christian readers have generally understood the servant to be Jesus. There was certainly no doubt about this in the mind of the librettist for Handel's *Messiah*.

The music and words of the fourth servant song which the Ethiopian was reading also ring in our ears:

He was despised and rejected . . . ;
a man of sorrows, and acquainted with grief.
(Isa. 53:3, RSV)

"Who is this man of sorrows?" pondered the Ethiopian. As many have before and many since, the Ethiopian wondered about the identity of the servant of God referred to in Isaiah. Was he Isaiah himself or some other person? For the first time in the book of Acts, this important Old Testament text is applied directly to Jesus. Philip proclaimed to the Ethiopian the good news about Jesus. *He* was the suffering servant of God of whom Isaiah wrote. The two men came to some water, the Ethiopian was baptized, and the Spirit whisked Philip away to Caesarea.

This is a simple and familiar story, and one might be tempted to turn quickly to the next scene. But the reader is advised to linger awhile here, and not rush on.

Imbedded in this passage are a number of interesting details. First, we are told that the Ethiopian—a black African—was the treasurer of "The Candace," the official title of the queen mother and real head of government in Ethiopia. Furthermore, he was probably a "God-worshiper" returning from a pilgrimage to Jerusalem (God-fearers or God-worshipers were Gentiles who accepted the theological and ethical teachings of Judaism, and worshiped with Jews in the synagogue without becoming full converts [proselytes] to Judaism).

Finally, Luke notes that the Ethiopian had been castrated; he was a eunuch. According to Deuteronomy 23, castrated males were not to be accepted into the Jewish community. The Ethiopian may have discovered just how rigidly this injunction was enforced as he attempted to worship at the temple in Jerusalem (Acts 8:27). The Ethiopian may have still had his experience of rejection in mind as he was reading Isaiah: "In his humiliation justice was denied him." While he was a God-worshiper, he wanted more. He had wanted to convert to Judaism, a privilege denied to him because of his physical condition.

In his mission to Samaria, Philip had already broken through the ancient barriers of religion and race which bred tremendous hostility between Jews and Samaritans. Now he was prepared to take on a third serious barrier—sexuality.

Philip's heroism and leadership is understated in the New Testament. He was an amazing man of deep faith and great courage. It is not at all difficult to make the leap of two millennia to see the need for just such heroes in our own time. The parallels are all too obvious. He not only baptized those whose race and religion were problems for the guardians of right religion in Jerusalem. Now he gladly received into the Christian sect of Judaism a man whose sexuality was a problem for the temple elite. Perhaps he and the eunuch read a bit further in Isaiah's prophecies, discover-

ing a passage that refers to foreigners (e.g., Samaritans, Ethiopians) and
eunuchs:

> Do not let the foreigner joined to the LORD say,
>   "The LORD will surely separate me from his people";
> and do not let the eunuch say,
>   "I am just a dry tree."
> For thus says the LORD:
> To the eunuchs who keep my sabbaths,
>   who choose the things that please me
>   and hold fast my covenant,
> I will give, in my house and within my walls,
>   a monument and a name better than sons and daughters;
> I will give them an everlasting name
>   that shall not be cut off.
> And the foreigners who join themselves to the LORD,
>   to minister to him, to love the name of the LORD,
>   and to be his servants,
> all who keep my sabbath, and do not profane it,
>   and hold fast my covenant—
> these I will bring to my holy mountain,
>   and make them joyful in my house of prayer;
> their burnt offerings and their sacrifices
>   will be acceptable on my altar;
> *for my house shall be called a house of prayer*
>   *for all peoples.*
> *Thus says the Lord GOD,*
>   *who gathers the outcasts of Israel.*
>
>   (Isa. 56:3–8a)

This is a powerful prophetic challenge that Philip accepted with utmost
seriousness.

Baptism was one of the rites of initiation into Judaism, and now the
Ethiopian may have found a way into the community of faith which he
loved. He may have thought to himself, I have been blocked from baptism
before as I have tried to become a Jew. Now, is there anything about me
that might prevent me from being baptized into this messianic sect of Judaism? Therefore, the question that pops out of the Ethiopian's mouth was
an honest one. "Look, here is water! What is to prevent me from being
baptized?" (v. 36). Philip responded to the Ethiopian's query with a bold
action. He baptized him. And with that, the eunuch "went on his way rejoicing," for at last he had become a full member of the household of faith.

Immediately after the Ethiopian was baptized, Philip was carried off by the Spirit of the Lord (reminiscent of Elijah; 2 Kings 2) and deposited in Azotus (Ashdod). According to the story, Philip continued his preaching mission along the Judean seacoast, from Ashdod, perhaps through Lydda and Joppa—"all the towns until he came to Caesarea" (v. 40). It may be that Luke is implying that Philip was founder of the Christian communities in those cities. With the arrival of the gospel in Caesarea, the reader is being prepared for the next great barrier to be broken by the followers of Jesus of Nazareth.

In 63 B.C., Pompey added Caesarea, along with other nearby coastal towns, to the Roman province of Syria. For the next six hundred years, Caesarea was the capital of Roman government in Palestine, seat of the Roman governor, and headquarters for the Roman legions stationed in Palestine. It is here that Peter will encounter a Gentile centurion of the Italian Cohort named Cornelius (Acts 10).

4. The Church Reaches Out to Gentiles
Acts 9:1–11:18

THE CALL OF SAUL OF TARSUS
Acts 9:1–22

9:1 Meanwhile Saul, still breathing threats and murder against the disciples of the Lord, went to the high priest [2] and asked him for letters to the synagogues at Damascus, so that if he found any who belonged to the Way, men or women, he might bring them bound to Jerusalem. [3] Now as he was going along and approaching Damascus, suddenly a light from heaven flashed around him. [4] He fell to the ground and heard a voice saying to him, "Saul, Saul, why do you persecute me?" [5] He asked, "Who are you, Lord?" The reply came, "I am Jesus, whom you are persecuting. [6] But get up and enter the city, and you will be told what you are to do." [7] The men who were traveling with him stood speechless because they heard the voice but saw no one. [8] Saul got up from the ground, and though his eyes were open, he could see nothing; so they led him by the hand and brought him into Damascus. [9] For three days he was without sight, and neither ate nor drank.

[10] Now there was a disciple in Damascus named Ananias. The Lord said to him in a vision, "Ananias." He answered, "Here I am, Lord." [11] The Lord said to him, "Get up and go to the street called Straight, and at the house of Judas look for a man of Tarsus named Saul. At this moment he is praying, [12] and he has seen in a vision a man named Ananias come in and lay his hands on him so that he might regain his sight." [13] But Ananias answered, "Lord, I have heard from many about this man, how much evil he has done to your saints in Jerusalem; [14] and here he has authority from the chief priests to bind all who invoke your name." [15] But the Lord said to him, "Go, for he is an instrument whom I have chosen to bring my name before Gentiles and kings and before the people of Israel; [16] I myself will show him how much he must suffer for the sake of my name." [17] So Ananias went and entered the house. He laid his hands on Saul and said, "Brother Saul, the Lord Jesus, who appeared to you on your way here, has sent me so that you may regain your sight and be filled with the Holy Spirit." [18] And immediately, something like

scales fell from his eyes, and his sight was restored. Then he got up and was baptized, [19] and after taking some food, he regained his strength.

For several days he was with the disciples in Damascus, [20] and immediately he began to proclaim Jesus in the synagogues, saying, "He is the Son of God." [21] All who heard him were amazed and said, "Is not this the man who made havoc in Jerusalem among those who invoked this name? And has he not come here for the purpose of bringing them bound before the chief priests?" [22] Saul became increasingly more powerful and confounded the Jews who lived in Damascus by proving that Jesus was the Messiah.

These few verses raise a host of important issues relating to Saul/Paul of Tarsus, beginning with his name. Luke uses the Jewish name Saul until Acts 13:9, at which point he switches to Saul's Roman name, Paul. In this study, we will follow Luke in this regard. Other more substantive issues must be addressed, including Saul's background as a Hellenistic and Pharisaic Jew, his persecution of the church, and his Damascus road experience (call or conversion?).

Before we begin a detailed look at these issues, we note that there are other accounts of this event in the New Testament, including two that occur later in the book of Acts (22:4–16 and 26:9–18) and Paul's own recollection which he recorded in his letter to the Galatians (1:11–24). It may be helpful to look at some of the points of agreement and disagreement between Paul and his biographer.

Both Paul and Luke agree that Saul/Paul was a zealous student in the Pharisaic tradition. The reader of Acts will come to discover in Paul's speeches that he "was a Jew, born in Tarsus of Cilicia, but brought up in this city [Jerusalem] at the feet of Gamaliel, educated strictly according to our ancestral law" (Acts 22:3; see 26:5). Paul, however, never mentioned Gamaliel in his letters. It could be that for Paul, Gamaliel and his teaching had become irrelevant in light of Jesus and his teaching. As a member of the Christian sect of Judaism, Paul was under the guidance of a new master teacher.

In reading the book of Acts, one has the impression that Paul began his persecution in Jerusalem and intended to carry it to the Jewish communities scattered outside of Palestine (i.e., the diaspora; Acts 26:9–12 supports this impression). By Paul's own account, he "was still unknown by sight to the churches of Judea [presumably including Jerusalem] that are in Christ; they only heard it said, 'The one who formerly was persecuting us is now proclaiming the faith he once tried to destroy'" (Gal. 1:22–23).

In the passage before us, Paul spent "several days . . . with the disciples in Damascus," while Paul himself says, "I went away *at once* into Arabia, and afterwards I returned to Damascus" (Gal. 1:17).

Finally, what about the letters from the chief priests? Paul himself said nothing about written authorization from the chief priests for his activity. If such were indeed the case, then Luke records the only known instance of interference by the Sanhedrin in the affairs of diaspora Judaism (remember, the letters are to synagogues asking their cooperation in handing over members of the messianic sect of Judaism who may be in their midst). It is highly unlikely that the Jerusalem council had the right to arrest and extradite Jews residing in foreign territories; an exception may be Jewish-Christian residents of Jerusalem who fled the Holy City during the persecution (see 1 Maccabees 15:15–21). Most likely, these "letters" from the high priest are part of the Lukan (or pre-Lukan) lore about the great apostle's pre-Christian days.

While such discrepancies may call into question how personally close Luke was to Paul, the core of the Lukan tradition about the apostle conforms with Paul's own account: Paul had been a superior, if overly enthusiastic, rabbinic student who persecuted the church outside Judea. Other aspects of the story appear to be the embellishments of a good storyteller.

And, of course, we must acknowledge that each account has its own peculiar thrust. Luke's concern was to show that a great change had come over Paul—from persecutor of the church to promoter of the gospel. Paul was primarily concerned to show that the gospel came to him through a direct revelation from Jesus, and was not mediated by any human source. Luke and Paul agree that Paul's violence directed against the church was the context for divine intervention.

Now let us consider some of the significant details embedded in this passage.

Saul, a Man of Tarsus

Saul is a Jewish name. The reader would link this name to the first prince of Israel, the mighty warrior Saul. Paul is Saul's Roman name. This double identity—Saul/Paul—leads us to consider Saul's background. In this passage, the reader is told, almost incidentally, that Saul is "a man of Tarsus" (v. 11). Later in Acts, Paul himself will fully establish his Roman pedigree: "I am a Jew, from Tarsus in Cilicia, a citizen of an important city; . . . I was born a [Roman] citizen" (21:39; 22:28).

These statements prick our curiosity about Saul/Paul. What was he taught in school? How was his daily life at home and in the city? How did Jews of Tarsus relate to the wider Greek culture? What impact did the wider culture make on the Jewish community in Tarsus, and in particular on Saul's family? How did the crosscurrents of Hellenism and Judaism influence Saul? Though we cannot obtain certain answers to any of these questions, we can make some educated guesses about how cultural and social forces might have influenced a Jew growing up in Tarsus.

Tarsus was a large, prosperous commercial city located in the Roman province of Cilicia about ten miles inland from the Mediterranean Sea. The worldwide traffic flowing through Tarsus carried, along with its goods, a steady stream of diverse peoples, philosophies, religions, and mystery cults. In particular, Tarsus was renowned for its intellectual life, second only to Athens as a center for the study of Stoic philosophy with its emphasis on duty, patriotism, reason, and honesty. Indeed, the founder of stoicism, Zeno, was a resident of Tarsus in the fourth century B.C.E. The ancient geographer Strabo notes that "the zeal which the men of Tarsus show for philosophy and culture in general is so great that even Athens and Alexandria are surpassed."

There is also evidence that Tarsus was the cultic center of a vegetation deity named Sandan. An annual ritual of this fertility religion included burning a figure of the god on a funeral pyre each fall with the expectation that the god (and new crops) would rise to new life each spring.

Was Saul influenced by any of this? Scholars of the "history of religions school" in the early part of the twentieth century speculated that Paul may have transferred the notion of a dying and rising god to his understanding of Jesus' resurrection. Others have seen an acquaintance with Stoic philosophy in some of his writings, for example, Paul's discussion of natural law in Romans 1—2. We can only speculate that young Saul may have seen the dying and rising ritual, and that he might have been impressed by Stoic scholars. We are on firmer ground, however, when we consider formative influences closer at hand for Saul.

Saul had been reared in the Jewish home of parents who had been Roman citizens (for a discussion of Paul's Roman citizenship, see comments on Acts 22:22–30). The Judaism that Saul experienced would have had a distinctly Hellenistic coloring. The everyday language of his parents was Greek and the text of scripture commonly used for study and worship in synagogue was a Greek translation of the Hebrew scriptures known as the Septuagint. It is probably the case that Saul learned to read the Hebrew text of the Bible as well; he was so well schooled in scripture that as a young man he was sent to Jerusalem to study with the great interpreters of (Hebrew) scripture.

Jews who lived outside of Palestine were in a situation that encouraged a certain amount of accommodation with the wider Hellenistic culture.

Everyday life, buying and selling in the market, maintaining good relations with one's neighbors, would encourage a modicum of goodwill between Jews and non-Jews in the community. There is evidence that Jews in the diaspora attempted not only to live in concord with others, but when possible they tried to win converts to their way of life. The prophet Isaiah had foreseen their role in history as "a light to the nations." Many in the diaspora took Isaiah seriously and lived in the Roman Empire with a genuine sense of mission. Members of Greek-speaking synagogues seem to have been quite liberal toward their Gentile neighbors. They were satisfied if the God-fearers who worshiped with them (see Acts 13:16) simply pledged themselves to confess belief in one God and to observe a minimum of ritual and ethical rules. No demand was made for circumcision; they were not required to become proselytes, full members of the Jewish people.

Perhaps this diaspora "liberality" was only exchanging favor for favor. Judaism had long been recognized as a legitimate religion and was treated with toleration and respect. Jews were free of work obligations on the sabbath, they were allowed to pay the annual temple tax which supported Jewish leadership in Jerusalem, they were exempted from serving in the military, and they were not required to sacrifice to the emperor—though they were encouraged to pray *for* him. These privileges may have made their Gentile neighbors jealous—sporadic clashes are recorded—but they also enticed some non-Jews to look more closely at Judaism as a possible way of life.

Through experience in his Hellenistic-Jewish home and synagogue, Saul's character was probably marked with the spirit of toleration toward his non-Jewish neighbors—as much out of deference toward the non-Jewish majority as from genuine missionary concern. Furthermore, we can surmise that Saul took full advantage of the education offered him. He did indeed surpass his colleagues. He not only developed rudimentary literary skills, but learned his philosophical, biblical, and rhetorical lessons well. We noted above that he understood the Stoic notion of discerning God and God's will through creation (Romans 1—2); he was also familiar with such Stoic virtues as patience, endurance, sobriety, and duty. Like the Hellenistic-Jewish philosopher Philo, he occasionally used the allegorical method of biblical interpretation, for instance, the allegory of Sarah and Hagar in Galatians 4. Paul also used the style of argument favored by itinerant preachers and philosophers of the time, the diatribe that advanced philosophical, moral, or religious ideas without long-winded deductions, speculative arguments, and technical language. Often in his letters Paul's diatribe takes the form of a lively debate, outlining an imaginary opponent's objections and bringing the reader into the discussion. Finally, Luke

notes that Paul was able to engage in lively constructive philosophical discussions with Stoic and Epicurean philosophers in Athens (Acts 17).

The young man Saul had a serious and well-educated attitude toward
his own religion. He may also have possessed a liberal perspective toward
human beings who stood outside Judaism and a deep concern that somehow they too might be included in the people of God.

During his teenage years Saul was sent by his parents to Jerusalem to
study with the rabbis of that great center of Jewish life. According to Luke
(though Paul himself never makes this claim), Saul became a disciple of the
Pharisaic teacher Gamaliel the Elder, one of the most respected and influential scholars of his day. Paul does claim, "I advanced in Judaism beyond many among my people of the same age, for I was far more zealous
for the traditions of my ancestors" (Gal. 1:14). It sounds as if the young
man Saul possessed the zeal of one who was a convert from the relaxed religion of his parents to the demanding life of a rabbinic scholar. Luke has
presented a significant contrast between Saul and his tolerant teacher
Gamaliel (see Acts 5). The reader of Acts has the impression that Saul took
a much more severe and rigid view of Pharisaic Judaism than his master
may have intended.

Zealous for his Pharisaic faith, Saul attempted to destroy the recently
organized sect of Judaism. In doing so, he was also destroying the more
tolerant tendencies deeply etched in his being. Saul the rigid Pharisaic Jew
had turned against Saul the tolerant Hellenistic Jew, so that in attempting
to destroy the church—mission-oriented messianic Hellenistic Judaism—
he was destroying part of himself.

Saul, Persecutor of the Church

The reader of Acts already knows that Saul had consented to the killing
of Stephen and had become a persecutor of the church. According to
Luke, this persecution was first carried out in Jerusalem (8:1). In Acts 9,
Luke offers more information about Saul's vicious deeds. Wishing to pursue his attack on the Christian community in Damascus, Saul has asked
the high priest for letters to the synagogues requesting their assistance in
reporting those belonging to "the Way"—one of the names the early
church took for itself (see Acts 19:9, 23; 22:4; 24:14, 22). According to a
later account in Acts, Saul had received authorization from the chief
priests not only to lock up Christians, but, he says, "I also cast my vote
against them when they were being condemned to death. By punishing
them often in all the synagogues I tried to force them to blaspheme; and

since I was so furiously enraged at them, I pursued them even to foreign cities" (26:10–11).

But Saul, on his way to one such foreign city, was suddenly stopped by a bright heavenly light. The voice of Jesus asked Saul, "Why do you persecute me?" Jesus commanded Saul to enter the city and wait for further instructions. Saul, blinded by the light, remained "in the dark" for three long days.

Why Damascus?

Both Paul and Luke agree that the revelation of Jesus took place near Damascus. This capital city of Syria was under the rule of Rome through a local Nabatean governor, Aretas IV (9 B.C.E.–40 C.E.; he is remembered for having given his daughter in marriage to King Herod's son Antipas, a political bond designed to heal strained Jewish-Nabatean relations. In 28 C.E., Antipas divorced his Nabatean wife in order to marry Herodias, occasioning a reproach from John the Baptist; Mark 6:17–29).

A large community of Jews resided in Damascus; note that Luke uses the plural "synagogues" (9:2). One of these synagogues may have been a community of strict "covenanters" which may have produced the so-called *Zadokite Fragments*, and maintained an affiliation with the Essene community at Qumran. (The *Zadokite Fragments*, a tenth-century C.E. document, came to light in Cairo in the late nineteenth century; however, discovery of very similar material among the scrolls at Qumran suggests that the contents of the *Fragments* are much older.) The community that produced this literature appears to have been a messianic community of the "New Covenant" in the "Land of Damascus" (metaphorical or the actual city?) awaiting a "Teacher of Righteousness" who would come to them "in the end of days." Such a community might have been quite hospitable to Jewish Christians from Jerusalem. And perhaps Saul, who heard the preaching of Stephen about a messiah called the Righteous One, was anxious to stop the spread of such a message to an obvious and easy target in Damascus.

Through an exchange of visions, Ananias and Saul were brought together. We are not told much about Ananias, only that he was a disciple, that is, a Christian, a "devout man according to the law and well spoken of by all the Jews" living in Damascus (22:12). It is impossible to tell whether he was a Christian who had fled from Jerusalem, or a native of Damascus. His statement, "I have heard from many about this man [Saul], how much evil he has done to your saints in Jerusalem," suggests the latter possibility.

Conversion or Call?

Acts 9:15 indicates the vocation that God has in mind for Saul. Jesus has called Saul as "an instrument whom I have chosen to bring my name before Gentiles and kings and before the people of Israel." This brings us to an issue that has evoked considerable discussion among contemporary Bible scholars. How shall we talk about Saul's experience on the Damascus road? Was it a conversion or a call? In spite of the headings found in many Bibles and commentaries (including the editors' notation in the Oxford annotated edition of the NRSV: "The Conversion of Saul of Tarsus"), a significant number of scholars prefer to understand this experience of Saul as his *calling* to preach the gospel.

Those who favor conversion language emphasize Saul's radical change. That Saul was transformed from an adversary of the Christian community into an advocate of their faith is certainly true. This, however, insufficiently accounts for the full scope of Saul's experience. As I noted above, the change from adversary to advocate is a secondary issue for Paul and only establishes the context for his profound experience.

Perhaps by conversion one might mean that Paul the Pharisee had become Paul the Christian. This, too, does not do justice to Paul. His letters nowhere indicate that he ceased to be a Pharisee (especially see his impassioned words in Romans 9—11). Luke also indicates that Paul never gave up his allegiance to the Pharisaic tradition. In addressing the Sanhedrin, Paul declared, "I am a Pharisee, a son of Pharisees" (23:6). To the end, Paul was both a Christian and a Pharisee.

Finally, it has been suggested that Paul was converted from legalistic Judaism to the freedom of Christianity. His conscience, crushed by the twin burdens of guilt and law, found blessed relief in God's grace. Yet, as we read above, Paul did not find the law oppressive nor did he sense guilt before it; "as to righteousness under the law, [I am] blameless" (Phil. 3:6). The reader needs to be careful about ascribing a bad conscience to Paul.

People often read Paul through the experience and interpretation of Saint Augustine and Martin Luther; both suffered from pangs of conscience and found relief in Paul's writings about finding righteousness before God apart from the law. One needs to read the apostle's discussion about sin and grace very carefully. When Paul cried out, "Wretched man that I am! Who will rescue me from this body of death?" his issue was not with the law of God (which "is holy, and the commandment is holy and just and good," Rom. 7:12). Rather, Paul's problem was a universal one; he is mortal—a member of the human race with all its built-in limitations ("the law is spiritual; but I am of the flesh"). Sin is the universal human condition that needs to be addressed on a universal scale. Only God can do this. In fact, God *had* given revealed law to Israel and natural law to the Gentiles, but both failed to comprehend, appropriate, and appreciate these gifts (Romans 1—3). So now, "apart from law, the righteousness of God has been disclosed, . . . the righteousness of God through faith in Jesus Christ for all who believe. For there is no distinction [between Jew and Gentile], since all have sinned and fall short of the glory of God; they are now justified by his grace as a gift, through the redemption that is in Christ Jesus" (Rom. 3:21–24).

Paul did not seem to be suffering from a bad conscience or from the oppressive weight of law. And consequently, it is difficult to hold that his Damascus road experience was a conversion from legalistic Judaism to freedom in Christ.

What contemporary readers do see in the Damascus road experience, from the perspective of both Paul and Luke, is a *call* from God. Rather than a negative "turn your back on the past," Paul received a positive "turn your face toward the future." Paul states, "God . . . called me through his grace, [and] was pleased to reveal his son to me, so that I might proclaim him among the Gentiles" (Gal. 1:15–16). And according to Luke, Paul "is an instrument whom I [Jesus] have chosen to bring my name before Gentiles" (Acts 9:15). Paul claims this revelation of Christ along the road; Luke puts words and purpose to this revelation: "For I [Jesus] have appeared to you for this purpose, to appoint you to serve and testify to the things in which you have seen me and to those in which I will appear to you" (Acts 26:16).

We, like Paul, are not called to turn our back on the past. Rather, we are to look fully at all aspects of our personal histories, to repent of (to change our minds about) the things we do that run counter to the inevitability of God's grace, and to turn our faces toward God's future. In doing this, we, like Paul, enter the process of completing God's joy by expanding God's love in the world. And as we reflect on the experience, we—like Paul—come to discover that God was there all along, transforming destructive anger into overflowing joy.

The young rabbi Saul now has his true vocation (*vocatus:* "call"). He will soon assume center stage in the book of Acts, bringing the name of Jesus "before Gentiles and kings and before the people of Israel" (v. 15).

Saul in Damascus

Saul, blinded by his experience, was led by his fellow travelers to the house of Judas (a common Jewish name) in Damascus. Ananias, a leader in the Jewish-Christian community of Damascus, was instructed in a vision to go to Judas's house to visit with Saul and heal him of his blindness. An understandably anxious Ananias did as he was told. Saul was healed (something like scales fell from his eyelids), he received the Holy Spirit, and he was baptized into the Christian community.

According to verses 20–22, Saul immediately entered the synagogues of Damascus not to persecute Christians but to proclaim that Jesus "is the Son of God" and to argue from scripture that Jesus is the Messiah. The reader has the impression that Saul spent considerable time in Damascus reconstructing his own theological perspective and developing his message, which for Saul the Pharisee was a theological shift of cosmic proportions. Luke's description of Saul's proclamation—"[Jesus] is the Son of God" (the only time this title occurs in the book of Acts)—conforms with the apostle's recollection that during his Damascus road experience, "God . . . was pleased to reveal his Son to me, so that I might proclaim him among the Gentiles" (Gal. 1:15–16).

SAUL ESCAPES FROM DAMASCUS AND ARRIVES IN JERUSALEM
Acts 9:23–31

9:23 **After some time had passed, the Jews plotted to kill him,** 24 **but their plot became known to Saul. They were watching the gates day and night so that they might kill him;** 25 **but his disciples took him by night and let him down through an opening in the wall, lowering him in a basket.**
26 **When he had come to Jerusalem, he attempted to join the disciples; and they were all afraid of him, for they did not believe that he was a disciple.** 27 **But Barnabas took him, brought him to the apostles, and described for them how on the road he had seen the Lord, who had spoken to him, and how in Damascus he had spoken boldly in the name of Jesus.** 28 **So he went in and out among them in Jerusalem, speaking boldly in the name of the Lord.** 29 **He spoke and argued with the Hellenists; but they were attempting to kill him.** 30 **When the believers learned of it, they brought him down to Caesarea and sent him off to Tarsus.**
31 **Meanwhile the church throughout Judea, Galilee, and Samaria had peace and was built up. Living in the fear of the Lord and in the comfort of the Holy Spirit, it increased in numbers.**

This section presents a few nasty problems if one attempts to reconcile the narrative of Luke and the memory of Paul. "For several days" and "after some time" indicate a significant stay in Damascus, whereas Paul says that after the revelation he *immediately* went to Arabia and sometime later returned to Damascus. Either Luke does not know about Paul's journey to Arabia or he simply omits it.

Furthermore, Luke's account of Saul's visit to Jerusalem after his escape from Damascus does not square with the apostle's words. Paul says, "*After three years* I did go up to Jerusalem *to visit Cephas* and stayed with him fifteen days; but *I did not see any other apostle except James the Lord's brother*" (Gal. 1:18–19). Luke indicates that Barnabas brought Paul to the apostles, that Paul "went in and out among them," spoke boldly in the name of the Lord, and argued with the Hellenists (Acts 9:27–29).

Perhaps some of these differences can be reconciled in the following way:

1. Acts 9:10–19a refers to Saul's short visit to Damascus for healing and baptism.
2. Saul immediately made a trip to Arabia, perhaps to contemplate his experience on the road to Damascus. This three-year sojourn is omitted by Luke.
3. Saul then returned to Damascus—the events recorded in Acts 9:19b–25 (also see Gal. 1:17). Perhaps it was during this visit that he was forced to escape from Damascus (also mentioned by Paul in 2 Corinthians 11:32–33) and went to Jerusalem to visit Peter and James.

What cannot be reconciled, however, is Luke's account of Saul's visit to Jerusalem which indicates that Saul "attempted to join the disciples," eventually going "in and out among [the disciples] in Jerusalem, speaking boldly in the name of the Lord" (9:26, 28). According to Paul, he saw *no one* in Jerusalem except *Peter and James*, the brother of Jesus (Gal. 1:18–19). After fifteen days, he left for Syria and Cilicia.

We shall simply have to conclude that Luke is dependent on a tradition that attempts to fill in the sketchy details of Saul's early days as a Christian, a tradition less concerned with historical accuracy than with advancing the story of the great missionary to the Gentiles.

In Jerusalem it is Barnabas who becomes Saul's advocate. The reader will recall meeting Barnabas in Acts 4. He was a priest (Levite), a diaspora Jew from Cyprus, and a generous Christian who fully shared his property with the community. Since Barnabas and Saul share similar backgrounds, it is not surprising that Barnabas should be an effective shepherd for Saul in Jerusalem's Christian community.

Like Stephen before him (Acts 6—7), Saul engages the Hellenists—fellow Greek-speaking Jews—in debate about Jesus. They react to Saul in the same negative way. To rescue him from Stephen's fate, the disciples spirit Saul out of Jerusalem and send him home to Tarsus.

Once again, Luke ends this section with an editorial summary that reminds the reader that the mission initiated by Jesus is well under way. "The church throughout Judea, Galilee, and Samaria had peace and was built up" (v. 9:31; this is the only mention in Acts of a Christian community in Galilee; it is strange that Luke does not record a mission in the home territory of Jesus and his apostles). The great persecutor has been won over so that Christians need no longer live in anxious fear of Saul, but "in the fear of the Lord and in the comfort of the Holy Spirit" (v. 31).

PETER IN LYDDA AND JOPPA
Acts 9:32–43

9:32 Now as Peter went here and there among all the believers, he came down also to the saints living in Lydda. 33 There he found a man named Aeneas, who had been bedridden for eight years, for he was paralyzed. 34 Peter said to him, "Aeneas, Jesus Christ heals you; get up and make your bed!" And immediately he got up. 35 And all the residents of Lydda and Sharon saw him and turned to the Lord.

36 Now in Joppa there was a disciple whose name was Tabitha, which in Greek is Dorcas. She was devoted to good works and acts of charity. 37 At that time she became ill and died. When they had washed her, they laid her in a room upstairs. 38 Since Lydda was near Joppa, the disciples, who heard that Peter was there, sent two men to him with the request, "Please come to us without delay." 39 So Peter got up and went with them; and when he arrived, they took him to the room upstairs. All the widows stood beside him, weeping and showing tunics and other clothing that Dorcas had made while she was with them. 40 Peter put all of them outside, and then he knelt down and prayed. He turned to the body and said, "Tabitha, get up." Then she opened her eyes, and seeing Peter, she sat up. 41 He gave her his hand and helped her up. Then calling the saints and widows, he showed her to be alive. 42 This became known throughout Joppa, and many believed in the Lord. 43 Meanwhile he stayed in Joppa for some time with a certain Simon, a tanner.

By now, the reader may have detected that Luke has stitched together a number of sources, perhaps independent traditions about the various leaders in the early church—Acts of Peter, Stephen, Philip, Paul. We return here to more acts of Peter.

As I noted in the Introduction, Luke typically writes double stories in his narrative. In this passage Luke narrates the healing of a paralyzed man and the raising of a dead woman. Moreover, these stories have interesting parallels in the Gospels.

The stories in Acts 9:32–11:18 are set in the context of a tour that Peter makes of Christian communities in Judea—Lydda, Joppa, and Caesarea. The first two stories return to the theme of Peter the miracle worker as he raises a paralyzed man and a dead woman (9:32–42). In the third story (10:1–11:18), Peter performs perhaps his greatest miracle—he brings the gospel to a Gentile.

The two short stories in this passage reflect early traditions about Peter's work in two Judean towns, Lydda and Joppa. The first story (9:32–35) is simply and briefly told. Using the name of Jesus, Peter healed a man who had been paralyzed for eight years. Luke had told a similar story about Jesus who healed a paralytic, telling him to "stand up and take your bed and go to your home. Immediately he stood up" (Luke 5:24–25). Likewise, Peter tells this paralytic, " 'Get up and make your bed!' And immediately he got up."

This story concludes with a bit of literary license: "*All* the residents of Lydda and Sharon saw him and turned to the Lord" (9:35). The coastal plain of Sharon extended from Caesarea thirty miles southward to Joppa, and from the Mediterranean Sea to the Judean hill country, about ten miles eastward, roughly three hundred square miles!

The second healing story (9:36–42) finds Peter at Joppa, called there by members of the church distressed with the death of Tabitha, a disciple. Luke notes for his Greek reader that the Aramaic name Tabitha is a translation of "Dorcas" (Greek for "gazelle"). Tabitha, a disciple "devoted to good works and acts of charity . . . became ill and died" (vv. 36–37). Luke paints a poignant scene: "All the widows stood beside [Peter], weeping and showing tunics and other clothing that Dorcas had made while she was with them" (v. 39). The poor widows offered Peter tangible evidence of her good works and charity. The following verse is reminiscent of Jesus raising the daughter of Jairus; in fact, the entire description closely parallels Mark's account (5:35–43; also Luke 8:40–56):

Mark	**Acts**
The people are weeping and wailing loudly.	The widows are weeping loudly.
Jesus put them all outside.	Peter put them all outside.
Jesus said to the girl (in Aramaic), "Talitha, cum!"— "Little girl, get up!"	Peter said to the woman (in Aramaic), "Tabitha, cum!"— "Tabitha, get up."

Notice the striking similarity even in the name given the girl or woman—a difference of only one letter. Mark translates the term "talitha" for the Greek reader as "little girl." Luke likewise translates "Tabitha" for his Greek reader as "Dorcas/gazelle." It is doubtful that Luke has confused the two stories. Rather, there was probably an early Christian tradition that intentionally attached to Peter, Jesus' chief apostle, the same kind of miracles as the master had performed. Peter, like Jesus, was remembered not only as a healer of infirmities, but he raised the dead as well.

Unlike his ending to the prior story set in Lydda, Luke's estimate of the impact of this miracle is somewhat more realistic (and perhaps ironic, given the nature of the two miracles): "This became known throughout Joppa, and *many* believed in the Lord." Finally, Luke notes that while in Joppa Peter stayed with Simon, a tanner. This detail regarding Simon's trade foreshadows the break Peter will make with more orthodox Judaism. Simon the tanner did work which, according to Jewish law, was defiling since it required handling animal carcasses. He was Peter's host "for some time."

PETER AND THE CONVERSION OF CORNELIUS
Acts 10:1–48

The Vision of Cornelius (Acts 10:1–8)

10:1 **In Caesarea there was a man named Cornelius, a centurion of the Italian Cohort, as it was called. 2 He was a devout man who feared God with all his household; he gave alms generously to the people and prayed constantly to God. 3 One afternoon at about three o'clock he had a vision in which he clearly saw an angel of God coming in and saying to him, "Cornelius." 4 He stared at him in terror and said, "What is it, Lord?" He answered, "Your prayers and your alms have ascended as a memorial before God. 5 Now send men to Joppa for a certain Simon who is called Peter; 6 he is lodging with Simon, a tanner, whose home is by the seaside." 7 When the angel who spoke to him had left, he called two of his slaves and a devout soldier from the ranks of those who served him, 8 and after telling them everything, he sent them to Joppa.**

These verses introduce the reader to an important figure in the early church—Cornelius. Luke tells us a great deal about this man. He was a Roman military officer, a centurion. His military company was the Italian Cohort stationed in Caesarea. He was a God-fearer. And he was generous with his money. This description may sound familiar to the reader of Luke's two volumes. In his Gospel, Luke described a similar centurion who was highly regarded by the Jews of Capernaum because he generously built a synagogue for them (Luke 7:1–10).

Originally, Caesarea had been a small anchorage on the Mediterranean coast called Strabo's Tower. Herod the Great built the town into a magnificent seaport, naming it Caesarea Maritima in honor of Caesar Augustus. The city served as the official residence of Roman governors of the province of Judea, as well as headquarters for the Roman army stationed in Judea.

Roman troops stationed in Palestine were auxiliary forces, volunteers largely drawn from the local population. An auxiliary cohort was a company of a thousand men. As a centurion, Cornelius was in charge of one-tenth of the Italian Cohort, a unit formed in Italy by freedmen (former slaves) who served in exchange for Roman citizenship.

Moreover, Cornelius had a significant relationship with Judaism. He was a "devout man who feared God" (v. 2). This indicates that Cornelius was a Gentile who took part in synagogue services, but did not adhere to all of the legal requirements of Judaism. That "all his household" is mentioned may indicate either that he was stationed for a long term (not unusual), or that he was close to the end of his active military career and planned to retire in the coastal town of Caesarea.

Luke's description of Cornelius's piety is couched in the language of Greek text of the Old Testament. He gave alms liberally and prayed constantly. During a traditional Jewish time of prayer, three P.M., an angel came to Cornelius and said, "Your prayers and your alms have ascended as a memorial before God" (v. 4; see Exod. 2:23; 17:14; Lev. 2:1). Acting on instructions from the angel, Cornelius commanded two slaves and a "devout soldier" (perhaps a fellow God-fearer) to find Peter and bring him to Caesarea.

The Vision of Peter (Acts 10:9–16)

10:9 **About noon the next day, as they were on their journey and approaching the city, Peter went up on the roof to pray.** [10] **He became hungry and wanted something to eat; and while it was being prepared, he fell into a trance.** [11] **He saw the heaven opened and something like a large sheet coming down, being lowered to the ground by its four corners.** [12] **In it were all kinds of four-footed creatures and reptiles and birds of the air.** [13] **Then he heard a voice saying, "Get up, Peter; kill and eat."** [14] **But Peter said, "By no means, Lord; for I have never eaten anything that is profane or unclean."** [15] **The voice said to him again, a second time, "What God has made clean, you must not call profane."** [16] **This happened three times, and the thing was suddenly taken up to heaven.**

At noon Peter climbed to the roof of Simon's house in order to pray. While there, Peter's thought turned to food. For Jews, noon was not a fixed mealtime. Breakfast was eaten midmorning and the main meal in late afternoon. (Greek and Roman practice also included a light meal at noon.) Nevertheless, Peter was hungry, he asked for something to eat, and his host set about to prepare a snack.

Peter's next experience came in a state of ecstasy. Our text says that he "fell into a trance" and had a vision. We can be certain that we are reading an often-repeated story, for Luke lapses into a favorite storyteller's idiom—verbs in the historical present tense. Our corrected English translation reads, "He *saw* the heaven opened . . . " (v. 11). The Greek text reads, "He *sees* the heaven opened. . . . "

The passage is clear about the vision. In the sheet that descended from heaven were "*all kinds of . . . creatures,*" including reptiles and birds. Peter was commanded to "kill and eat" these creatures. Biblical tradition is quite clear that this would be a violation of Mosaic law (Leviticus 11 offers a lengthy and detailed list of clean and unclean creatures). Peter may have been hungry, but he refused to violate traditional food laws.

The story indicates that Peter, in spite of his powerful miracles and sermons, had not changed much since his days with Jesus. That strong stubborn streak was still there. With empty bravado, Peter earlier had said to Jesus, "Lord, I am ready to go with you to prison and to death!" Jesus responded, "I tell you, Peter, the cock will not crow this day, until you have denied *three times* that you know me" (Luke 22:33–34). In the passage under consideration here, Peter was told *three times* by a heavenly voice, "What God has made clean, you must not call profane." Later on Peter will be instructed *three times* by an angel to do as he is told (Acts 12)! Jesus' pun on Peter's name—"the rock"—was well deserved!

Peter was naturally perplexed by his dream (v. 17). The fact that he felt compelled to challenge the message of the dream three times indicates just *how extraordinary* the message was. In modern psychological terms, we would call Peter's experience cognitive dissonance. That is, he has heard a voice commanding him to do something that ran counter to an established set of beliefs and values which he firmly held to be true—and not just true in human valuation, but divinely ordained as absolutely and eternally true. Can he trust that this really is the voice of God?

As I noted above, Israel's food laws were part of the legal tradition given to Moses by God. According to the rabbis of Peter's time, Moses not only received the Ten Commandments on Mount Sinai, but the whole of the law (Torah) codified in the first five books of Moses (the Pentateuch; additionally, the Pharisees taught that Moses also received the oral law preserved in the Pharisaic legal tradition). Therefore, Leviticus 11 and oral interpretation of that text were understood by pious (and even semipious) Jews to be God's law for their lives. How can Peter, a humble fisherman from Galilee, receive a contradictory message from God some twelve hundred years later? It is not at all surprising that Peter should challenge this message three times. In fact, it is surprising that he challenged it *only* three times!

Peter and Cornelius Meet
(Acts 10:17–33)

10:17 Now when Peter was greatly puzzled about what to make of the vision that he had seen, suddenly the men sent by Cornelius appeared. They were asking for Simon's house and were standing by the gate. 18 They called out to ask whether Simon, who was called Peter, was staying there. 19 While Peter was still thinking about the vision, the Spirit said to him, "Look, three men are searching for you. 20 Now get up, go down, and go with them without hesitation; for I have sent them." 21 So Peter went down to the men and said, "I am the one you are looking for; what is the reason for your coming?" 22 They answered, "Cornelius, a centurion, an upright and God-fearing man, who is well spoken of by the whole Jewish nation, was directed by a holy angel to send for you to come to his house and to hear what you have to say." 23 So Peter invited them in and gave them lodging.

The next day he got up and went with them, and some of the believers from Joppa accompanied him. 24 The following day they came to Caesarea. Cornelius was expecting them and had called together his relatives and close friends. 25 On Peter's arrival Cornelius met him, and falling at his feet, worshiped him. 26 But Peter made him get up, saying, "Stand up; I am only a mortal." 27 And as he talked with him, he went in and found that many had assembled; 28 and he said to them, "You yourselves know that it is unlawful for a Jew to associate with or to visit a Gentile; but God has shown me that I should not call anyone profane or unclean. 29 So when I was sent for, I came without objection. Now may I ask why you sent for me?"

30 Cornelius replied, "Four days ago at this very hour, at three o'clock, I was praying in my house when suddenly a man in dazzling clothes stood before me. 31 He said, 'Cornelius, your prayer has been heard and your alms have been remembered before God. 32 Send therefore to Joppa and ask for Simon, who is called Peter; he is staying in the home of Simon, a tanner, by the sea.' 33 Therefore I sent for you immediately, and you have been kind enough to come. So now all of us are here in the presence of God to listen to all that the Lord has commanded you to say."

While Peter was trying to figure out the meaning of the dream, the emissaries from Cornelius arrived in Joppa where he was staying. The Spirit, still speaking with Peter, instructed him to go with the men "without hesitation."

The scene sounds very much like the story of the centurion in Luke's Gospel. In Luke 7, Jewish elders came to Jesus saying that a centurion stationed in Capernaum "is worthy" to have Jesus heal his slave, for "he loves our people, and it is he who built our synagogue for us." Even as Jesus was going with them, a second group (the centurion's friends) was sent to appeal to Jesus for help. According to this story, Jesus never actually met the Gentile centurion (perhaps to preserve Jesus' "orthodoxy"), though the friends do return to the centurion's house to find the centurion's slave in good health.

In the Acts account, the centurion's lieutenant and two slaves intercede with Peter on behalf of their master. "Cornelius, a centurion, an upright and God-fearing man, who is well spoken of by the whole Jewish nation, was directed by a holy angel to send for you to come to his house and to hear what you have to say" (v. 22). Unlike the Gospel story where Jesus does not deal directly with the centurion, here Peter is instructed by the Spirit to have face-to-face contact with an officer of the Roman army in the Gentile's home.

The actual meeting of the two men is very strange. In preparation for the meeting, Cornelius has gathered together his relatives and friends. According to Luke, when Peter arrived at Cornelius's door, the first thing the centurion did was prostrate himself at Peter's feet to worship him. The image presented by Luke is vivid. The term Luke uses in describing Cornelius's action—"falling" at Peter's feet—is an act of obeisance reserved for divine beings and human authorities of the highest order. A Roman officer lying prostrate before a Galilean peasant would certainly make exciting reading for the early Christian community. However, this might cause the reader to wonder about the depth of this God-fearer's understanding of the worship of God.

Peter, recognizing what was happening, immediately corrected the centurion and commanded him to stand up. Peter's response was, "I am only a mortal"—I am not divine!

Peter then walked into the house and saw the assembled crowd—Gentile relatives and friends of Cornelius. Peter's first comment to them calls attention to the difference between him and these Gentiles. Peter's statement is perhaps an exaggeration; it is not true that Jews were forbidden "to associate with or to visit a Gentile" (v. 28). Cornelius, after all, was a God-fearer "well spoken of by the whole Jewish nation." Perhaps Luke understood that Jewish law forbade Jews from actually entering the homes of Gentiles; thus, Jesus did not go to the home of the centurion in Luke 7 (Jesus did not even talk with the centurion, but only with Jewish intermediaries; in Matthew's parallel account [8:5–13] the centurion had direct contact with Jesus).

It is apparent that we are dealing with a story that touches on an issue of tremendous importance. Luke has been quite careful in his presentation of social interactions between Jews and Gentiles. As we shall come to see in Acts 11, the real problem may have been Peter's participation in a meal with Gentiles (Acts 11:2; see Paul's description of the issue in Galatians 2:12: "until certain people came from James, [Peter] used to eat with the Gentiles").

It is with gradual clarity to Peter and to the reader that the meaning of Peter's dream unfolds. In spite of the taboo (this is one meaning of the Greek word translated here as "unlawful") of visiting with Gentiles, Peter interpreted his dream as God's instruction "not to call anyone profane or unclean." The dream of various creatures on a four-sided sheet was interpreted metaphorically to represent all the world's people gathered within the four corners of the earth (people of antiquity imagined the earth as a rectangular plane supported by four pillars). Peter's claim that he first understood the meaning of the dream and then came in response (v. 29) seems a bit forced. However, during the two-day journey from Joppa to Caesarea, Peter may have had ample time to discern an interpretation of the dream, an interpretation confirmed when he walked through the door of Cornelius's house.

This is still a rather astounding event, even as we modern readers reflect on this scene. Here is Peter, a fisherman from Galilee, claiming that he now knows, because of a dream and his interpretation of it, that God has changed a millennium of divinely ordered regulations regarding social interactions between Jews and Gentiles. Like the stories of Philip in Acts 8, this is a profound episode, greatly underappreciated and underappropriated in the collective Christian consciousness. For early Jewish Christians to use this story to make such a claim about God's will for the future of Jewish and Gentile relations was audacious, to say the least.

Peter now understands why God has brought him from Joppa to Caesarea. This gathering of Gentiles waits with high expectation to hear Peter's message.

Peter's Sermon to the Gentiles
in Caesarea (Acts 10:34–43)

> 10:34 **Then Peter began to speak to them: "I truly understand that God shows no partiality, [35] but in every nation anyone who fears him and does what is right is acceptable to him. [36] You know the message he sent to the people of Israel, preaching peace by Jesus Christ—he is Lord of all. [37] That message spread throughout Judea, beginning in Galilee after the baptism that John announced: [38] how God anointed Jesus of Nazareth with the Holy Spirit and with power, how he went about doing good and healing all who were oppressed by the devil, for God was with him. [39] We are witnesses to all that he did both in Judea and in Jerusalem. They put him to death by hanging him on a tree; [40] but God raised him on the third day and allowed him to appear, [41] not to all the people but to us who were chosen by God as witnesses, and who ate and drank with him after he rose from the dead. [42] He commanded us to preach to the people and to testify that he is the one ordained by God as judge of the living and the dead. [43] All the prophets testify about him that everyone who believes in him receives forgiveness of sins through his name."**

The story moves ever more deeply into the realm of audacious claims. Not only has God revealed to a Galilean fisherman that God has changed the rules of the game which determine social interactions between Jews and Gentiles. This fisherman-preacher now boldly announces that "God shows no partiality, but in every *nation* [not in the sense of the modern nation-state, but in terms of ethnic groups] *anyone* who fears him and does what is right is acceptable to him" (vv. 34–35). To a first-century Jewish reader, this would have been close to blasphemy. This message flies in the face of ancient tradition that the Lord has set his heart on Israel and chosen her above all the *nations* (Exod. 19:5–6; Deut. 7:6–8) to be his special people.

If Philip scaled the wall that kept Jews and Samaritans apart, now Peter smashes that barrier completely. Anyone—Jew, Samaritan, Roman, Greek—anyone who fears God and does what is right is acceptable to God. That which was implicit in Jesus' message of peace is now explicit in the preaching of Peter and the early church.

> You know the message [God] sent to the people of Israel, preaching peace by Jesus Christ—he is Lord of all. (Acts 10:36)

Unfortunately, the NRSV translation does not do justice to this important verse.

This passage deserves to be read very carefully. It begins bluntly and boldly: "You know the message [literally, "word," *logos*] [God] sent to the people of Israel, preaching peace by Jesus Christ—he is Lord of *all* [everything that is—cosmic in scope]." The first key word reminds the reader of John 1:1, "In the beginning was the Word (*logos*)"—God's creative word that brings about all that is (also see Gen. 1:1). God's word to the people of Israel is the good news of peace through Jesus Christ. Luke's narrative is intentionally ambiguous here. Jesus not only brought the good news of peace, he *is* the good news of peace. Jesus both proclaimed God's *logos* and he is the *logos* of God. As such, Jesus is Lord of all that is—of everything and everyone in the created order. This is a powerful christological statement. Everyone—Jew, Samaritan, Roman, Greek, African, European, Asian, American—is under the Lordship of Jesus Christ! And if this is the case, then God does not show preference for any one people.

The good news of Jesus and the message of Peter is inclusive. As Paul deftly put it, "All of you are one in Christ" (Gal. 3:28). Jesus, Peter, and Paul give voice to a radical new revelation of God who yearns for unity, wholeness, inclusiveness, and peace for God's creation—a conviction expressed in the Hebrew concept Shalom.

Peter continues with a historical explication of this message, some of which is familiar to his hearers. He tells them, "You know the message. . . ." What follows is a sketch of the life of Jesus, beginning with his baptism by John and his anointing by God (note the parallelism), and continuing with the good deeds and healings Jesus performed. In mentioning the crucifixion of Jesus, Peter does not implicate the Romans (Peter's hearers). Peter uses the ambiguous pronoun "they" in identifying those who put Jesus to death (in his Gospel, Luke also used the third-person plural pronoun in his presentation of the crucifixion, Luke 23:13–35; see comments on Acts 2:22–36).

The next part of Peter's presentation is most interesting, and the reader is encouraged to consider the passage very carefully. The statement, "God raised him on the third day," conforms with the Gospel accounts of Jesus' resurrection. The next phrase, however, is striking in its careful delineation of who actually experienced the resurrection. According to Peter, God allowed Jesus to appear, "*not to all the people but to us who were chosen by God as witnesses, and who ate and drank with him after he rose from the dead*" (vv. 40–41).

The modern reader must confront in all seriousness what this sentence means. We begin by asking a question: Was Jesus' resurrection universally available? Did everyone, believer and unbeliever alike, experience the resurrection? Peter's (and Luke's) answer seems to be No. He is quite emphatic: Jesus did *not* appear to just anyone, but only to those chosen to be Jesus' witnesses, and who ate and drank with him after the resurrection.

Again, we are reminded of the resurrection appearances narrated in Luke's Gospel. The women who were devoted to Jesus were the first to discover an empty tomb—Jesus' body was not there (Luke 24:1–12). The women were told that Jesus had risen from the dead, as he had promised. The women then told the eleven apostles (and others) of their experience, but they were not believed.

The next scene finds two disciples on the road to Emmaus. A stranger joins them and enters into their discussion about recent events in Jerusalem: the death of Jesus and the empty tomb. The stranger speaks to them of the necessity of a suffering Messiah, interpreting scripture in this light. They come to an inn where the stranger agrees to share a meal with the disciples. "When he was at the table with them, he took bread, blessed and broke it, and gave it to them"—these certainly sound like eucharistic words. "Then their eyes were opened, and they recognized him; and he vanished from their sight" (Luke 24:30–31). When the two disciples later tell the Eleven what had happened to them, they report that "he had been made known to them in the breaking of the bread" (24:35). They had become "witnesses of these things" (24:48).

Back to the passage in Acts: Peter's description is in perfect agreement with the description of the resurrection of Jesus given in Luke's Gospel. Jesus did not appear to just anyone; he was even unknown to his own disciples until they broke bread with him. Jesus became known to those who ate and drank with him, those who were chosen by God as witnesses to testify about their experience of the risen Christ to others.

This does not sound like an objectively verifiable experience. But it was subjectively attested by those who had the experience of being with their risen master through eating and drinking with him after his death. For them, this extraordinary experience of the resurrection transcended the ordinary routine of everyday life in such a radical way that it virtually defied description. What this was really like for those original followers of Jesus we shall never know. We can only speculate that somehow, in their grieving—like the downcast disciples on the Emmaus road—Jesus came to share a meal with them, to stir their memories of scripture and his own words, and to ask them to bear witness to their full experience of him. They knew that Jesus was alive in their midst, just as we know that he is alive among us who continue to eat and drink with him.

According to Peter, the content of the testimony is that Jesus "is the one ordained by God as judge of the living and the dead"—he is "Lord of all," Lord of *everyone, everything, everywhere!* Peter continues in this vein: "All the prophets testify about him that *everyone who believes in him receives forgiveness of sins* through his name" (v. 43). This is yet another audacious claim which stands in sharp contrast with Peter's own Jewish tradition. Jesus of Nazareth is not only a historical figure (a good man who did wonderful deeds), and not only God's Messiah (a crucified man whom God exalted). In addition to these truths, *belief in him brings forgiveness of sins!* This is a quantum leap from the Judaism that Peter had lived and loved. Peter has bluntly challenged the efficacy of the sacrificial system in Jerusalem in which priests offer sacrifices for the forgiveness of sins. It is remarkable that all of this revolutionary thought and language came in a dream and its interpretation. A dream that changed the world! This claim cannot and, as we shall see, will not be allowed to stand unchallenged by other Jews and Jewish Christians.

The Holy Spirit Comes to the Gentiles (Acts 10:44–48)

> 10:44 **While Peter was still speaking, the Holy Spirit fell upon all who heard the word.** [45] **The circumcised believers who had come with Peter were astounded that the gift of the Holy Spirit had been poured out even on the Gentiles,** [46] **for they heard them speaking in tongues and extolling God. Then Peter said,** [47] **"Can anyone withhold the water for baptizing these people who have received the Holy Spirit just as we have?"** [48] **So he ordered them to be baptized in the name of Jesus Christ. Then they invited him to stay for several days.**

Like the Jews of Jerusalem who received the Holy Spirit, now these Gentiles of Caesarea have received the same gift and symbol of God's presence and power. At Peter's order, Cornelius along with his family and friends are baptized with water, and now they constitute the first Gentile-Christian community. Among those who witness these astounding events are Jewish Christians who had accompanied Peter. As this mix of people gathers in Cornelius's home, they smash the final barrier. This group of Christians, both Gentile and Jew, stand together as witnesses that *Jesus is the good news of peace—he is the Lord of all!*

THE JEWISH-CHRISTIAN RESPONSE TO PETER'S ACCEPTANCE OF GENTILES INTO THE CHURCH Acts 11:1–18

> 11:1 **Now the apostles and the believers who were in Judea heard that the Gentiles had also accepted the word of God.** [2] **So when Peter went up to Jerusalem, the circumcised believers criticized him,** [3] **saying, "Why did you**

go to uncircumcised men and eat with them?" [4] Then Peter began to explain it to them, step by step, saying, [5] "I was in the city of Joppa praying, and in a trance I saw a vision. There was something like a large sheet coming down from heaven, being lowered by its four corners; and it came close to me. [6] As I looked at it closely I saw four-footed animals, beasts of prey, reptiles, and birds of the air. [7] I also heard a voice saying to me, 'Get up, Peter; kill and eat.' [8] But I replied, 'By no means, Lord; for nothing profane or unclean has ever entered my mouth.' [9] But a second time the voice answered from heaven, 'What God has made clean, you must not call profane.' [10] This happened three times; then everything was pulled up again to heaven. [11] At that very moment three men, sent to me from Caesarea, arrived at the house where we were. [12] The Spirit told me to go with them and not to make a distinction between them and us. These six brothers also accompanied me, and we entered the man's house. [13] He told us how he had seen the angel standing in his house and saying, 'Send to Joppa and bring Simon, who is called Peter; [14] he will give you a message by which you and your entire household will be saved.' [15] And as I began to speak, the Holy Spirit fell upon them just as it had upon us at the beginning. [16] And I remembered the word of the Lord, how he had said, 'John baptized with water, but you will be baptized with the Holy Spirit.' [17] If then God gave them the same gift that he gave us when we believed in the Lord Jesus Christ, who was I that I could hinder God?" [18] When they heard this, they were silenced. And they praised God, saying, "Then God has given even to the Gentiles the repentance that leads to life."

In the final scene of this short story, Peter and his fellow travelers return to Jerusalem. News travels fast, even in the first century, so that by the time Peter arrived in Jerusalem he was met by Jewish Christians who were upset by his dealings with Gentiles. It is worth noting, as we did above, that the real complaint against Peter may have been about his dining with Gentiles. "Why did you go . . . and eat with them?" (v. 3). Jewish Christians would probably have been less concerned about Peter's preaching to Gentiles than about his violation of kosher regulations.

Peter's explanation is contained in the next thirteen verses (11:5–17), and essentially is a retelling of the vision, though Luke notes that he explained it very carefully "step by step." A few details toward the end of Peter's explanation deserve examination, particularly the addition of the "word of the Lord" (v. 16). This is one of the few quotes from Jesus found outside the Four Gospels. It is worth noting that Peter introduces this quote with "I remembered."

The function of memory was critical in the early church. Frequently the disciples remembered the words of Jesus and linked them to some new experience in their community. An outstanding example of this linkage may be found in the resurrection narrative in which women discovered Jesus' tomb to be empty. They were perplexed (just as Peter was perplexed about his dream). In the midst of their confusion two men in dazzling clothes appeared to them and asked, "'Why do you look for the living among the dead? He is not here, but has risen. *Remember* how he told you, while he was still in Galilee, that the Son of Man must be handed over to sinners, and be crucified, and on the third day rise again.' Then they *remembered* [Jesus'] words, and returning from the tomb, they told all this to the eleven and to all the rest" (Luke 24:5–9). The role of memory in the early church (the Greek word for "memory" is related to the word "tomb," a place of memories) cannot be overemphasized.

Memory of the words of Jesus provided one set of structural materials in building the church's tradition about Jesus' life and ministry, death and resurrection. The other set of materials came from scripture—passages in the Old Testament that point to Jesus (e.g., Psalms 22; 110; Isaiah 9; 53). The combination of Jesus' words and scriptural references led to the development of stories about Jesus. These stories were first transmitted orally, then committed to writing. Finally, the stories were developed into the Gospel accounts with which we are familiar.

In this passage of Acts, Peter has remembered the word of the Lord, "John baptized with water, but you will be baptized with the Holy Spirit" (v. 16). This promise can be traced to the words of the risen Lord given to the apostles in the upper room (Acts 1:5). The promise was also on the lips of John the Baptist at the beginning of Jesus' ministry (Luke 3:16).

The authorization for Peter's action is unmistakable. He had received a vision from God which called him to minister to all people—there are no unclean people. The words of the risen Jesus, recently spoken to the apostles, provided confirmation that Peter's baptism of these Gentiles was in accordance with the will of God. The Gentiles who had gathered in Cornelius's house were not only baptized with water, but they also received the Holy Spirit just as had these Jerusalem Jewish Christians. Peter drew the obvious conclusion, "God gave them the same gift that he gave us when we believed in the Lord Jesus Christ" (v. 17). Peter would not, and he could not, "hinder God."

The response of Peter's Jewish-Christian hearers was unmistakably enthusiastic. They glorified God, concluding: "Then God has given *even to the Gentiles* the repentance that leads to life" (v. 18). The strange rooftop dream of a Galilean fisherman has led to a religious turn of events that will be nothing short of revolutionary in the history of humankind.

5. Mission and Persecution
Acts 11:19–12:25

THE MISSION TO ANTIOCH
Acts 11:19–30

11:19 Now those who were scattered because of the persecution that took place over Stephen traveled as far as Phoenicia, Cyprus, and Antioch, and they spoke the word to no one except Jews. 20 But among them were some men of Cyprus and Cyrene who, on coming to Antioch, spoke to the Hellenists also, proclaiming the Lord Jesus. 21 The hand of the Lord was with them, and a great number became believers and turned to the Lord. 22 News of this came to the ears of the church in Jerusalem, and they sent Barnabas to Antioch. 23 When he came and saw the grace of God, he rejoiced, and he exhorted them all to remain faithful to the Lord with steadfast devotion; 24 for he was a good man, full of the Holy Spirit and of faith. And a great many people were brought to the Lord. 25 Then Barnabas went to Tarsus to look for Saul, 26 and when he had found him, he brought him to Antioch. So it was that for an entire year they met with the church and taught a great many people, and it was in Antioch that the disciples were first called "Christians."

27 At that time prophets came down from Jerusalem to Antioch. 28 One of them named Agabus stood up and predicted by the Spirit that there would be a severe famine over all the world; and this took place during the reign of Claudius. 29 The disciples determined that according to their ability, each would send relief to the believers living in Judea; 30 this they did, sending it to the elders by Barnabas and Saul.

This passage focuses on the mission to Antioch in Syria. Located on the Orontes River about sixteen miles from the Mediterranean Sea, Antioch was the third largest city in the Roman Empire (about 500,000 residents) and the capital of the Roman province of Syria, which included Galilee and Judea. The city was predominantly Gentile, though it contained a large Jewish colony.

Luke gives the clear impression that a bit of tension exists between the Christian mission to the Jews and the mission to the Gentiles. Our English translation may be a source of unnecessary confusion in this regard. Verse 19 notes that the missionaries who came from Jerusalem worked only among Jews. Verse 20 notes that some missionaries turned up in Antioch who were from Cyprus and Cyrene (the latter is far to the west, on the North African Mediterranean coast). These missionaries worked with the "Greeks"—Gentiles. By using the term "Hellenists," the translators of the NRSV may have injected a note of confusion. It seems clear from the context that here Luke is distinguishing between Jews and Gentiles, not Hebrews and Hellenists, that is, Aramaic-speaking and Greek-speaking Jews (see Acts 6:1). Presumably, both Jews and Gentiles in this thoroughly Hellenistic city were Greek-speaking.

Again, news of a mission to the Gentiles reached the church in Jerusalem and the leaders there felt the need to investigate. It may have been the case that (1) no recognized church leaders such as Peter or Philip were identified among the missionaries and/or (2) the mission to Gentiles may have been to pagans completely unrelated to the local synagogue, a step removed from God-fearers like Cornelius and his household. Therefore, Barnabas, a Levite and a native of Cyprus (see 4:36), was sent by the Jerusalem leaders to check on work being carried out by his fellow Cypriots. Barnabas was pleased with what he found in Antioch and joined the work among the Gentiles there. This work was going so well that he took a short trip to Tarsus (just northwest of Antioch) to find Saul and secure his help in the mission. According to the text, the two men worked together for a year.

Luke notes that in Antioch the followers of Jesus of Nazareth were first called Christians. This name was given by those outside the faith and the term seems to have distinguished these believers as a particular sect of Judaism. Normally in Acts, Christians call themselves disciples, the Way, saints, brethren (which the NRSV often translates "believers"), and Nazarenes. It appears that Christ was understood by the residents of Antioch as a proper name, not a title: Jesus Christ, not Jesus *the* Christ. The tag sticks; these folks are followers of a man named Christ—Christians (see also Acts 26:28 where the thoroughly Hellenistic King Agrippa asks Paul, "Are you so quickly persuading me to become a Christian?"; 1 Peter 4:16 contains the only other occurrence of the word in the New Testament).

The prophets who came to Antioch from Jerusalem appear to have constituted a distinct order of leadership in the early church (see Acts 13:1 where "prophets and teachers" are mentioned). Paul also identifies discrete groups known as "apostles," "prophets," "teachers," "miracle workers," and so on (1 Cor. 12:28–29). Among these prophets, Agabus is remembered as one who offered an accurate prophecy of a severe empirewide famine that took place during the reign of Claudius (41–54 C.E.). We know that an es- pecially severe famine occurred in Palestine between 46 and 48 C.E. Ac- cording to Luke, the famine occasioned a collection among the Christians of Antioch to be sent as relief for the Christian community in Judea. This gift would help pay for higher food costs caused by short supplies. How- ever, there is a problem reconciling the date of this famine (46–48 C.E.) with Acts 12, which narrates the death of King Herod Agrippa. Herod died in 44 C.E., two years prior to the famine. Luke's order of events appears to be reversed.

A final term deserves our attention. Barnabas and Saul brought the col- lection to the "elders" (*presbyterous*) of the Jerusalem church. Luke does not tell the reader how this particular office came into being. In his narrative they stand alongside the apostles as persons in authority in the church (see Acts 15:6, 22). Perhaps they were heads of families whose homes were gathering places for house churches and they may have had some admin- istrative responsibilities (including the administration of common funds). It could also be the case that the administrative structure of the church evolved following the pattern of the local synagogue whose members elected a council of elders to facilitate the business of the synagogue.

HEROD AGRIPPA'S PERSECUTION OF THE CHURCH IN JERUSALEM
Acts 12:1–25

12:1 **About that time King Herod laid violent hands upon some who be- longed to the church.** [2] **He had James, the brother of John, killed with the sword.** [3] **After he saw that it pleased the Jews, he proceeded to arrest Peter also. (This was during the festival of Unleavened Bread.)** [4] **When he had seized him, he put him in prison and handed him over to four squads of sol- diers to guard him, intending to bring him out to the people after the Passover.** [5] **While Peter was kept in prison, the church prayed fervently to God for him.**

[6] **The very night before Herod was going to bring him out, Peter, bound with two chains, was sleeping between two soldiers, while guards in front of the door were keeping watch over the prison.** [7] **Suddenly an angel of the Lord ap- peared and a light shone in the cell. He tapped Peter on the side and woke him, saying, "Get up quickly." And the chains fell off his wrists.** [8] **The angel said to him, "Fasten your belt and put on your sandals." He did so. Then he**

said to him, "Wrap your cloak around you and follow me." [9] Peter went out and followed him; he did not realize that what was happening with the angel's help was real; he thought he was seeing a vision. [10] After they had passed the first and the second guard, they came before the iron gate leading into the city. It opened for them of its own accord, and they went outside and walked along a lane, when suddenly the angel left him. [11] Then Peter came to himself and said, "Now I am sure that the Lord has sent his angel and rescued me from the hands of Herod and from all that the Jewish people were expecting."

[12] As soon as he realized this, he went to the house of Mary, the mother of John whose other name was Mark, where many had gathered and were praying. [13] When he knocked at the outer gate, a maid named Rhoda came to answer. [14] On recognizing Peter's voice, she was so overjoyed that, instead of opening the gate, she ran in and announced that Peter was standing at the gate. [15] They said to her, "You are out of your mind!" But she insisted that it was so. They said, "It is his angel." [16] Meanwhile Peter continued knocking; and when they opened the gate, they saw him and were amazed. [17] He motioned to them with his hand to be silent, and described for them how the Lord had brought him out of the prison. And he added, "Tell this to James and to the believers." Then he left and went to another place.

[18] When the morning came, there was no small commotion among the soldiers over what had become of Peter. [19] When Herod had searched for him and could not find him, he examined the guards and ordered them to be put to death. Then Peter went down from Judea to Caesarea and stayed there.

[20] Now Herod was angry with the people of Tyre and Sidon. So they came to him in a body; and after winning over Blastus, the king's chamberlain, they asked for a reconciliation, because their country depended on the king's country for food. [21] On an appointed day Herod put on his royal robes, took his seat on the platform, and delivered a public address to them. [22] The people kept shouting, "The voice of a god, and not of a mortal!" [23] And immediately, because he had not given the glory to God, an angel of the Lord struck him down, and he was eaten by worms and died.

[24] But the word of God continued to advance and gain adherents. [25] Then after completing their mission Barnabas and Saul returned to Jerusalem and brought with them John, whose other name was Mark.

Luke's editorial hand is clearly seen in chapter 12. In the midst of a narrative about the mission in Antioch, he has inserted a cycle of stories about Herod Agrippa's persecution, Peter's imprisonment, and Agrippa's death. Famine relief is the vehicle that provides a transition in Luke's narrative, shifting the attention of the reader from Antioch to Jerusalem and back again to Antioch (11:27–30 and 12:25, though the latter verse contains a serious problem which, as we shall see, may be overcome by a common-sense interpretation of the passage).

The story of Herod's persecution and Peter's imprisonment and escape seems to be another self-contained piece of tradition which Luke had before him, and which he skillfully wove into his narrative. Even in its written form, Luke has retained the charm and humor of a story that must have made the rounds in early Christian communities, told in part as an affectionate lampoon on Peter. The original storyteller was able to break the tension of a serious tale (Herod's execution of James and his threat against Peter) with traces of humor at Peter's expense.

The "King Herod" of this passage was the grandson of Herod the Great (the King Herod who ruled Palestine at the time of Jesus' birth) and nephew of Herod Antipas (tetrarch of Galilee during the ministry of Jesus). This Herod is Herod Agrippa I (11–44 C.E.), who ruled over much of Palestine as a vassal of Rome. The Jewish leadership of Jerusalem had great disdain for Herod because of his strong Roman allegiance and his non-Jewish Idumean ancestry. Perhaps it was in order to placate them that he attacked a relatively easy target—the Jerusalem church. We note that his attack was aimed at "some" of the Christians, and only James the brother of John and Peter are specifically mentioned. This, in contrast to the persecution recorded in Acts 8:1, was the more usual form of social control; attack the leadership and the followers will drift away.

In addition to executing James (by beheading; one recalls how Herod's uncle similarly executed John the Baptist), Herod had Peter arrested and put in prison. Luke notes that, as with Jesus, Peter's arrest occurred during Passover. Bowing to religious scruples, Herod did not intend to deal with Peter until after the holy days had passed.

Peter must have been considered as either dangerous or slippery. Perhaps Herod had heard about Peter's earlier escape from prison (Acts 5:17–21). Luke notes that Herod ordered four squads of soldiers to guard Peter. Sixteen soldiers were assigned to Peter and their watch was limited to three hours per group of four in order to ensure that they would remain alert.

The scene that Luke describes is vivid. Peter was bound with chains on each wrist; he was asleep with a guard on either side of him and two more guards "keeping watch" at his cell door. Escape would be impossible. Only divine intervention could rescue Peter: "Suddenly an angel of the Lord appeared and a light shone in the cell." The reader is not told how the guards responded. The focus is on the dialogue between Peter and the angel.

Peter was told to get dressed and follow the angel outside the prison. Peter was incredulous about this turn of events and he could not believe what was happening to him. He was confused, and did not know whether his experience was real, or was he dreaming? As in a dream-state, Peter and the angel simply walked past a first set of guards, and then a second. The large iron gate of the prison swung open by itself, and suddenly Peter and the angel were in the night air of Jerusalem walking down a lane. Then the angel disappeared.

It was only when Peter was in the midst of the city that he realized his experience was not a dream: *"Now I am sure* that the Lord has sent his angel and rescued me from the hands of Herod"* (v. 11). Doubting Thomas must take a back seat to Peter. Again, as in the vision of the creatures where he must be told three times not to contradict God, it takes a miracle of outstanding proportions to convince Peter that God is at work in his life. Peter, the greatest of the Lord's apostles, is remembered by the early church not only as the one who denied Jesus, but as the one who consistently doubted—in the face of overwhelming evidence to the contrary—that he was indeed called by God to be a servant of Christ. Perhaps his own humble background as a Galilean fisherman prevented him from fully recognizing and accepting the fact that God had a significant mission for him. In this is a reminder that God has important work for each one of us to do regardless (and often in spite of) the circumstances of our lives.

In verse 12 the storyteller informs the reader or hearer that Peter finally got things clear in his mind: "As soon as he realized [that] this [was a real experience and not a dream], he went to the house of Mary, the mother of John whose other name was Mark." This verse also reminds the reader that the church, meeting in Mary's house, had been praying fervently for Peter (see v. 5).

Mary's house must have been of considerable size. It had a gateway that opened from the street and led into a courtyard; passing through this courtyard one would reach the house proper. There must have been some smiles and laughter from those who first heard the next portion of this story. Peter knocked at the gate. Mary's maid Rhoda went to see who was there. Excited by hearing Peter's voice, she left him at the locked gate— a fugitive running from the authorities—while she hurried back to the house shouting that Peter was standing outside. Those in the house were incredulous: "You are out of your mind!" they chided Rhoda. And a lively debate ensued, while Peter was still on the outside, knocking on the gate and looking around nervously for any sign of Herod's soldiers. The believers finally came out of the house to see for themselves. This failure to believe the word of the servant girl is reminiscent of the women who discovered the empty tomb, reported their finding to the disciples, and were summarily dismissed as telling "an idle tale" (Luke 24:11). In this story, the joke is not only on Peter, but on all who discount the witness of women.

Peter was indeed nervous about being spotted by the police. "He motioned to them with his hand to be silent" (v. 17). The story quickly comes to a close as Peter described his escape and asked that this be told to James (the first mention of another James, referring here to Jesus' brother, the new head of the Jerusalem church; see below, Acts 15) and other believers. Not surprisingly, Peter left quickly and "went to another place."

In an editorial conclusion, Luke recounts the aftermath among the soldiers of Herod who had allowed Peter to escape. The guards were questioned about this amazing escape; then they were executed for allowing it to happen. Almost as a footnote, Luke records that Peter fled to Caesarea where he probably placed himself under the protection of Cornelius.

The next passage (vv. 20–23) appears unconnected with the story of Peter's miraculous escape. Without a transition of any kind, Luke abruptly shifts to the tale of Herod's death. This vignette gives the impression that Herod had been waging war (he was more than "angry" as the NRSV indicates; he was "raging violently") against the cities of Tyre and Sidon. Fearing defeat, these cities finally "sued for peace" (a more literal translation than "asked for reconciliation"; NRSV).

There is a historical problem imbedded in this account. It is highly unlikely that Herod would wage war on Tyre and Sidon, cities within the Roman province of Syria—not if he wished to stay in power. And if Herod were withholding food from these cities, he could have been commanded by the Roman legate of Syria to give assistance to these people. The entire sentence seems inaccurate in historical substance, and one wonders what it was intended to add to the account of Herod's demise.

Josephus offers an account of Herod's death which adds some helpful details to Luke's narrative (*Jewish Antiquities* 19.343–52). According to Josephus, Herod's "royal robes" were "woven completely of silver so that its texture was wondrous." The morning sun had just begun to fill the outdoor amphitheater in Caesarea not far from the shimmering waters of the Mediterranean. Herod's entrance was spectacular:

> There the silver, illumined by the touch of the first rays of the sun, was wondrously radiant and by its glitter inspired fear and awe in those who gazed intently upon it. Straightway his flatterers raised their voices from various directions—though hardly for his good—addressing him as a god.

Likewise, Luke recounts that the people kept shouting, "The voice of a god, and not of a mortal!" Then, because Herod had not ascribed his "glory" (shining apparel is often the sign of a divine visitor; recall Jesus' transfiguration) to God, "an angel of the Lord struck him down, and he was eaten by worms and died" (v. 23).

Almost as an afterthought, Luke has added a strange last verse to the story of King Herod. He reminds us that Saul and Barnabas are in Jerusalem. Luke writes: "Then after completing their mission Barnabas and Saul returned *to* Jerusalem and brought with them John, whose other name was Mark" (v. 25). The little preposition "to" presents us with a bit of a problem. We last met Barnabas and Saul while they were in Antioch and about to bring a collection *to* Jerusalem (11:29). Mention of Barnabas and Saul serve as "bookends" standing at each side of the story about Herod's persecution and Peter's escape: (1) 11:19, Barnabas and Saul *go to Jerusalem*; (2) 12:1–24, events in Jerusalem; (3) 12:25, Barnabas and Saul *return to (?) Jerusalem!* Couple this last verse with the next verse and the problem, and perhaps the solution as well, becomes clear. Acts 13:1 reads: "Now in the church at Antioch there were prophets and teachers: Barnabas . . . and Saul." Barnabas and Saul are back in Antioch!

Even though there is no sound manuscript evidence for reading 12:25 in any way other than the way it appears in our text, common sense would change the preposition from "to" to "from." Barnabas and Saul, having brought the collection to Jerusalem, are now prepared to return *from* Jerusalem to Antioch, where Acts 13 resumes the story. One of the more reasonable explanations for our problematic text has been the suggestion that an early scribe added "to Jerusalem" to his manuscript. Remove these two words and the meaning of this transitional verse becomes clear. Barnabas and Saul, having visited the Jerusalem church that met in the home of Mary the mother of John Mark, left Jerusalem after depositing the collection with the church, and took John Mark with them.

Luke's story about the death of King Herod brings to an end the first section of the Acts of the Apostles. The church has survived the birth pangs of a new creation. The euphoria of Pentecost led to God's gifts of tongues and miraculous healing powers. The inspired preaching of the apostles led to challenges from more orthodox religious leaders in Jerusalem. The fulfillment of Jesus' commission to take the good news to *all* people, including Samaritans and Gentiles, led to serious questions and concerns within the infant body of believers. And finally, Luke brings down the curtain on this section of Acts with a note of great irony: a great and godlike king, intent on destroying this young movement, cannot even defeat the likes of

Peter, a somewhat bumbling and very fallible Christian leader. Instead, God put an end to the king. The infant church has fulfilled the prophecy of Mary even as she bore the prenatal church in her womb:

> [God] has brought down the powerful from their thrones,
> and lifted up the lowly.
>
> (Luke 1:52)

Luke adds his own grace note: "But the word of God continued to advance and gain adherents" (Acts 12:24).

2. Paul's Missionary Journeys

Acts 13:1–21:16

6. Paul's First Missionary Journey
Acts 13:1–14:28

SAUL AND BARNABAS
ARE COMMISSIONED AS MISSIONARIES
Acts 13:1–3

13:1 **Now in the church at Antioch there were prophets and teachers: Barnabas, Simeon who was called Niger, Lucius of Cyrene, Manaen a member of the court of Herod the ruler, and Saul.** 2 **While they were worshiping the Lord and fasting, the Holy Spirit said, "Set apart for me Barnabas and Saul for the work to which I have called them."** 3 **Then after fasting and praying they laid their hands on them and sent them off.**

With this passage, we begin the second large section of the Acts of the Apostles, which focuses on Paul's mission to the Gentiles: Acts 13—20. A map of the Mediterranean world will help us trace the travels of Paul and his companions. We begin in Syrian Antioch which appears to be headquarters for the Christian mission to the Gentiles (see 14:26; 15:30–35; 18:22–23).

A group of prophets and teachers has gathered in Antioch. We have already met Barnabas and Saul. Luke also mentions Simeon "who was called Niger," which means "black"; some have conjectured that he was Simon of Cyrene (North Africa) who carried Jesus' cross (Luke 23:26). We know nothing more about Lucius of Cyrene. According to the NRSV, Manaen (Greek for the Hebrew "Manachem") had been "a member of the court of Herod the ruler [13:1, marginal note, "tetrarch"]." The term translated as "member of the court" is a title of honor given to certain children reared in the court of Herod the Great, father of Herod Antipas. Manaen, therefore, had been a playmate of young Herod Antipas (who became tetrarch of Galilee during Jesus' lifetime). In his Gospel, Luke mentioned another member of Herod's court, Joanna, the wife of Herod's steward, Chuza (Luke 8:3). Some scholars have speculated that members of

Herod's court may have been responsible for a special Herodian source of information which Luke used (particularly the scenes of Jesus before Herod Antipas [Luke 23:7–12] and Paul before Herod Agrippa II [Acts 25:13–26:32]).

It is in Antioch that the Holy Spirit called Barnabas and Saul to become missionaries. The three leaders who would be left behind—Simeon, Lucius, and Manaen—placed their hands on the heads of Barnabas and Saul and sent them off to Cyprus.

THE MISSION TO CYPRUS
Acts 13:4–12

13:4 **So, being sent out by the Holy Spirit, they went down to Seleucia; and from there they sailed to Cyprus. 5 When they arrived at Salamis, they proclaimed the word of God in the synagogues of the Jews. And they had John also to assist them. 6 When they had gone through the whole island as far as Paphos, they met a certain magician, a Jewish false prophet, named Bar-Jesus. 7 He was with the proconsul, Sergius Paulus, an intelligent man, who summoned Barnabas and Saul and wanted to hear the word of God. 8 But the magician Elymas (for that is the translation of his name) opposed them and tried to turn the proconsul away from the faith. 9 But Saul, also known as Paul, filled with the Holy Spirit, looked intently at him, 10 and said, "You son of the devil, you enemy of all righteousness, full of all deceit and villainy, will you not stop making crooked the straight paths of the Lord? 11 And now listen—the hand of the Lord is against you, and you will be blind for a while, unable to see the sun." Immediately mist and darkness came over him, and he went about groping for someone to lead him by the hand. 12 When the proconsul saw what had happened, he believed, for he was astonished at the teaching about the Lord.**

Barnabas and Saul began their long journey by walking from Antioch sixteen miles along the Orontes River to the port city of Seleucia. From there they sailed westward to the island of Cyprus, Barnabas's home. Luke notes that they confined their preaching mission to the synagogues (in conformance with Saul's belief that the gospel must be brought to Jews first). Luke traces their journey across the island, about ninety miles, beginning with Salamis, a commercial seaport (Cyprus was a major source of copper for the Roman Empire) at the eastern end of the island, and ending with the capital city of Paphos located on the island's western shore.

Luke's narration of the work of Barnabas and Saul in Paphos is full of interesting names; one suspects that Luke was having fun playing name games in this section. The missionaries encountered a Jewish magician named Bar-Jesus. Luke's suggestion that Bar-Jesus is to be translated as "Elymas" does not make much sense; the obvious translation of Bar-Jesus is "Son of Jesus." Perhaps Luke simply means that Bar-Jesus went by another name, Elymas. It may also be the case that Luke has lost sight of an original wordplay embedded in this story. In confronting this magician, Saul, instead of addressing him by his name, Bar-Jesus (Son of Jesus), called him "son of the devil." Elymas was clearly no "Son of Jesus."

We also note that for the first time in the book of Acts, Saul is called by his Roman name, Paul. It is not incidental that at the start of Paul's first missionary journey, on a Roman island in the middle of the Mediterranean Sea, Saul the Jewish Christian is now known as Paul the Roman citizen—a status that becomes increasingly important as Luke's story unfolds. Paul now steps forward into Luke's spotlight. As if to underscore the importance of this shift to a Roman name, Luke notes that the Roman proconsul was also named Paul, Sergius Paulus (v. 7).

The miracle that Paul performed on Elymas is an interesting reversal of other miracles in Acts. Ordinarily, one expects a follower of Jesus to restore sight to blind eyes. In this case, Paul took away the magician's sight. Because of Elymas's attempts to undermine the work of the missionaries, he was temporarily blinded.

Verse 12, the final verse of this section, like many Lukan conclusions, is somewhat odd: "When the proconsul saw what had happened, he believed, for he was astonished at the teaching about the Lord." The reader is left to ponder the connection between the anti-miracle and the "teaching about the Lord." For the ancient reader, a teaching based on fear might induce belief—did "the teaching about the Lord" include such a message as "Watch out, you may be next"? Seeing the effects of a rather harsh lesson taught to Elymas, Paulus the proconsul believed. That such a lesson should compel belief, however, seems odd to modern readers. Faith and fear make strange bedfellows. Nevertheless, the Christian movement can now claim a high-ranking Roman official among its members. What better defense for the faith could there be than the conversion of two officers of the Roman government: Cornelius, led to Christ by Peter, and Sergius Paulus, converted through the word and work of Paul.

THE MISSION IN ANTIOCH OF PISIDIA
Acts 13:13–52

Paul, Barnabas, and John Arrive in Antioch (Acts 13:13–162)

13:13 **Then Paul and his companions set sail from Paphos and came to Perga in Pamphylia. John, however, left them and returned to Jerusalem;** [14] **but they went on from Perga and came to Antioch in Pisidia. And on the sabbath day they went into the synagogue and sat down.** [15] **After the reading of the law and the prophets, the officials of the synagogue sent them a message, saying, "Brothers, if you have any word of exhortation for the people, give it."** [16a] **So Paul stood up and with a gesture began to speak:**

Note that Paul has suddenly become the primary focus of attention. Until this point Luke's listing has been "Barnabas and Saul"; now the text reads "Paul and his companions," presumably Barnabas and John. Their journey by ship took them about 120 miles northwest to the mainland, arriving at the Roman province of Pamphylia. After they landed, John Mark left his two companions and returned to Jerusalem. No reason is given for Mark's departure, though Paul was not happy with Mark's decision. Later in Acts, Luke notes that Paul decided not to take Mark on his second missionary journey because he "had deserted them in Pamphylia and had not accompanied them in the work" (15:38).

Paul and Barnabas traveled one hundred miles northward on winding and treacherous mountain paths to the province of Galatia, finally arriving at another city named Antioch in the mountainous region known as Pisidia. "Antioch" was a popular city name used throughout southern Asia Minor and Syria, a name that was derived from the Syrian dynasty of Antiochus, which ruled the area from the time of Alexander the Great (fourth century B.C.E.).

It has been speculated that the missionaries sought the higher ground of Pisidian Antioch (elevation 3,600 feet) for health reasons. There may be some confirmation for this speculation in Paul's letter to the Galatians. He reminds his readers, "You know that it was because of a physical infirmity that I first announced the gospel to you; though my condition put you to the test, you did not scorn or despise me, but welcomed me as an angel of God, as Christ Jesus" (Gal. 4:13–14). Paul may have contracted a serious fever from the malaria-ridden swampy coast, and then traveled to higher ground in order to seek relief.

As was the custom for Paul and Barnabas, they went to the synagogue on the sabbath day. Worship in the synagogue began with recital of the creed, the Shema ("Hear, O Israel: The LORD our God is one LORD"), followed by prescribed prayers. Next came a reading from the Torah and appropriate passages from the prophets. A sermon was then offered by one competent in the interpretation of scripture. Finally, a blessing was pronounced by the leader of the synagogue and the congregation departed.

This passage indicates that after the Law and the Prophets were read, officials of the synagogue invited Paul and Barnabas to offer a "word of exhortation" to the gathering. Certainly these men were competent to comment on the scripture readings: Paul was a respected Pharisaic teacher educated in biblical interpretation in Jerusalem, and Barnabas was a Levite qualified to perform priestly duties in Jerusalem. They would be highly honored guests of the synagogue and the congregation would eagerly wish to hear from them.

It was Paul who accepted the invitation to speak. Ordinarily, the preacher in the synagogue would sit to address the congregation. Luke, however, offers his own interpretation of this scene by having Paul pose as a Hellenistic orator; he stands and begins his speech with the wave of an outstretched hand. Luke has already given his readers sample sermons from Peter (Acts 2:14–40; 3:12–26) and Stephen (7:1–53), and now he offers one that he considered typical of Paul.

It would be nice to know which biblical passages had been read, and therefore which passages Paul was commenting on. Unfortunately, Paul's sermon does not give us any clear-cut clues, though Habakkuk may be a good candidate (see p. 132).

Paul's Sermon in the Synagogue
(Acts 13:16b–41)

13:16b **"You Israelites, and others who fear God, listen. [17] The God of this people Israel chose our ancestors and made the people great during their stay in the land of Egypt, and with uplifted arm he led them out of it. [18] For about forty years he put up with them in the wilderness. [19] After he had destroyed seven nations in the land of Canaan, he gave them their land as an inheritance [20] for about four hundred fifty years. After that he gave them judges until the time of the prophet Samuel. [21] Then they asked for a king; and God gave them Saul son of Kish, a man of the tribe of Benjamin, who reigned for forty years. [22] When he had removed him, he made David their king. In his testimony about him he said, 'I have found David, son of Jesse, to be a man after my heart, who will carry out all my wishes.' [23] Of this man's posterity God has brought to Israel a Savior, Jesus, as he promised; [24] before his coming John had already proclaimed a baptism of repentance to all the people of Israel. [25] And as John was finishing his work, he said, 'What do you** suppose that I am? I am not he. No, but one is coming after me; I am not worthy to untie the thong of the sandals on his feet.'

26 "My brothers, you descendants of Abraham's family, and others who fear God, to us the message of this salvation has been sent. 27 Because the residents of Jerusalem and their leaders did not recognize him or understand the words of the prophets that are read every sabbath, they fulfilled those words by condemning him. 28 Even though they found no cause for a sentence of death, they asked Pilate to have him killed. 29 When they had carried out everything that was written about him, they took him down from the tree and laid him in a tomb. 30 But God raised him from the dead; 31 and for many days he appeared to those who came up with him from Galilee to Jerusalem, and they are now his witnesses to the people. 32 And we bring you the good news that what God promised to our ancestors 33 he has fulfilled for us, their children, by raising Jesus; as also it is written in the second psalm,

'You are my Son;
today I have begotten you.'

34 As to his raising him from the dead, no more to return to corruption, he has spoken in this way,

'I will give you the holy promises made to David.'

35 Therefore he has also said in another psalm,

'You will not let your Holy One experience corruption.'

36 For David, after he had served the purpose of God in his own generation, died, was laid beside his ancestors, and experienced corruption; 37 but he whom God raised up experienced no corruption. 38 Let it be known to you therefore, my brothers, that through this man forgiveness of sins is proclaimed to you; 39 by this Jesus everyone who believes is set free from all those sins from which you could not be freed by the law of Moses. 40 Beware, therefore, that what the prophets said does not happen to you:

41 'Look, you scoffers!
Be amazed and perish,
for in your days I am doing a work,
a work that you will never believe, even if someone tells you.'"

Luke's setting for Paul's sermon is a synagogue in the Gentile town of Antioch located in the heart of Galatia. The congregation consists of both Jews and Gentiles—"You Israelites, and others who fear God" (v. 16b, also v. 26). The modern reader may remember that the heart of the diaspora Jew was liberal in reaching out to the Gentile neighbor; the synagogue was indeed "a light for the Gentiles" (Acts 13:47). Perhaps Paul's short history of Israel from the matriarchs and patriarchs to David was intended for the benefit of Gentiles in the congregation. This brief sketch of Israel's history also set the historical context for the life and work of Jesus, information that would be important to Paul's Jewish listeners. Note the flow of this historical survey, from the ancestors of antiquity up to the present time: "And we bring you the good news that what God promised to our ancestors he has fulfilled for us, their children, by raising Jesus" (vv. 32–33).

This sermon is similar to others we have read in Acts (especially Stephen's speech in Acts 7). Luke has constructed a condensation of the kind of sermon Paul preached in a diaspora synagogue. Paul's christological interpretation of scripture is fueled by several Old Testament "testimonies." He guides his hearers through a short history of Israel (vv. 17–22) leading up to Israel's Savior, Jesus of Nazareth. Paul even includes a word about the last of the prophetic voices in pre-Christian Israel: as John the Baptist was "finishing his work" among "all the people of Israel," he declared that he was not the messiah, but "one is coming after me" (vv. 24–25). To identify the turning point of Israel's history with John the Baptist may remind the reader, both ancient and modern, of Luke 16:16: "The law and the prophets were in effect until John came; since then the good news of the kingdom of God is proclaimed, and everyone tries to enter it by force." Paul's recital of Israel's history now turns to more recent events.

Paul continues: "My brothers, you descendants of Abraham's family [Jews by birth], and others who fear God, to us the message of this salvation has been sent" (v. 26). The next part of Paul's sermon, which describes the trial and death of Jesus, is similar to the accounts given by Peter (3:13–15; 4:8–10; 5:30–31; 10:37–41). Notice, however, how the personal pronoun used of those responsible for Jesus' death shifts from "you" (3:13; 4:10; 5:30) to "they" (10:39; 13:28–29), indicating that the "Israelites" of Jerusalem ("they"), and not the "Israelites" of the diaspora ("you"), had something to do with the death of Jesus.

Here, as in previous passages in Acts, Paul's (Luke's) description of Jesus' trial attempts to shift responsibility for Jesus' crucifixion away from Pontius Pilate, the Roman governor, and onto "the residents of Jerusalem and their leaders. . . . Even though they found no cause for a sentence of death, they asked Pilate to have him killed" (vv. 27–28). The reader is not told that the Roman governor actually carried out the death penalty. Rather, Paul continues, "When *they* [presumably the Jewish leaders in Jerusalem] had carried out everything that was written about him, *they* took him down from the tree and laid him in a tomb" (v. 29; also see the discussion on 2:22–36; 3:11–16; 4:1–12; 5:17–42; 10:34–43).

It is interesting to note that both Paul and Peter choose not to fix the blame, but to fix the problem—a good practice for modern church leaders. Peter said, "I know that you acted in ignorance, as did your rulers"

(3:17), and then proceeds to offer his hearers correct information about Jesus. Likewise, Paul declares that "the residents of Jerusalem and their leaders did not recognize [Jesus] or understand the words of the prophets" (v. 27). The rest of his sermon is intended to teach, through scriptural interpretation, that Jesus of Nazareth is God's Messiah.

Verses 33–37 reiterate the fact that Jesus is of the lineage of David, and therefore the Messiah of Israel, though with a significant difference from the kings who preceded him. Even mighty David, a man after God's own heart, "after he had served the purpose of God in his own generation, died, was laid beside his ancestors, and experienced corruption" (v. 36). Paul suggests that David was limited in two senses: (1) he served a limited purpose and (2) his physical body was limited—it died and decomposed (which might have been an offensive thought for a pious Jew, and somewhat out of place in an exhortation). Jesus, on the other hand, "experienced no corruption," for God raised him from the dead. Paul's proof text is taken from David himself: "You will not let your Holy One experience corruption" (v. 35; see Psalm 16:10; also see Acts 3:14 on "Holy One").

Now Paul draws his conclusion: "Let it be known to you therefore, my brothers, that through this man forgiveness of sins is proclaimed to you; by this Jesus everyone who believes is set free from all those sins from which you could not be freed by the law of Moses" (vv. 38–39). This is an important sentence and should be looked at carefully. The English (NRSV) translation of the last half of this sentence hides an important Pauline concept. The Greek word, which is translated as "free" and "freed," is a courtroom term that means "acquitted," "justified," "made right," or "made righteous." With this sentence Luke was attempting to be faithful to Paul's theology: Jesus has brought about God's forgiveness, but more than this, those who believe in Jesus are now made righteous with a justification that the law of Moses could not provide. Through Christ it is at long last possible for human beings to be in right relationship with God. The consequences of humanity's fall from grace have been overcome in Christ.

It is appropriate that Luke should have Paul close his sermon with a quote from the prophet Habakkuk. Twice at strategic points in Paul's letters the apostle quotes this prophet in support of his understanding that those who are righteous live by faith (Hab. 2:4; Rom. 1:17; Gal. 3:11; also see Phil. 3:9). In this sermon, Paul quotes a passage that challenges his hearers not to be surprised that God is doing some radically new things: raising a dead carpenter as Messiah, granting forgiveness of sins through this man, and offering righteousness apart from the law of Moses. In his letters, Paul brought his full intellectual powers to bear on these items: now that God has declared

Jesus as Messiah and the promised messianic age has come, what is the relationship between human sin, Mosaic law, and God's requirement for righteousness? What does it mean to proclaim that Jesus of Nazareth, whom God has declared to be the Messiah, "is the end of the law"? In this sermon, Paul has rehearsed the history of God's gracious work among God's people, culminating in righteousness and freedom for all in Christ Jesus.

Paul warns his audience not to scoff at his message. According to Paul, Habakkuk had predicted this day in Antioch. "In your days I am doing a work," said God to the prophet. God's amazing work in Jesus Christ is "a work that you will never believe, even if someone tells you" (v. 41). Paul recognized that he was that "someone."

THE DISCUSSION IS CONTINUED
Acts 13:42–52

> 13:42 **As Paul and Barnabas were going out, the people urged them to speak about these things again the next sabbath. [43] When the meeting of the synagogue broke up, many Jews and devout converts to Judaism followed Paul and Barnabas, who spoke to them and urged them to continue in the grace of God.**
>
> [44] **The next sabbath almost the whole city gathered to hear the word of the Lord. [45] But when the Jews saw the crowds, they were filled with jealousy; and blaspheming, they contradicted what was spoken by Paul. [46] Then both Paul and Barnabas spoke out boldly, saying, "It was necessary that the word of God should be spoken first to you. Since you reject it and judge yourselves to be unworthy of eternal life, we are now turning to the Gentiles. [47] For so the Lord has commanded us, saying,**
>> **'I have set you to be a light for the Gentiles,**
>> **so that you may bring salvation to the ends of the earth.'"**
>
> [48] **When the Gentiles heard this, they were glad and praised the word of the Lord; and as many as had been destined for eternal life became believers. [49] Thus the word of the Lord spread throughout the region. [50] But the Jews incited the devout women of high standing and the leading men of the city, and stirred up persecution against Paul and Barnabas, and drove them out of their region. [51] So they shook the dust off their feet in protest against them, and went to Iconium. [52] And the disciples were filled with joy and with the Holy Spirit.**

Quite naturally, Paul's hearers wanted to know more. Luke pictures the Jews of the synagogue following Paul and Barnabas out of the synagogue and into the street, wanting to continue the discussion. The missionaries suggest that the discussion be put on hold until the next sabbath; in the meantime, they urge these folks to "continue in the grace of God"—a peripatetic benediction offered by a couple of weary missionaries ready for a bit of rest.

Luke's note that "almost the whole city" gathered in the synagogue on the next sabbath may be somewhat of an exaggeration. At any rate, the crowd of visitors, probably Gentiles, was large enough to be of concern to the Jewish members of the congregation. It is impossible to know why the Jews were "filled with jealousy" over Paul (v. 45). Had they, during the intervening week, thoroughly considered the implications of Paul's sermon? Were they jealous of the positive impact Paul had made on the non-Jewish portion of the congregation, who apparently told their friends about this powerful teacher and orator?

Whatever the case may have been, this scene offers Luke an opportunity to convey a significant theological message to the reader. This was the great turning point for the early Christian mission. In the next sentence Paul articulates the approach that will guide his missionary activity: "Since you reject [the word of God] and judge yourselves to be unworthy of eternal life, we are now turning to the Gentiles" (v. 46). It is of divine necessity that he must always preach the gospel to Jews first. If they reject his message, then he is free to move on to Gentiles (see also Acts 18:5–6; 28:25–28; Rom. 1:16; 2:9–10). In v. 47 Paul cites the prophet Isaiah (49:6) for support:

> I have set you to be light for the Gentiles,
>   so that you may bring salvation to the ends of the earth.

In using this passage, Paul has selected a verse that has been the subject of a variety of interpretations: this verse was originally addressed to the Servant of Yahweh (Isaiah himself?), then applied to diaspora Judaism, and finally Christians suggested that Jesus himself was "a light to the Gentiles" (Luke 2:32; Acts 26:23). Now Paul applied the text to himself and to those who were part of his mission. "The Lord has commanded *us*, saying, 'I have set *you* to be a light for the Gentiles . . . '" (v. 47).

According to Luke, when the Gentiles heard this, "they were glad." Then Luke describes these Gentiles in terms that are unusual in Acts. "As many as had been *destined for eternal life* became believers" (v. 48). The reader has already been told that those who rejected the word of God "judge[d themselves] to be unworthy of eternal life" (v. 46; see a similar idea in John 3:18).

It would be a mistake to read verse 48 in a narrowly predestinarian way. The Greek term translated in the NRSV as "destined" is a word usually used in a military or political context, and might be better rendered as "appointed"—one is "appointed" to a post or position. Furthermore, Luke puts an odd twist on the phrase. One would ordinarily expect the passage to read: "those who became believers were destined for eternal life." Why does he reverse this formula? It may be that Luke was simply using a traditional rabbinic phrase that fit this context. Paul, the rabbi from Jerusalem, considered that those "appointed to the life of the age to come" (an awkward, but literal translation of the phrase "eternal life") have become believers.

Luke notes that the Jews incited both devout women of high standing and leading men against Paul and Barnabas—city leaders with a close connection to the synagogue. The missionaries were expelled from Antioch, and on their way out of town they "shook the dust off their feet in protest against them," a gesture that signified a complete break with the region (v. 51; see Luke 9:5; 10:11). This gesture notwithstanding, a community of believers was left behind, "filled with joy and with the Holy Spirit" (v. 52). The next stop for the missionaries was Iconium, about eighty miles southeast of Antioch, in the province of Galatia.

THE MISSION TO ICONIUM, LYSTRA, AND DERBE
Acts 14:1–28

Iconium (Acts 14:1–7)

14:1 The same thing occurred in Iconium, where Paul and Barnabas went into the Jewish synagogue and spoke in such a way that a great number of both Jews and Greeks became believers. 2 But the unbelieving Jews stirred up the Gentiles and poisoned their minds against the brothers. 3 So they remained for a long time, speaking boldly for the Lord, who testified to the word of his grace by granting signs and wonders to be done through them. 4 But the residents of the city were divided; some sided with the Jews, and some with the apostles. 5 And when an attempt was made by both Gentiles and Jews, with their rulers, to mistreat them and to stone them, 6 the apostles learned of it and fled to Lystra and Derbe, cities of Lycaonia, and to the surrounding country; 7 and there they continued proclaiming the good news.

Fleeing Pisidian Antioch, Paul and Barnabas made their way eighty miles southeast to the city of Iconium. A second-century apocryphal romance, *The Acts of Paul and Thecla*, elaborates on Paul's visit to Iconium, including the earliest physical description of Paul:

A man named Onesiphorus, who heard that Paul was come to Iconium . . .
went along the royal road which leads to Lystra, and stood there waiting for
him, and looked at (all) who came, according to Titus' description. And he
saw Paul coming, a man small of stature, with a bald head and crooked legs,
with eyebrows meeting and nose somewhat hooked, full of friendliness; for
now he appeared like a man, now he had the face of an angel.

As usual, the missionaries began their work in the local synagogue. The
reader is told that the mission was highly successful. Paul and Barnabas
were able to work in the city for a considerable length of time, developing
a strong congregation to which Paul returned from time to time (16:1–6;
18:23). This is undoubtedly one of the congregations Paul had in mind as
he wrote his letter to the churches of Galatia.

As with the Twelve (5:12), Paul and Barnabas give evidence of God's
grace by performing "signs and wonders" among the Iconians (see comments on 2:22–24). The phrase "signs and wonders" is contained in an odd
sentence (v. 3). Paul and Barnabas spoke "boldly for the Lord [God or
Jesus?], who testified to the word of his grace by granting signs and wonders to be done through them." Similarly, in his letter to the churches of
Galatia, Paul notes that God had worked miracles among them because
they believed the word that they heard (Gal. 3:5). In both cases miracles
are related to the spoken word. God's confirmation that Paul's words were
true could be seen in the miracles he performed. Again, the awesome
power of God is at work in the church.

Throughout the book of Acts, Luke encourages us to keep that power
alive in our congregations. Where the word of God is proclaimed boldly we
can expect confirmation of God's grace through "signs and wonders." Miracles will come upon us in small and large ways, not because of anything that
we do, but through "believing what [we have] heard" (Gal. 3:5).

Even though these Iconian Christians were living among miracles,
Luke's language indicates that trouble between the missionaries and mal-
content non-Christians had been brewing for some time. Sensing that the
situation was about to reach the boiling point, Paul and Barnabas left for
Lystra, eighteen miles to the south.

Lystra and Derbe (Acts 14:8–20)

14:8 **In Lystra there was a man sitting who could not use his feet and had
never walked, for he had been crippled from birth. ⁹ He listened to Paul as
he was speaking. And Paul, looking at him intently and seeing that he had
faith to be healed, ¹⁰ said in a loud voice, "Stand upright on your feet." And**

the man sprang up and began to walk. [11] When the crowds saw what Paul had done, they shouted in the Lycaonian language, "The gods have come down to us in human form!" [12] Barnabas they called Zeus, and Paul they called Hermes, because he was the chief speaker. [13] The priest of Zeus, whose temple was just outside the city, brought oxen and garlands to the gates; he and the crowds wanted to offer sacrifice. [14] When the apostles Barnabas and Paul heard of it, they tore their clothes and rushed out into the crowd, shouting, [15] "Friends, why are you doing this? We are mortals just like you, and we bring you good news, that you should turn from these worthless things to the living God, who made the heaven and the earth and the sea and all that is in them. [16] In past generations he allowed all the nations to follow their own ways; [17] yet he has not left himself without a witness in doing good—giving you rains from heaven and fruitful seasons, and filling you with food and your hearts with joy." [18] Even with these words, they scarcely restrained the crowds from offering sacrifice to them.

[19] But the Jews came there from Antioch and Iconium and won over the crowds. Then they stoned Paul and dragged him out of the city, supposing that he was dead. [20] But when the disciples surrounded him, he got up and went into the city. The next day he went on with Barnabas to Derbe.

Those who have read the book of Acts from the beginning may notice something interesting in this passage. The story of the man, crippled from birth, healed by two followers of Jesus is almost identical with the healing story in Acts 3. Note the similarities:

Acts 14:8–10	Acts 3:1–8
Paul and Barnabas encounter "a man . . . crippled from birth." "Paul [note that Paul is the main actor], looking at him intently and seeing that he had faith to be healed, said in a loud voice, 'Stand upright on your feet.' And the man sprang up and began to walk."	Peter and John encounter "a man lame from birth." "Peter [note that Peter is the main actor] looked intently at him, . . . [mention of faith comes later in the passage] and said, . . . 'Stand up and walk.' . . . Jumping up, he stood and began to walk."
This is followed by a response of amazement from the crowd and a speech by Paul.	This is followed by a response of amazement from the crowd and a speech by Peter.

It could be that among Luke's sources were parallel narratives which re-counted the "acts of Peter" and the "acts of Paul," which Luke wove into our canonical Acts of the Apostles. It is clear that these miracle stories share several features, including the response of the crowd; the Jews of Jerusalem and the Gentiles of Lystra were amazed. However, from this point forward the stories take radically divergent paths as each tale evolves into its respective Jewish and Greek ethos. In the earlier account, Peter used this opportunity to address the crowd, offering them a sermon on Jesus the suffering Messiah. The leaders of the Jewish temple were not amused, so they arrested Peter and John, and compelled them to explain their actions.

In Acts 14, the astonished onlookers take Paul and Barnabas to be gods who have come to earth. They identify Barnabas and Paul as Zeus and Hermes respectively. The priest of the temple to Zeus gives a warm wel-come to Paul and Barnabas, bringing garlands (used to adorn sacrificial an-imals) and oxen to sacrifice before them.

Here the two healing stories could not be more diverse. In Acts 3, Peter and John try to convince the authorities that their power is indeed from God. In Acts 14, Paul and Barnabas must argue that they themselves are *not* gods!

Note that verse 14 contains the single occurrence of the term "apostles" applied to persons other than the Twelve (see 1:1–5). When "the apostles Barnabas and Paul" heard what was about to take place, they tore their clothes as a sign of horror at the blasphemy. They were men, not gods!

The brief speech of Acts 14:15–17 reminds us that the missionaries are dealing only with Gentiles in Lystra—Gentiles who apparently have no understanding of Jewish teachings about God. There has been no mention of a visitation to a synagogue or of a community of Jews and God-fearers. In this speech, Paul and Barnabas cannot assume any understanding of Judaism and its traditions. Furthermore, they cannot even assume that their hearers are well-educated *Hellenistic* Lystrians, for they have addressed Paul and Barnabas in the Lycaonian language (v. 11); apparently the words of Paul and Barnabas were translated from Greek into Lycaonian.

The speech begins with a typical biblical theme: "Turn from these worthless things [idols] to the living God, who made the heaven and the earth and the sea and all that is in them" (v. 15; the last phrase is borrowed directly from Exodus 20:11; also see Isaiah 44 and 1 Thessalonians 1:9). Verse 16 bears echoes of Paul's letter to the Romans 1:20ff. "In past gen-erations he allowed all the nations [Gentiles] to follow their own ways." The final sentence of this short speech is drawn from popular Hellenistic natural theology: "Yet [God] has not left himself without a witness in doing good—giving you rains from heaven and fruitful seasons, and filling you with food and your hearts with joy" (v. 17). Paul has used just the right words to link his Old Testament–Christian message with the Hellenistic mind-set of his hearers. The missionaries have argued that neither they nor the idols in the temple to Zeus are divine. There is only one God who lives, and yet this God cannot be seen except through the gifts of God's abundance in nature.

It is clear, even to the casual reader, that this speech is only loosely connected with any of the speeches already recorded in Acts. There is no mention of Jesus, Messiah, crucifixion, resurrection, or any other specifically Christian theme. The speech does call for the hearers to "turn to the living God," as did Peter's speech of Acts 3:19.

According to Luke, the speech barely achieved its purpose of dissuading the crowd from honoring Paul and Barnabas as gods. The reader can infer from the end of this story that the crowd quickly gained a new perspective of these Christian missionaries.

When Luke finally mentions Jews in Lystra, they are identified as outside agitators who have followed Paul and Barnabas from Pisidian Antioch and Iconium, intent on turning the crowds against the Christian missionaries. Again, Luke closes this scene with a note of irony. The Gentile crowds who once hailed Paul as a god now attempt to kill him. "They stoned Paul and dragged him out of the city," like the carcass of a sacrificed animal.

Apparently, Paul and Barnabas had made some headway in Lystra, for a community of disciples came out to surround Paul as he lay unconscious on the ground. According to this passage, Paul was finally able to get up and was helped back to Lystra where he spent the night. The next day he and Barnabas left town and moved eastward to Derbe.

PAUL AND BARNABAS VISIT THE CHURCHES OF GALATIA AND PAMPHYLIA BEFORE RETURNING TO SYRIAN ANTIOCH
Acts 14:21–28

14:21 **After they had proclaimed the good news to that city and had made many disciples, they returned to Lystra, then on to Iconium and Antioch. ²² There they strengthened the souls of the disciples and encouraged them to continue in the faith, saying, "It is through many persecutions that we must enter the kingdom of God." ²³ And after they had appointed elders for** them in each church, with prayer and fasting they entrusted them to the Lord in whom they had come to believe.

²⁴ Then they passed through Pisidia and came to Pamphylia. ²⁵ When they had spoken the word in Perga, they went down to Attalia. ²⁶ From there they sailed back to Antioch, where they had been commended to the grace of God for the work that they had completed. ²⁷ When they arrived, they called the church together and related all that God had done with them, and how he had opened a door of faith for the Gentiles. ²⁸ And they stayed there with the disciples for some time.

In spite of the troubles encountered in Lystra, Iconium, and Antioch, Paul and Barnabas made a return visit to these cities. Since they left each place under a cloud of bitter disagreement, they probably felt the need to reassure themselves that their mission churches had survived the bad feelings which had been generated. Luke suggests that this indeed was the case: Paul and Barnabas "strengthened the souls [psyche; the inner life of a human being which would include one's feelings and emotions; our term "psychology" is derived from this Greek word] of the disciples and encouraged them to continue in the faith." The brief admonition seems appropriate to the situation the missionaries faced in each of these cities: "It is through many persecutions that we must enter the kingdom of God" (v. 22).

To ensure that a modicum of order would be maintained in each congregation, the missionaries appointed elders [presbyteroi] and "entrusted them to the Lord [Jesus] in whom they had come to believe." While it is too early in the life of the church to detect a fixed order of congregational leadership, the mention of "elders" may indicate that local church organization was modeled along the lines of the synagogue. The older members of the congregation would be chosen to oversee worship, instruction, discipline, and charitable works.

Retracing their steps back to the Mediterranean coast, Paul and Barnabas sail from Attalia to Syrian Antioch where their mission began. There they gave a progress report to the church. God had "opened a door of faith for the Gentiles," and Paul and Barnabas bravely walked through. The walk across this threshold, as we shall soon see, was the beginning of a one-way journey into a totally new understanding of what God had willed for the human race.

7. The First Christian Council
Acts 15:1–41

Acts 15 marks the midpoint of the Acts of the Apostles and a great turning point in the life of the early Christian community. The church which began as a tiny Jewish sect in Jerusalem has opened it doors to Gentiles living far from the Holy City. The prophecy of Isaiah has been fulfilled. Israel, through her Jewish-Christian missionaries, had indeed become a light to the Gentiles. So successful was this mission that some of the churches in Asia Minor may have been predominantly Gentile. Church leaders in Jerusalem, headquarters for the Christian movement, must have felt pressure (internal and external) to come to terms with the growing enthusiasm of Gentile Christians for this new sect of Judaism. Now the question is raised: What exactly is the status of Gentiles in the church? This question leads to others: What is the relationship between Gentile Christians and Jewish Christians? What is the relationship of Gentile Christians with Judaism? What is the relationship of Jewish Christians with Judaism?

In order to deal with some of these questions, a council of Christian leaders was convened in Jerusalem in about 48 C.E. This is the first of several important Christian councils which gathered to address critical theological issues that challenged Christian unity.

We are fortunate that in addition to Acts 15 another narrative of this event comes from one of the participants. In Galatians 2, Paul the apostle recounts his own recollection of this meeting. While I will focus on Acts 15, occasionally I will compare the two accounts. At the end of the chapter I make some concluding observations about the perspectives of Luke and Paul regarding the first Christian council.

THE ISSUE
Acts 15:1–5

> 15:1 **Then certain individuals came down from Judea and were teaching the brothers, "Unless you are circumcised according to the custom of**

Moses, you cannot be saved." [2] And after Paul and Barnabas had no small dissension and debate with them, Paul and Barnabas and some of the others were appointed to go up to Jerusalem to discuss this question with the apostles and the elders. [3] So they were sent on their way by the church, and as they passed through both Phoenicia and Samaria, they reported the conversion of the Gentiles, and brought great joy to all the believers. [4] When they came to Jerusalem, they were welcomed by the church and the apostles and the elders, and they reported all that God had done with them. [5] But some believers who belonged to the sect of the Pharisees stood up and said, "It is necessary for them to be circumcised and ordered to keep the law of Moses."

Paul and Barnabas had been in Antioch for some time when they were visited by a group from Judea whose mission was to "correct" Paul. A letter from the leaders of the Jerusalem church describes these visitors as interlopers (see below, 15:24). Unlike the earlier Christian emissary, Barnabas, who considered the initial work among Jews and Gentiles in Antioch to be an acceptable witness to the grace of God (11:22–23), this group found the church of Antioch lacking in its adherence to Judaic tradition. They put the issue bluntly: "Unless you are circumcised according to the custom of Moses, you cannot be saved" (v. 1). The group sounds very much like the Judaizers who followed Paul into the churches of Galatia in order to "bewitch" the Gentile Christians into accepting circumcision as a condition for membership in the body of Christ (Gal. 1:6–9; 3:1; 6:12–16).

Luke's chronology indicates that the church of Antioch had been in existence for several years. According to Acts, King Herod died in 44 C.E., shortly after the successful Christian mission in Antioch (Acts 11:19–12:23). The date usually assigned to the first Christian council in Jerusalem is 48 C.E. Therefore, the reader can assume that for four or five years this church of Jewish Christians and Gentile Christians has functioned smoothly. Smoothly yes, but inadequately and dangerously according to the emissaries from Judea (Jerusalem?).

Paul and Barnabas, fresh from a successful missionary journey among the Gentiles of Asia Minor, took offense at these self-appointed guardians of the faith who taught that belief in Jesus as God's Messiah was not sufficient for salvation. Circumcision "according to the *custom* of Moses" was also required. It is worth noting that at the end of this section Luke also connects circumcision with the "*law* of Moses" (vv. 1, 5). For Luke, "custom" and "law" were synonymous (Luke 2:27; Acts 6:11–14; 21:21), which may indicate that Luke was a writer who looked at Judaism from a non-Jewish perspective. Luke seems to have had a flexible understanding toward Jewish law, honoring the right of Jews (including Jewish Christians) to follow their legal traditions. On the other hand, Luke may have come to the conclusion that since these traditions were only *customary*, it would be unnecessary to impose on the Gentiles a Jewish *custom* (circumcision) with the force of *law*.

According to Luke, Paul and Barnabas had "no small dissension and debate" (v. 2, NRSV; the translation in Today's English Version comes closer to the passion of the moment—"a fierce argument") with the Judean emissaries over the issue of salvation through circumcision. Since the issue could not be resolved, both parties were summoned to Jerusalem for a general discussion with the apostles and elders (note that in Galatians 2:2 Paul went to Jerusalem in response to a divine revelation).

On their way to Jerusalem, Paul and Barnabas did a bit of public relations work: "They reported the conversion of the Gentiles, and brought great joy to all the believers" (v. 3). When they finally arrived in Jerusalem, they were welcomed warmly "by the church and the apostles and the elders" (v. 4).

Among the members of the Jerusalem church were a number of Pharisees. Quite appropriately, these Pharisees raised serious questions about how much of the Jewish legal tradition should be maintained in the Christian sect of Judaism. According to the Christian Pharisees, it is "*necessary*" for Gentile Christians to be circumcised and "to keep the law of Moses" (v. 5). If Christianity is to remain within Judaism, then, according to the Christian Pharisees, the Mosaic law pertains to Jews and Gentiles within this Jewish sect, and circumcision is a crucial test of conformance to the "law of Moses." This is the issue to be debated before the church leaders in Jerusalem.

PETER'S RESPONSE TO THE ISSUE
Acts 15:6–11

15:6 **The apostles and the elders met together to consider this matter.**
7 After there had been much debate, Peter stood up and said to them, "My brothers, you know that in the early days God made a choice among you, that I should be the one through whom the Gentiles would hear the message of the good news and become believers. 8 And God, who knows the human heart, testified to them by giving them the Holy Spirit, just as he did to us; 9 and in cleansing their hearts by faith he has made no distinction between

them and us. [10] Now therefore why are you putting God to the test by placing on the neck of the disciples a yoke that neither our ancestors nor we have been able to bear? [11] On the contrary, we believe that we will be saved through the grace of the Lord Jesus, just as they will."

Peter refers back to the "early days" of the church when he was chosen by God through a dream to bring the gospel to Gentiles, beginning with the household of the Roman centurion Cornelius (10:9–48). As proof that this work was acceptable to God, the Holy Spirit came upon these Gentiles just as it had previously descended upon Jewish Christians.

To persist in distinguishing between Jews and Gentiles in the church would be to "put God to the test," a phrase borrowed from the Old Testament (see Exod. 17:2; Deut. 6:16). Therefore, Peter asks, "Why are you putting God to the test by placing on the neck of the disciples a yoke that neither our ancestors nor we have been able to bear?" The words "test" and "yoke" are linked to a rabbinic concept which suggested that the law is a "yoke" of obligation that "tests" the faithful. The rabbis also taught, however, that to bear the yoke of the law was a privilege and blessing.

Even the Christian Pharisee Paul can affirm that "the law is holy, and the commandment is holy and just and good. . . . For I delight in the law of God in my inmost self" (Rom. 7:12, 22). Paul, however, like Peter came to see that for Gentiles the yoke of the law may be an unnecessary burden, and certainly unnecessary for salvation.

Finally, both Peter and Paul have Jesus himself as their predecessor in questioning the burden of the legal yoke. "Woe also to you lawyers! For you load people with burdens hard to bear, and you yourselves do not lift a finger to ease them" (Luke 11:46). Jesus the teacher offers his own interpretation of the rabbinic metaphor "yoke." "Come to me, all you that are weary and are carrying heavy burdens, and I will give you rest. Take *my yoke* upon you, and *learn from me;* for I am gentle and humble in heart, and you will find rest for your souls. *For my yoke is easy, and my burden is light*" (Matt. 11:28–30).

Peter and Paul did learn from Jesus. They did indeed want to lighten the burden for Gentiles by replacing the yoke of the law with the yoke of Jesus.

Peter's message was clear: Do not put God to the test by placing on the Gentiles a burden that even we Jews cannot bear (v. 10). This would indeed be hypocrisy. In this Peter and Paul agree: "We believe that we [Jews] will be saved through the grace of the Lord Jesus [and not by the law of Moses], just as they [the Gentiles] will" (v. 11).

PAUL AND BARNABAS MAKE A STATEMENT
Acts 15:12

15:12 **The whole assembly kept silence, and listened to Barnabas and Paul as they told of all the signs and wonders that God had done through them among the Gentiles.**

This is one of the strangest sentences in Luke's narrative. In this story of the first general meeting of Christian leaders which is devoted to a critical aspect of Paul's message—that God's reconciling work in Jesus Christ has brought freedom from the law—only one sentence is given to Paul and Barnabas. Moreover, in their address to the leadership of the Jerusalem church, these missionaries to the Gentiles talked only about the "signs and wonders that God had done through them among the Gentiles"! According to Luke, it was Peter who carried the banner of freedom from the law. Paul, however, indicates in his letter to the Galatians that this was a defining moment for his apostleship. He had argued against circumcision persuasively and *privately* with James, Peter, and John. Furthermore, Paul recalls that instead of being a champion of the Gentiles, Peter who used to eat with them discontinued the practice under pressure from "certain people . . . from James" (Gal. 2:12). Paul reserves an especially bitter comment for Peter—he was a hypocrite! This hardly reflects the glowing picture of Acts.

THE DECISION OF JAMES
Acts 15:13–21

15:13 **After they finished speaking, James replied, "My brothers, listen to me. 14 Simeon has related how God first looked favorably on the Gentiles, to take from among them a people for his name. 15 This agrees with the words of the prophets, as it is written,**
> 16 '**After this I will return,**
> **and I will rebuild the dwelling of David, which has fallen;**
> **from its ruins I will rebuild it,**
> **and I will set it up,**
> 17 **so that all other peoples may seek the Lord—**
> **even all the Gentiles over whom my name has been called.**
> **Thus says the Lord, who has been making these things**
> 18 **known from long ago.'**
19 **Therefore I have reached the decision that we should not trouble those Gentiles who are turning to God, 20 but we should write to them to abstain**

only from things polluted by idols and from fornication and from whatever has been strangled and from blood. [21] For in every city, for generations past, Moses has had those who proclaim him, for he has been read aloud every sabbath in the synagogues."

After Peter, Paul, and Barnabas have finished speaking, James responded with a definitive judgment. This action suggests that he possessed singular authority in the Christian community. Why was James such an important figure in the early church? Mark 6:3 indicates that Jesus' family consisted of Mary, his mother, and his brothers James, Joses, Judas, and Simon. Unnamed sisters are also mentioned. The order of brothers in Mark's list indicates that James was the next oldest male after Jesus (Mary's firstborn son).

After the death of Jesus, the mantle of leadership in the family, in this patriarchal culture, fell on James. It has been suggested that this familial patriarchate also extended to the first followers of Jesus. Even as early as the persecution by King Herod (44 C.E.), and perhaps because of that persecution, James was recognized as a significant Christian figure (Acts 12:17). By the time one reaches the end of Acts, James has emerged as the undisputed head of the church. In Acts 21:18, Paul reports the results of his missionary journeys to James and the elders; "the twelve apostles" have drifted completely from view (after 16:4, the apostles are not mentioned again).

In the midpoint of Acts, James takes center stage as leader of the predominantly Jewish-Christian Jerusalem church, while Peter (onetime champion of the Gentile mission) and the apostles step aside. At the same time, Paul emerges as the genuine leader of the Christian mission among the Gentiles.

James renders the decision: "Therefore *I have reached the decision* that we should not trouble those Gentiles who are turning to God" (v. 19). Paul, on the other hand, remembers that it was James, Peter, and John—the real leaders of the church in Jerusalem—who, far from making a decision, "recognized the grace" given him and simply offered him the right hand of fellowship as a sign of agreement on the division of missionary labor among the Jews (Peter) and Gentiles (Paul) (Gal. 2:9).

According to Paul these pillars of the church "asked only one thing, that we remember the poor" (Gal. 2:10). Luke records that James asked for considerably more than this. On the one hand, Gentile-Christian men need not be circumcised (a decision that can only be inferred from the text; they are not to be "troubled"). On the other hand, James declared that the Gentile Christians are to be given written instructions containing four prohibitions (v. 20). They are to abstain from:

1. Things polluted by idols; that is, eating meat sold in shops that had been offered in sacrifice to heathen idols.
2. Fornication; the meaning could be sexual intercourse outside of marriage, or marriage within forbidden degrees of relationship (e.g., first cousins), or both.
3. Whatever has been strangled; that is, eating meat from animals that were not ritually slaughtered.
4. Blood; this might mean murder, or using blood as food, or it might be a reference to heathen sacrifice.

Verse 21 offers a justification for these four prohibitions. "In *every* city, *for generations past*, Moses has had those who proclaim him, for he has been read aloud *every sabbath* in the synagogues." The implication is that Gentiles everywhere in the world have consistently heard some such basic rules proclaimed. These prohibitions, therefore, are not new and not unknown to the Gentiles.

There was a tradition in early rabbinic Judaism that the sons of Noah, and therefore all humankind, received from God a set of universal rules which may be used to regulate the life of any community—the Noachian commands. The rabbis eventually arrived at seven basic rules (derived from the Pentateuch = "Moses") which could be expected of Gentiles living among Jews. Perhaps this passage in Acts allows the reader to glimpse an early Christian attempt to develop a similar set of basic rules, narrowed to four, which would be applicable and acceptable to both Jewish-Christian and Gentile-Christian communities. The next section considers the problem posed by this reductionist approach to observing Mosaic law.

THE LETTER TO THE GENTILES
Acts 15:22–35

15:22 **Then the apostles and the elders, with the consent of the whole church, decided to choose men from among their members and to send them to Antioch with Paul and Barnabas. They sent Judas called Barsabbas, and Silas, leaders among the brothers,** 23 **with the following letter: "The brothers, both the apostles and the elders, to the believers of Gentile origin in Antioch and Syria and Cilicia, greetings.** 24 **Since we have heard that certain persons who have gone out from us, though with no instructions from us, have said things to disturb you and have unsettled your minds,** 25 **we have decided unanimously to choose representatives and send them to you, along**

with our beloved Barnabas and Paul, [26] **who have risked their lives for the sake of our Lord Jesus Christ.** [27] **We have therefore sent Judas and Silas, who themselves will tell you the same things by word of mouth.** [28] **For it has seemed good to the Holy Spirit and to us to impose no further burden than these essentials:** [29] **that you abstain from what has been sacrificed to idols and from blood and from what is strangled and from fornication. If you keep yourselves from these, you will do well. Farewell."**

[30] **So they were sent off and went down to Antioch. When they gathered the congregation together, they delivered the letter.** [31] **When its members read it, they rejoiced at the exhortation.** [32] **Judas and Silas, who were themselves prophets, said much to encourage and strengthen the believers.** [33] **After they had been there for some time, they were sent off in peace by the believers to those who sent them.** [35] **But Paul and Barnabas remained in Antioch, and there, with many others, they taught and proclaimed the word of the Lord.**

The council sent two men—Judas Barsabbas and Silas—from the Jerusalem church to accompany Paul and Barnabas. These men were to bring a letter from the apostles and elders of the Jerusalem church addressed to "the believers of Gentile origin in Antioch and Syria and Cilicia" (v. 23). Antioch, the capital of the joint provinces of Syria and Cilicia, was apparently also the headquarters of the Gentile mission. While Luke did not narrate a mission of Paul to these provinces, Paul himself indicates that he had worked there very early in his missionary career (Gal. 1:21).

After the greeting, the letter harks back to recent events (15:1). Some persons, unauthorized by the church in Jerusalem, had come from Judea with a disturbing message to the Gentile Christians of Antioch indicating that they must be circumcised in order to be saved. This letter assures the believers in Antioch that its bearers are authentic representatives of the Christian leadership in Jerusalem commissioned to convey their decision, a decision that countermanded the message of those who insisted on circumcision for Gentile Christians.

According to the letter, the Jerusalem church will "impose no further burden [a reminder of the heavy yoke of the law; 15:10] than these essentials" (v. 28). The last word, "essentials," raises the question of whether there was in the early church a search for some minimal, but universal, guiding principles, some short form of the Mosaic law, which might be applied to the mixed body of Jewish and Gentile believers. Could the law be reduced to the Ten Commandments? To seven rabbinic Noachian commands? To four essentials of the Jerusalem Christian council? To one necessary rite of circumcision? One wonders if this might be the issue behind

Paul's letter to the Galatians: Can the law be reduced to some manageable size? Paul's answer was, Not at all. One maintains either the whole law of Moses or none of the law. Does Acts 15 portray the early church slipping ever so gently into the waters of legalism without disturbing the antilegalistic gospel of Paul? Finally, one must wonder why the commands of Jesus were not selected as "essentials"—to love God and love your neighbor (Luke 10:27; see John 13:34 and Gal. 5:14).

The four essentials (v. 29) are repeated along with an injunction that the Gentile Christians will "do well" if they maintain them. This last phrase finally saves these essentials from the force of legalism. No sanctions are mentioned if the essentials are *not* maintained. Only the promise of unspecified blessing—doing well—is offered as a reward for keeping them. Paul says nothing about these "essentials." In fact, he explicitly states that the leaders in Jerusalem "asked only one thing, that we remember the poor, which was actually what I was eager to do" (Gal. 2:10).

Luke reports that the members of the church in Antioch received the letter with joy and they were encouraged by the message of Judas and Silas. Eventually, the emissaries returned to Jerusalem "in peace," leaving behind Paul and Barnabas and a harmonious church.

PREPARATIONS FOR THE
SECOND MISSIONARY JOURNEY
Acts 15:36–41

> 15:36 **After some days Paul said to Barnabas, "Come, let us return and visit the believers in every city where we proclaimed the word of the Lord and see how they are doing." 37 Barnabas wanted to take with them John called Mark. 38 But Paul decided not to take with them one who had deserted them in Pamphylia and had not accompanied them in the work. 39 The disagreement became so sharp that they parted company; Barnabas took Mark with him and sailed away to Cyprus. 40 But Paul chose Silas and set out, the believers commending him to the grace of the Lord. 41 He went through Syria and Cilicia, strengthening the churches.**

We have already noted that Paul wanted Barnabas to accompany him on a visitation to the congregations which they established on their first journey (see 13:13–16). According to Luke, Paul did not take Barnabas on his second missionary journey because Barnabas insisted on bringing John Mark along. Paul rejected this idea because John Mark had "deserted" him in Pamphylia (Acts 13:13, though no mention is made of desertion in this verse). In his letter to the Galatians, however, Paul recalls that Barnabas (like Peter) had gone over to the side of the Judaizers, and therefore would not be an effective companion on the Gentile mission (Gal. 2:13).

The disagreement between Paul and Barnabas over Mark was so bitter that they parted company. Barnabas and Mark sailed away to Cyprus and are no longer mentioned in the book of Acts. Paul chose Silas as his missionary partner, and together they set out on foot through the provinces of Syria and Cilicia, traveling westward to the churches of Galatia.

SOME CONCLUDING OBSERVATIONS REGARDING LUKE'S NARRATIVE AND PAUL'S RECOLLECTION OF THE FIRST CHRISTIAN COUNCIL

A number of explanations have been put forward to account for the differences between Luke's historical narrative in Acts and Paul's personal recollection in Galatians: (1) Paul wrote just after the heat of the moment and he may have exaggerated his own point of view. (2) Luke wrote several decades after the meeting in Jerusalem and he may have embellished parts of the story, or he (or his sources) may have simply gotten some of it wrong. (3) Luke (or his sources) may have taken the "rough edges" off Paul and the "pillars," bringing them theologically closer together. (4) Galatians 2 and Acts 15 may be referring to different meetings in Jerusalem; some scholars suggest that the meeting Paul describes occurred during his visit to Jerusalem recorded in Acts 11:29, though the text of Acts offers no details regarding that visit. (5) Galatians 2 may be a record of a private conference between Paul and the "pillars" which occurred prior to the public meeting with the "apostles and elders."

Scholars have suggested two basic ways of resolving the differences between Luke (Acts 15) and Paul (Galatians 2): (1) Most accept Paul's version of the story as the more accurate. He was, after all, a major participant in the conversations. (2) Some suggest that Luke (or his source), through the distance of time, has a view of the meeting that is more balanced and objective than Paul's.

We might consider a third solution: Paul and Luke have left their readers two accounts that are ancient, authoritative, and sometimes conflicting. The truth may lie somewhere in between and it is helpful simply to identify those items of agreement between Paul and Luke: (1) The conversion of the Gentiles posed a theological problem for Jews who believed Jesus was the Messiah. Are these converts required to maintain the law of Moses?

What are the guidelines for table fellowship between Jewish and Gentile Christians? (2) There was a group of Christians who insisted that circumcision was necessary for salvation and table fellowship. (3) Paul conferred with church leaders about these problems. (4) Paul's perspective was upheld by the leaders; they all agreed that circumcision was not essential for salvation, and that table fellowship could take place between Gentiles and Jews in the Christian community. (5) In spite of the decision supporting Paul's point of view, those opposed to Paul continued to agitate against him.

In the final analysis, it is likely that the real Paul lies somewhere between Paul's self-disclosures and Luke's portrait. That which we disclose to others (through conversation and letter) is only partial truth. That which others see in us is also partial truth. Paul was not as crusty and rigid as he appears in his letters, nor was he quite as malleable as he appears in the book of Acts. The quest for the historical Paul, like quests for the historical Jesus, eventually end up in dark caverns that yield shadowy outlines (largely theologically framed) about the life and work of this great apostle. Luke's reconstruction may not be any farther off the mark than any of our own.

8. Paul's Second Missionary Journey
Acts 16:1–18:22

THE JOURNEY THROUGH ASIA
Acts 16:1–5

16:1 **Paul went on also to Derbe and to Lystra, where there was a disciple named Timothy, the son of a Jewish woman who was a believer; but his father was a Greek. [2] He was well spoken of by the believers in Lystra and Iconium. [3] Paul wanted Timothy to accompany him; and he took him and had him circumcised because of the Jews who were in those places, for they all knew that his father was a Greek. [4] As they went from town to town, they delivered to them for observance the decisions that had been reached by the apostles and elders who were in Jerusalem. [5] So the churches were strengthened in the faith and increased in numbers daily.**

Luke has briefly recorded the initial stage of Paul's second missionary journey. From Antioch, headquarters for the Gentile mission, he went north through Syria and west through Cilicia. Crossing the border into the province of Galatia he soon came to Derbe (see 14:20–21). Continuing westward, he finally arrived at Lystra, whose fickle citizens had treated him so badly during his first visit (14:8–20). Residing in this town was a young Hellenistic Jewish Christian named Timothy. According to 2 Timothy 1:5 both his mother, Eunice, and grandmother, Lois, were also Jewish Christians. Perhaps all three had come under the influence of Paul's missionary work during his previous visit (see 14:8ff.).

It may seem strange that Paul, one who championed freedom from the law, should have Timothy circumcised. The text of Acts indicates that Timothy was circumcised for pragmatic and political reasons, not out of religious conviction. Circumcision had nothing to do with Timothy's salvation. It was done to legitimate his status as Paul's fellow missionary. If they were to go "to the Jews first," then it would be helpful, perhaps imperative, that Timothy should be Jewish in every way. Luke notes that

Timothy's mother was Jewish, but his father was Gentile. Therefore, circumcision would eliminate endless disputes about Timothy's Jewishness. Additionally, this was Paul's way of being consistently above reproach—"under the law, blameless" (Phil. 3:6; see 1 Cor. 9:20). Had Timothy been fully Gentile, as was Titus, Paul would not have had him circumcised (Gal. 2:3; Titus was a Gentile Christian, Timothy a Jewish Christian, and the regulations pertaining to observation of Mosaic law was different for each community—admittedly a source of tension in the early church). From this point on, Timothy became Paul's constant companion (the opening words of most of Paul's letters refer to Timothy as a missionary partner: 2 Corinthians, Philippians, Colossians, 1 and 2 Thessalonians, and Philemon; additionally, two pastoral letters are also addressed to Timothy).

Luke suggests that the missionaries were expected to attend to an important piece of business among the Christian communities: "they *delivered* to them *for observance* the *decisions* that had been reached by the apostles and elders who were in Jerusalem" (v. 4). The text of the NRSV understates the importance of this task, and a closer look at the emphasized words will reveal why this is so.

The Greek word for "deliver" is the same used by rabbis of the first century, including Paul, for the passing on of a sacred tradition. A rabbinic teacher would "deliver" an interpretation of scripture to his students, often the same interpretation "delivered" to the teacher by his own rabbi—a chain of oral tradition. According to the rabbis, this chain of tradition had originated with Moses himself and constituted the oral law. Paul, the Jewish-Christian rabbi, offers a powerful illustration of this concept in 1 Corinthians 11. Paul tells the church at Corinth, "I *received* (in Greek, a technical term for receiving authorized teaching) from the Lord what I also *handed on* (a technical term for passing on authorized teaching; "delivered" in the RSV) to you, that the Lord Jesus on the night when he was betrayed took a loaf of bread, and when he had given thanks, he broke it and said, 'This is my body that is for you. Do this in remembrance of me'" (1 Cor. 11:23–24). Paul has received from his new teacher, Jesus, instructions for life in the community.

Furthermore, Paul is to "deliver" the authoritative teachings—the "decisions"—which the Christian council formulated in Jerusalem. The Greek term for "decisions" is *dogmata*, the same word used of imperial decrees (Luke 2:1; Acts 17:7). The decisions were to be taken seriously; after all, they were authorized by the apostles and elders in Jerusalem. These "decisions" were contained in the letter James and the leaders of the Jerusalem church wanted Paul to carry with him and read to the newly formed

Gentile churches. This letter included the four "essential" rules for living in community (15:22–29).

Finally, Luke notes that the churches were to "observe" the decisions. The usual meaning of this term is "to guard, to be on guard, to watch over, to defend." By extension, the word had also come to mean "to keep" a law from being broken; thus, "to observe, to follow" the law (in ancient literature the term refers to both Jewish and Roman law).

Thus, Luke portrays Paul as a delegate from Jerusalem who is to deliver to the diaspora churches a written copy of the decree authorized by the apostles and elders of the Jerusalem church. This decree is to be observed by the diaspora churches. There seems little doubt that Luke has placed a high value on the church of Jerusalem. This community is not only the mother church, giving birth and nurture to all others; she is the queen church giving guidance, advice, and direction to churches beyond Jerusalem's walls. Again, in light of Galatians, something seems wrong with this picture. It is doubtful that Paul (the determined and independent person we know from his letters) would have agreed to such a mission. Nor would he have viewed himself as an emissary of the Jerusalem church. Nor would this messenger of freedom in Christ have delivered such binding decisions for observance. Nevertheless, Luke has given us *his* portrait of Paul, a more even tempered and agreeable apostle to the Gentiles—and perhaps this is how Paul really was viewed by those who knew and loved him.

Verse 5 is another of Luke's editorial summaries indicating that the church continued to grow in faith and numbers.

THE CALL TO VISIT MACEDONIA
Acts 16:6–10

16:6 **They went through the region of Phrygia and Galatia, having been forbidden by the Holy Spirit to speak the word in Asia.** [7] **When they had come opposite Mysia, they attempted to go into Bithynia, but the Spirit of Jesus did not allow them;** [8] **so, passing by Mysia, they went down to Troas.** [9] **During the night Paul had a vision: there stood a man of Macedonia pleading with him and saying, "Come over to Macedonia and help us."** [10] **When he had seen the vision, we immediately tried to cross over to Macedonia, being convinced that God had called us to proclaim the good news to them.**

To understand better the movements of Paul and his company in this passage, it will be helpful to follow a map printed in the back of most

Bibles. From Lystra, Paul and his companions probably had planned to follow the main highway which led to Iconium and Pisidian Antioch, and then continue westward to the great city of Ephesus, capital of the Roman province of Asia. "Asia" in verse 6 does not refer to the modern continent of Asia; rather, it was a province in the westernmost part of Asia Minor. For some reason, the Holy Spirit informed Paul that this was not the time to proclaim the gospel in this province. The missionaries then traveled northward through Asia and attempted to enter the province of Bithynia. Once again, the divine Spirit, "the Spirit of Jesus," did not allow this. Turning westward, they followed the northern border of Asia until they came to Troas on the Aegean Sea which divides Asia Minor from Greece.

Troas provides the setting for Paul's dream in which a Macedonian man pleads with him to sail across the Aegean to begin a mission to the Roman province of Macedonia (the northern part of ancient Greece; Achaia lay to the south). Paul was convinced by the dream and set sail for a challenging mission in the cradle of western culture—the home of Homer and Hesiod, of Socrates and Plato, of Aristotle and Alexander the Great.

Some have conjectured that Luke was the man in Paul's dream, a conjecture based on the first-person plural pronoun ("we . . . us") which occurs for the first time in the book of Acts in this passage. "When he had seen the vision, *we* immediately tried to cross over to Macedonia, being convinced that God had called *us* to proclaim the good news to them" (v. 10). While this conjecture is an attractive possibility, it cannot be more than that.

You will notice that in the rest of the book of Acts, some of Luke's narrative describing Paul's travels is presented in the language of an eyewitness. As I noted in the Introduction, the existence of the "we passages" has been used to support the traditional claim that the author of the Third Gospel and the Acts of the Apostles was a traveling companion of Paul, probably Luke, Paul's "fellow worker" (Philemon 24). It could be that Luke has joined Paul and Silas during the mission to Philippi in Macedonia. It could also be the case that the author has "cut and pasted" a section from one of his several sources—a travel diary, perhaps written by Silas. The author's use of "we" abruptly drops out after verse 17 and reappears at 20:5. The final two we passages in Acts occur in 20:5–21:18 (Paul's journey from Philippi to Jerusalem) and 27:1–28:16 (Paul's journey from Caesarea to Rome).

In whatever way one might account for this sudden shift in the narrative from third person to first person, the shift is effective in bringing additional life to the story. The reader, along with the writer, is now part of the action; *we* are going with Paul on this important mission which leads from Judaism's religious center into Greece's intellectual center, and eventually to Rome's political center.

THE MISSION TO PHILIPPI
Acts 16:11–40

Lydia and the Slave Girl (Acts 16:11–18)

16:11 We set sail from Troas and took a straight course to Samothrace, the following day to Neapolis, 12 and from there to Philippi, which is the leading city of the district of Macedonia and a Roman colony. We remained in this city for some days. 13 On the sabbath day we went outside the gate by the river, where we supposed there was a place of prayer; and we sat down and spoke to the women who had gathered there. 14 A certain woman named Lydia, a worshiper of God, was listening to us; she was from the city of Thyatira and a dealer in purple cloth. The Lord opened her heart to listen eagerly to what was said by Paul. 15 When she and her household were baptized, she urged us, saying, "If you have judged me to be faithful to the Lord, come and stay at my home." And she prevailed upon us.

16 One day, as we were going to the place of prayer, we met a slave girl who had a spirit of divination and brought her owners a great deal of money by fortune-telling. 17 While she followed Paul and us, she would cry out, "These men are slaves of the Most High God, who proclaim to you a way of salvation." 18 She kept doing this for many days. But Paul, very much annoyed, turned and said to the spirit, "I order you in the name of Jesus Christ to come out of her." And it came out that very hour.

At last Paul has reached the goal of his vision. Luke tells us that Philippi was "a leading city in the district of Macedonia and a Roman colony." It was founded in 356 B.C.E. by Philip of Macedon (father of Alexander the Great), and later Caesar Augustus established Philippi as a Roman colony for retired army veterans following the battle of Actium (31 B.C.E.). It was also the city in which Paul formed one of his favorite and most supportive congregations (Phil. 1:3–5)—a congregation that received Paul's "joyful epistle."

It is not certain why Paul and his companions wandered to the River Gangites, a stream that runs near Philippi. Perhaps they had been given directions to a synagogue located by the river, and, in their search, they came upon a group of women gathered by the riverside. It is significant that these women were Paul's first hearers in Philippi.

Luke indicates that Paul "sat down and spoke to the women" (v. 13). Sitting was the typical posture for the rabbi to assume when he was teaching (see Matt. 5:1). That Paul the Pharisee should sit to teach a group of women is nothing less than astonishing. This detail reminds us how significantly Paul had changed. He now disregarded such traditional Pharisaic maxims as "Talk not much with a woman. . . . Everyone that talks much with a woman causes evil to himself, and desists from the words of Torah, and his end is he inherits Gehinnom [Hell]" (*Pirke Aboth* 1:5). Yet, in Acts 16, Luke narrates an amazing story about the great apostle of Jesus and how that apostle demonstrated one of his profound theological conclusions: For those who have been baptized in Christ, "there is no longer Jew or Greek, there is no longer slave or free, there is no longer male and female; for all of you are one in Christ Jesus" (Gal. 3:28).

Paul's first convert at Philippi was Lydia, a wealthy Gentile and God-fearer. Luke notes that she was the local retailer of purple cloth which was sold only to members of the upper class in this Roman colony. Furthermore, she appears to be head of the household; as was typical for the time, when she accepted a new religion, all of her household would be expected to do likewise. She implored Paul and his companions to enjoy her hospitality while they were in Philippi. We can assume that a house-church was established in Lydia's home (see Acts 16:40).

Verse 16 suggests that Paul eventually found the synagogue he had been looking for. On the way to "the place of prayer," he met a slave girl "who had a spirit of divination," literally "a spirit, a python." This phrase is an allusion to the snake that symbolized the Greek god Apollo at Delphi. Those who were members of the guild of Delphic oracle readers (usually young women) were thought to have the spirit of the god inside them offering divinely inspired answers to petitioners' questions. While in a frenzy or trance, the oracle would speak in the spirit of the snake-god.

The modern reader might consider this girl to be mentally unbalanced or schizophrenic. For the ancient reader, she would have been accepted as a more or less ordinary member of society serving a useful function for people in that culture. Those who owned this slave certainly found her gifts profitable. Paul, however, found her just plain annoying. For days she would follow Paul, screaming out, "These men are slaves of the Most High God!" The theological comparison is obvious to the reader: a slave to the god Apollo recognized that she was in the company of servants of a higher divinity. The term she used, "Most High God," was the typical way for a non-Jew to speak of the God of Israel (see Num. 24:16; Psalm 46:4; Isa. 14:14; Dan. 3:26; the God of Abraham was remembered as God Most High, Gen. 14:22). Paul alleviated his annoyance by exorcising the spirit from her. While we are not told how the girl felt about this, we are informed about the response of her owners.

Paul and Silas Are Imprisoned
(Acts 16:19–34)

16:19 But when her owners saw that their hope of making money was gone, they seized Paul and Silas and dragged them into the marketplace before the authorities. [20] When they had brought them before the magistrates, they said, "These men are disturbing our city; they are Jews [21] and are advocating customs that are not lawful for us as Romans to adopt or observe." [22] The crowd joined in attacking them, and the magistrates had them stripped of their clothing and ordered them to be beaten with rods. [23] After they had given them a severe flogging, they threw them into prison and ordered the jailer to keep them securely. [24] Following these instructions, he put them in the innermost cell and fastened their feet in the stocks.

[25] About midnight Paul and Silas were praying and singing hymns to God, and the prisoners were listening to them. [26] Suddenly there was an earthquake, so violent that the foundations of the prison were shaken; and immediately all the doors were opened and everyone's chains were unfastened. [27] When the jailer woke up and saw the prison doors wide open, he drew his sword and was about to kill himself, since he supposed that the prisoners had escaped. [28] But Paul shouted in a loud voice, "Do not harm yourself, for we are all here." [29] The jailer called for lights, and rushing in, he fell down trembling before Paul and Silas. [30] Then he brought them outside and said, "Sirs, what must I do to be saved?" [31] They answered, "Believe on the Lord Jesus, and you will be saved, you and your household." [32] They spoke the word of the Lord to him and to all who were in his house. [33] At the same hour of the night he took them and washed their wounds; then he and his entire family were baptized without delay. [34] He brought them up into the house and set food before them; and he and his entire household rejoiced that he had become a believer in God.

The owners of the slave girl were exceedingly unhappy to see their source of income suddenly ended by Paul. They first dragged Paul and Silas into the marketplace where the courthouse was located. Here they brought complaints to the city magistrates, charging Paul and Silas with disturbing the peace. Beyond that, it is difficult to detect any specific Roman laws that Paul and Silas might have violated. The complaint that "they are Jews and are advocating customs that are not lawful for us as Romans to adopt or observe" may have been a piece of anti-Jewish sentiment tossed in to sway the Roman magistrates against these Jewish Christians. Even the charge of disturbing the peace is ironic. It was the slave girl who had been disturbing the peace with her rantings and ravings at Paul! Nevertheless, Paul and Silas were stripped and beaten as roving troublemakers.

The narrative of Paul and Silas in prison is simply told: the prison holding the missionaries was shaken to the foundations by an earthquake so that their chains fell off and the locked doors sprung open. The jailer, who had been specifically ordered to keep the prisoners secure, was ready to commit suicide rather than be executed for allowing prisoners to escape. Paul quickly intervened by assuring the jailer that the prisoners had not fled. The jailer's plaintive cry is probably one of the best known appeals in human history: "What must I do to be saved?" Paul, Silas, and the jailer had a short conversation about Jesus, belief, and salvation, and the scene ends with the missionaries and their jailer sharing a meal.

This story is full of incidents that defy logic: How did the stocks fall from the missionaries' feet? How did Paul know the jailer was about to fall on his sword when it was pitch-dark? Why did the other prisoners not escape? Why did the jailer bring the missionaries outside? Could the jailer and his whole household be convinced to believe in Jesus in the span of a few hours in the middle of the night? Why didn't the magistrates note the damage to the prison when they visited there the next day? Where was Timothy when all this was taking place? But the modern reader needs to remember that this is a story meant to be told orally with less stress on logical details and more emphasis on conveying the miraculous deeds of the early Christian servants of God.

The heart of this story is about the salvation of the jailer and his household. The jailer's question, "What must I do to be saved?" may have been a commonsense plea: "How will I survive this mess?" While the jailer's concern was for the moment, the missionaries offered him the opportunity of a lifetime; they offered him salvation that transcended the current crisis: "Believe on the Lord Jesus, and you will be saved, you and your household" (v. 31).

Luke was at his literary best when he wrote that the jailer took Paul and Silas to his home and washed the wounds they had received from the beating. Then the jailer and his family were baptized. The jailer had washed the physical and temporal wounds of the missionaries; he, in turn, received from their hands a spiritual and eternal washing.

Just as Lydia instructed all who belonged to her household (relatives and servants) to be baptized, so also the jailer had his entire household join the faith through baptism. With the entrance of these two households into the faith, Luke has put into story form what Paul expressed in his succinct theological statement of Galatians 3:28: *All are one through baptism in Christ Jesus:*

Jew and Gentile:	Paul and Silas and Lydia and the jailer
slave and free:	Lydia and the slave girl (though we do not know that the latter became a Christian); the household of Lydia may have contained "slave and free"
male and female:	the jailer and Lydia

Yes, Luke and Paul do present different pictures of the same events. However, Acts 15—16 and Galatians 2—3 illustrate that these differences may have more to do with form than content. Paul offered his readers tightly wound theological themes; Luke unrolls these themes and weaves them into stories.

Paul and Silas Receive an Apology
(Acts 16:35–40)

> 16:35 **When morning came, the magistrates sent the police, saying, "Let those men go."** [36] **And the jailer reported the message to Paul, saying, "The magistrates sent word to let you go; therefore come out now and go in peace."** [37] **But Paul replied, "They have beaten us in public, uncondemned, men who are Roman citizens, and have thrown us into prison; and now they are going to discharge us in secret? Certainly not! Let them come and take us out themselves."** [38] **The police reported these words to the magistrates, and they were afraid when they heard that they were Roman citizens;** [39] **so they came and apologized to them. And they took them out and asked them to leave the city.** [40] **After leaving the prison they went to Lydia's home; and when they had seen and encouraged the brothers and sisters there, they departed.**

The next morning the city magistrates were ready to expel Paul and Silas from town. This would be the normal course of events for troublemakers: beat them, put them in stocks (having one's legs stretched wide apart for the night was an additional painful punishment), and kick them out of town. Luke inserts a bit of humor into the story as the timid jailer is sent to deliver the news to Paul that they are free to go quietly ("go in peace"). He has had enough trouble for one night, and while Paul and Silas brought blessings to his household, it would be just fine with him if they were to leave now. But Paul, not to be dismissed as common riffraff, boldly (and probably loudly) demanded his due as a Roman citizen (why didn't he mention this in the first place? or is this question just more wooden modern logic?). Paul declared, "They have beaten us in public, uncondemned, men who are Roman citizens, and have thrown us into prison; and now are they going to discharge us in secret? Certainly not!" Even across the span of two thousand years one can feel the heat of Paul's anger at this injustice!

Paul—and Luke—knew Roman judicial process well, and they certainly recognized when it was absent. Paul should not have been beaten before he had an opportunity to answer the charges, and before a trial had taken place with all the attendant witnesses, cross examinations, verdict, and, if necessary, appeal. He was not even allowed to post bond prior to a hearing. He was simply beaten and thrown into jail as a common drifter. But Luke wants his reader to know that Paul of Tarsus had status. His hero was not just some itinerant preacher. He was Paul the Pharisee, student of Gamaliel, missionary for Jesus Christ, and a citizen of Rome. Luke has begun to lay out Paul's impressive credentials, in case one should doubt the credibility of this missionary to the Gentiles. These credentials become ever more important as Luke's story progresses toward its conclusion.

The city officials quickly realized the error of their ways, and, fearful that Paul might raise a loud complaint to the Roman provincial governor in Thessalonica (his next stop), they apologized to the missionaries and politely asked them to leave the city. Luke rounds out his account of Paul and Silas in Philippi by having them pay a last visit to Lydia, their benefactor. After offering some final encouraging remarks to the church gathered in Lydia's house, they left for the provincial capital, Thessalonica.

THE MISSION TO THESSALONICA
Acts 17:1–10a

17:1 **After Paul and Silas had passed through Amphipolis and Apollonia, they came to Thessalonica, where there was a synagogue of the Jews. 2 And Paul went in, as was his custom, and on three sabbath days argued with them from the scriptures, 3 explaining and proving that it was necessary for the Messiah to suffer and to rise from the dead, and saying, "This is the Messiah, Jesus whom I am proclaiming to you." 4 Some of them were persuaded and joined Paul and Silas, as did a great many of the devout Greeks and not a few of the leading women. 5 But the Jews became jealous, and with the help of some ruffians in the marketplaces they formed a mob and set the city in an uproar. While they were searching for Paul and Silas to bring them out to the assembly, they attacked Jason's house. 6 When they could not find them, they dragged Jason and some believers before the city authorities, shouting,**

"These people who have been turning the world upside down have come here also, ⁷ and Jason has entertained them as guests. They are all acting contrary to the decrees of the emperor, saying that there is another king named Jesus."
⁸ The people and the city officials were disturbed when they heard this, ⁹ and after they had taken bail from Jason and the others, they let them go.
¹⁰ᵃ That very night the believers sent Paul and Silas off to Beroea;

In 146 B.C.E. Thessalonica was made capital of the Roman province of Macedonia. Like other large Mediterranean cities, Thessalonica could boast of a rich cultural and religious life. Religious cults were in abundance, including shrines dedicated to various Greek gods and goddesses. A civic cult also appears to have flourished in the city; regularly scheduled divine honors were paid to Roman benefactors, rulers, and the emperor (Augustus had been acclaimed as a divine being). Inscriptions have been found to indicate that there were also a Jewish and a Samaritan synagogue in Thessalonica.

Paul's first stop was a visit to the Jewish synagogue, "as was his custom." It might be a mistake to assume from our English text that Paul was an argumentative person. Luke's phrase that Paul "argued with them from the scriptures" (v. 2) means that he was holding discussions with this congregation which would have been partly teaching and partly preaching. Luke has attempted to capture the style of a rabbi at work with a congregation: Paul was "explaining and proving" from scripture (see Luke 23:32, 45–46) "that it was necessary for the Messiah to suffer and to rise from the dead" (v. 3).

Luke lists three groups of people who were persuaded by Paul and Silas: Jewish members of the synagogue, devout Greeks, and leading women. Usually when Gentiles are part of the synagogue community they are identified as God-fearers or worshipers of God. These "devout Greeks" were probably drawn from the ranks of pious (and consequently patriotic) Gentiles who were deeply involved in some of the many cults available in Thessalonica (involvement in more than one cult was not only acceptable, but encouraged). Luke is fond of mentioning the conversion of upper-class Gentiles (though neither in Thessalonica nor in Beroea [Acts 17:12ff.] do they come to Paul's aid in averting persecution).

Once again the Jews are jealous of the success of Paul's mission—a pattern we encounter often in Acts. Here, Luke has presented a picture of a mob out of control, wildly searching all over Thessalonica for Paul and Silas. When the missionaries could not be found, they took out their frustration on Jason, who had offered hospitality to the missionaries, and a few other Christians by dragging them before the city authorities. The mob charged them (Paul and Silas? Jason and the believers?) with crimes that echo those brought against Jesus:

Acts 17:6–7	Luke 23:2
These people have been turning the world upside down.	This man was perverting our nation.
They are all acting contrary to the decrees of Caesar.	He was forbidding us to pay taxes to Caesar.
They say there is another king, Jesus.	He says that he himself is the Messiah, a king.

All three charges were quite serious in a Roman court. The first, "turning the world upside down," is literally "rebelling against the Roman order" and punishable by deportation to an island. The second two charges were direct challenges to Roman imperial authority and punishable by death. It is not surprising that the city authorities "were disturbed" when they heard these charges. The authorities allowed Jason and the others to post bond and let them go. Nor is it surprising that Paul and Silas were secreted out of town at night. They would not want to cause further serious damage to the small community of believers (see 1 Thessalonians 2:13–16 which may be Paul's own recollection of this event).

THE MISSION TO BEROEA
Acts 17:10b–15

17:10b **And when they arrived [in Beroea], they went to the Jewish synagogue. ¹¹ These Jews were more receptive than those in Thessalonica, for they welcomed the message very eagerly and examined the scriptures every day to see whether these things were so. ¹² Many of them therefore believed, including not a few Greek women and men of high standing. ¹³ But when the Jews of Thessalonica learned that the word of God had been proclaimed by Paul in Beroea as well, they came there too, to stir up and incite the crowds. ¹⁴ Then the believers immediately sent Paul away to the coast, but Silas and Timothy remained behind. ¹⁵ Those who conducted Paul brought him as far as Athens; and after receiving instructions to have Silas and Timothy join him as soon as possible, they left him.**

A pattern has emerged in Luke's narratives describing Paul's mission to the Gentiles:

1. Paul arrives in town.
2. He explores the scriptures (especially messianic texts) with Jews of the local synagogue in his teaching and preaching about Jesus the Messiah.
3. Some Jews become convinced.
4. A large number of Gentiles become believers.
5. But those opposed to Paul incite persecution against him.
6. They force Paul to move on to his next mission.

Luke says little about the day-to-day work of Paul and his companions between the founding of the churches and the persecution of the missionaries. It is obvious that Luke has compressed time substantially and skips over the details.

In this scene, Paul and Silas were warmly received by the Jews of the Beroean synagogue. As in Lystra (Acts 14:19), Jews from out of town have followed the missionaries in order to stir up trouble against them. Luke's irony may be unintended, but it is interesting to note that those who accused Paul of disturbing the peace of the empire were themselves doing just that!

Timothy has reemerged on the scene (we last read about him in 16:1–3) and, with Silas, remained in Beroea while Paul went on to Athens. Even though Paul wanted them to join him as soon as possible, they did not get together again until Paul was well into his work at Corinth (18:5).

PAUL AND THE PHILOSOPHERS OF ATHENS
Acts 17:16–34

17:16 **While Paul was waiting for them in Athens, he was deeply distressed to see that the city was full of idols. ¹⁷ So he argued in the synagogue with the Jews and the devout persons, and also in the marketplace every day with those who happened to be there. ¹⁸ Also some Epicurean and Stoic philosophers debated with him. Some said, "What does this babbler want to say?" Others said, "He seems to be a proclaimer of foreign divinities." (This was because he was telling the good news about Jesus and the resurrection.) ¹⁹ So they took him and brought him to the Areopagus and asked him, "May we know what this new teaching is that you are presenting? ²⁰ It sounds rather strange to us, so we would like to know what it means." ²¹ Now all** the Athenians and the foreigners living there would spend their time in nothing but telling or hearing something new.

22 Then Paul stood in front of the Areopagus and said, "Athenians, I see how extremely religious you are in every way. 23 For as I went through the city and looked carefully at the objects of your worship, I found among them an altar with the inscription, 'To an unknown god.' What therefore you worship as unknown, this I proclaim to you. 24 The God who made the world and everything in it, he who is Lord of heaven and earth, does not live in shrines made by human hands, 25 nor is he served by human hands, as though he needed anything, since he himself gives to all mortals life and breath and all things. 26 From our ancestor he made all nations to inhabit the whole earth, and he allotted the times of their existence and the boundaries of the places where they would live, 27 so that they would search for God and perhaps grope for him and find him—though indeed he is not far from each one of us. 28 For 'In him we live and move and have our being'; as even some of your own poets have said,

'For we too are his offspring.'

29 Since we are God's offspring, we ought not to think that the deity is like gold, or silver, or stone, an image formed by the art and imagination of mortals. 30 While God has overlooked the times of human ignorance, now he commands all people everywhere to repent, 31 because he has fixed a day on which he will have the world judged in righteousness by a man whom he has appointed, and of this he has given assurance to all by raising him from the dead."

32 When they heard of the resurrection of the dead, some scoffed; but others said, "We will hear you again about this." 33 At that point Paul left them. 34 But some of them joined him and became believers, including Dionysius the Areopagite and a woman named Damaris, and others with them.

One of the high points of Paul's missionary career was the opportunity to participate in a theological discussion with the philosophers of Athens. While the five thousand citizens of this small town proudly lived in the glow of its great past, for Luke, Athens was still the pride of high Hellenic culture. Luke notes two gathering places in Athens where Paul held frequent discussions: in the synagogue with fellow Jews and pious Greeks and in the marketplace with Stoic and Epicurean philosophers. The Epicureans were pragmatic atheists who taught that belief in the gods is not particularly useful, especially in light of life's inevitable sufferings. Even if gods do exist, they obviously do not care much about human beings. The Stoics, on the other hand, had a well-developed theology that taught that "the mind of Zeus [the greatest and highest of the gods] is reason/*logos* itself." We shall discuss Stoic logos theology, and some of its impact on early Christian thought, later in this section.

We are already familiar with Luke's presentation of Paul the Pharisee teaching in the synagogues; now we are treated to a portrait of Paul the first Christian philosopher conversing on the Areopagus.

According to Luke, Paul's debates with the philosophers attracted a great deal of attention in the bustling marketplace of Athens. Luke's parenthetical remark (v. 18) suggests that Paul's hearers understood him to be speaking of two separate divinities, Jesus and Anastasis (Greek for "resurrection"). The latter, they supposed, was a female deity. A small group of philosophers bring Paul away from the bustling center of town to the quiet sanctuary of Mars' Hill (the Areopagus) for a more intimate conversation. An older interpretation suggests that Paul was actually under arrest and being questioned about his teachings. It is true that at one time Mars' Hill was the site of murder trials, and Luke may have had the trial of Socrates in mind as he constructed this scene. However, there is little in this scene to indicate a trial; it is much more like a colloquium of philosophers politely hearing Paul's "new teaching." Luke offers a side, and perhaps snide, remark that those in Athens had leisure for nothing more than listening to the latest idea (v. 21).

Paul begins his address to the philosophers by complimenting them; perhaps this was tongue in cheek, given his initial anger about the many idols in Athens. His compliment, however, seems genuine; by the time he has reached Mars' Hill his response is measured and polite. Paul notes that while walking through Athens he saw an altar in which there was carved an inscription: "To an unknown God" (v. 23; the remains of such an altar have not been discovered, nor is this inscription quoted in other ancient literature). That this inscription provided Paul with a text for interpretation and discussion reminds the reader that Paul is far removed from the world of the Bible. Ordinarily, we hear him interpreting scripture. In Athens, however, Paul speaks to his Gentile audience as he begins to interpret the inscription: "What therefore you worship as unknown, this I proclaim to you."

Paul's initial assertion echoes Stephen's speech: God, who created the universe, "does not live in shrines made by human hands" (v. 24; Acts 7:48). Paul's speech has a distinctly Stoic tone and sounds very much like typical Hellenistic Jewish missionary preaching. A central theme in Stoic teaching was an understanding that the universe was created by means of God's reason. God, the source of all reason (*logos* = "reason, word"), has created an orderly cosmos, and each human being has a direct link with God through his or her divinely implanted "seed of reason" (see James 1:21).

Paul's address was a reflection on Stoic theology. God has given all mortals "life and breath and all things"; furthermore, God has "allotted the time of [each nation's] existence and the boundaries of the places where they would live, so that they would search for God and perhaps grope for him and find him—though indeed he is not far from each one of us" (vv. 26–27). Paul's next sentence clarifies what he means by "not far." "In [God] we live and move and have our being" (v. 28). Scholars have searched in vain among ancient philosophical writings for this theological formula. Perhaps it was Paul's (or Luke's) own summary of Stoic theology. The next quote, "For we too are his offspring," can be found in a work by the hymn writer Aratus (third century B.C.E.). With this colloquium of Greek philosophers, Paul uses quotes from their poets just as he would cite supporting biblical references in a synagogue discussion.

While Paul never mentions Jesus by name, he does use another Stoic theological concept to describe him. God has overlooked the past times of human ignorance regarding his will for the world. The seed of reason each human being contains was not quite enough to clearly discern God's will. Therefore, God sent "a man whom he has appointed." This "man" is God's intermediary *logos*/reason which God (the fullness of reason itself) sent into the world in order to inform the seed of reason that resides in each human being. This theological argument echoes the thought of Philo of Alexandria, a first-century Hellenistic Jewish theologian who developed a philosophical understanding of divine and human reason, and how they are linked. God has created a great chain of reason: God ↔ intermediaries (including Torah, angels, the Holy Spirit, and Messiah) ↔ humankind.

The philosophical colloquium ends with Paul's hearers divided. Some scoff at him; Luke probably had Epicureans in mind as those who were not impressed with theological arguments. Others (Stoics?) want further conversation with Paul. Some of the latter group even became believers, including Dionysius and Damaris. Presumably, both this man and woman were philosophers, which follows the Lukan pattern of identifying a believer of each gender.

As the scene ends, the ancient reader might have breathed a sigh of relief. As we noted above there are elements in this passage intended to remind the reader of that premiere philosopher of Athens, Socrates. Paul, like his predecessor, speaks openly in the marketplace to anyone who will listen. The people think that Paul, like Socrates, is introducing new gods into Athens. And finally, both Paul and Socrates had been brought before the court on the Areopagus to explain their teachings. The reader would also remember the fate of Socrates in Athens, and would be pleased to see Paul depart unharmed for Corinth.

THE MISSION TO CORINTH
Acts 18:1–17

The Corinthian Church Is Established
(Acts 18:1–11)

18:1 After this Paul left Athens and went to Corinth. [2] There he found a Jew named Aquila, a native of Pontus, who had recently come from Italy with his wife Priscilla, because Claudius had ordered all Jews to leave Rome. Paul went to see them, [3] and, because he was of the same trade, he stayed with them, and they worked together—by trade they were tentmakers. [4] Every sabbath he would argue in the synagogue and would try to convince Jews and Greeks.

[5] When Silas and Timothy arrived from Macedonia, Paul was occupied with proclaiming the word, testifying to the Jews that the Messiah was Jesus. [6] When they opposed and reviled him, in protest he shook the dust from his clothes and said to them, "Your blood be on your own heads! I am innocent. From now on I will go to the Gentiles." [7] Then he left the synagogue and went to the house of a man named Titius Justus, a worshiper of God; his house was next door to the synagogue. [8] Crispus, the official of the synagogue, became a believer in the Lord, together with all his household; and many of the Corinthians who heard Paul became believers and were baptized. [9] One night the Lord said to Paul in a vision, "Do not be afraid, but speak and do not be silent; [10] for I am with you, and no one will lay a hand on you to harm you, for there are many in this city who are my people." [11] He stayed there a year and six months, teaching the word of God among them.

It has long been observed that Christianity, beginning with the Day of Pentecost in Jerusalem, was an urban movement. Roman satirists caricatured Judaism and Christianity as noxious plagues, spreading especially among the lower classes of urban culture. To be sure, the setting of Luke's first volume, the Gospel, is more pastoral in orientation; Jesus was, after all, an itinerant teacher-preacher who worked with people beside the Sea of Galilee, on the hillsides of central Palestine, and along the dusty roads of Judea. With the Acts of the Apostles, the gospel is brought indoors and to the cities.

Paul's itinerary through the ancient world brings him to major centers of religious, intellectual, and political power: Jerusalem, Antioch, Philippi, Thessalonica, Athens, Corinth, Ephesus, and finally Rome. In his first missionary journey, Paul's focus was on the cities of Asia Minor, especially in the province of Galatia. The goal of the second journey is proclamation of the gospel to Greece—in Paul's time the Roman provinces of Macedonia (in the north) and Achaia (in the south). He had already worked in Thessalonica (the governmental capital of Macedonia) and Athens (the intellectual capital of all Greece). Now Paul has come to Corinth (the capital of Achaia) where he will establish a significant community of believers.

You are invited to read Paul's own account of the founding of the Corinthian church in his first letter to the Corinthians (1—4). We shall refer to Paul's Corinthian correspondence when it provides helpful clarification.

Corinth is remembered historically, and perhaps unfairly, as a city of sexual excesses—an opinion based on a comment by the ancient geographer Strabo, who refers to a thousand priestess-prostitutes attached to the cult of Aphrodite. More reflective contemporary historians conclude that Corinth was neither more nor less perverse than most cosmopolitan cities of antiquity. The Athenians may have been lobbing snobbish stereotypic volleys at their powerful neighbor fifty miles to the west.

Corinth was not only a provincial capital but also a major commercial center. The city was well situated with seaports opening to the Aegean Sea (and Asia Minor to the east) and the Adriatic Sea (and Italy to the west). Cargoes were often unloaded at one port, transported on a crude rail system across the isthmus, and reloaded at the opposite port—a maneuver that saved a dangerous and difficult journey around the southern coast Greece. Along with commercial goods from all over the world came a wide variety of peoples who made their home in Corinth, including a large colony of Jews.

It was just such an immigrant Jewish couple that quickly befriended Paul after his arrival in Corinth. Aquila and Priscilla themselves must have recently settled in the community, having left Rome by order of the emperor Claudius (49 C.E.; the Roman historian Suetonius also recorded this event: "Since the Jews constantly made disturbances at the instigation of Chrestus, he expelled them from Rome" [*Lives of the Caesars*, Claudius 25]. This is probably a reference to disturbances caused by controversies between Jews and Christians of Rome over *Christos*, the Messiah).

Priscilla and Aquila were Jewish Christians who had been expelled from Rome (the likely losers in a debate with more orthodox Jews about whether or not Jesus is the Messiah). They chose not to treat this expulsion as a defeat, but as an opportunity to bear witness to the good news in a new setting. They established a house church in Corinth from which they effectively used their time in exile (see 1 Cor. 16:19). By the time Paul wrote his letter to the Roman church (between 55 and 58 C.E.), the couple had returned to the imperial capital; in this letter, Paul included greetings to Aquila and Priscilla, acknowledging their long and significant ministry (Rom. 16:3).

Paul had much in common with this couple. All three were recent immigrants, they were Hellenistic Jewish Christians, and they held a trade in common as tentmakers. As a rabbi, Paul was expected to support himself and to offer his teaching without charge (1 Corinthians 9, especially v. 18). Therefore, Paul worked daily with his hands, but on the sabbath he would sit in the synagogue and teach Jews and Gentiles gathered there.

By the time Silas and Timothy arrived in Corinth, Paul was deeply engaged in proclaiming to the Jews that the Messiah was Jesus. When the Jews rejected his message, Paul responded in kind. He ceremoniously (shaking the dust out of his clothing; Acts 13:51) and formally (using a formula similar to the curse in 2 Samuel 1:16—"Your blood be on your head"; see Matt. 27:25) repudiated the Jews of Corinth, declaring that he will now work among the Gentiles. It is certainly not the case that Paul has turned his back on Judaism in general; he continued to work in synagogues (Acts 18:19; 19:8; Romans 9—11 details Paul's agonizing discussion about God's concern for his Jewish brothers and sisters). Rather, Paul left this particular synagogue and went next door to the house of one of the congregation's Gentile God-fearers, Titius Justus.

Luke also mentions Crispus, who must have been a significant convert to Christianity. The NRSV understates his position. More than an "official" of the synagogue, he is the "leader, ruler, or chief of the synagogue" (v. 8). The NRSV of the next half of this verse presents even more of a problem. The NRSV indicates that Paul's preaching was the reason that many Corinthians became believers. That may have been the case, but the Greek text says nothing about Paul here. Rather, the text indicates that when the Corinthians heard about the conversion of Crispus, many of them became believers. In his letter to the Corinthians, Paul, with a hint of pride, reminded the church that he himself baptized Crispus (1 Cor. 1:14). The conversion of a synagogue president would have made a significant impact on the Jewish community in Corinth.

Finally, Paul was encouraged through a dream to speak out even more boldly in Corinth. Paul himself acknowledges that some in the Corinthian church see him as a weak presence and "his speech contemptible" (2 Cor. 10:10). Perhaps the dream reflects Paul's own adjustment to this very difficult Christian community. Or the dream may have anticipated anger from the Jewish community against Paul that eventuates in his hearing before the provincial governor, Gallio.

Paul before Gallio (Acts 18:12–17)

18:12 **But when Gallio was proconsul of Achaia, the Jews made a united attack on Paul and brought him before the tribunal.** [13] **They said, "This man is** persuading people to worship God in ways that are contrary to the law." [14] Just as Paul was about to speak, Gallio said to the Jews, "If it were a matter of crime or serious villainy, I would be justified in accepting the complaint of you Jews; [15] but since it is a matter of questions about words and names and your own law, see to it yourselves; I do not wish to be a judge of these matters." [16] And he dismissed them from the tribunal. [17] Then all of them seized Sosthenes, the official of the synagogue, and beat him in front of the tribunal. But Gallio paid no attention to any of these things.

Sometime during his stay of eighteen months in Corinth, Paul was brought by an angry mob to Gallio, the proconsul of Achaia. From an inscription found at Delphi we know that Gallio was proconsul at Achaia in 51–52 C.E. This evidence has been valuable in helping to establish a chronology for Paul's activities (see the Introduction).

The charge against Paul was clear: "This man is persuading the people to worship God in ways that are contrary to the law" (v. 13). This is a charge that will be repeated later in Jerusalem (21:28). It was loosely related to a Roman law that forbade the teaching of "new religious doctrines . . . by which the minds of men are influenced" (Paulus, *Sentences* 5.21.12). Gallio, however, seemed impatient with the charge. Perhaps he thought it was frivolous and did not want to waste time with such pettiness. Roman law was designed, in part, to protect the majesty of Rome. As long as the civic cults were well maintained and not threatened, governors were not likely to interfere with the practices of small indigenous religious associations. Quite accurately Gallio judged that this was not a matter of Roman law, but of Jewish law—"your own law" (v. 15). He offered his own stereotypic view of Judaism as a religion primarily concerned with "words and names and your own law." It is interesting to note that Christianity was not yet distinguished from Judaism. As long as Christianity remained a sect of Judaism it was protected by Roman law as a legitimate religion. Toward the end of the first century, when Christianity and Judaism finally went separate and distinct ways, Christians found themselves belonging to a religion without statutory protection.

As soon as the case was dismissed, a miniriot broke out right in front of Gallio's judgment bench ("tribunal"). In the fracas, the mob (it is impossible to tell from the text whether the mob was composed of Jews or Greeks, though there is some manuscript evidence for the latter; see NRSV Marginal note at v. 17) grabbed Sosthenes and beat him up while Gallio looked on disinterestedly; some ancient manuscripts read, "Gallio pretended not to see."

The identity of Sosthenes has been a subject of speculation by readers of Acts. We are told that he, like Crispus (v. 8), was a leader of the synagogue.

Was he Crispus's successor? Was he a fellow leader with Crispus? Was he a Jewish Christian (see 1 Corinthians 1:1, where Paul presents him as coauthor of the letter)? Whatever the case may be, Sosthenes was either beaten up by an anti-Semitic mob of Gentiles, or by fellow Jews who were outraged (1) that he sided with Paul or (2) that he as their leader did not present a strong enough case against Paul.

Paul appears to have been unaffected by the hearing and its aftermath. According to Luke, he continued to stay in Corinth "for a considerable time" (v. 18). In those eighteen months Paul developed one of the liveliest and strongest churches of the first century, and, as we know from reading Paul's letters to the Corinthians, a church burdened with all manner of difficulties from serious challenge to Paul's authority to divisive internal partisanship, from harmful inequities between rich and poor to hurtful relationships between the sexes—stresses and strains that reveal the complexity and the vitality of a truly cosmopolitan church.

PAUL RETURNS TO ANTIOCH
Acts 18:18–22

> 18:18 **After staying there for a considerable time, Paul said farewell to the believers and sailed for Syria, accompanied by Priscilla and Aquila. At Cenchreae he had his hair cut, for he was under a vow.** [19] **When they reached Ephesus, he left them there, but first he himself went into the synagogue and had a discussion with the Jews.** [20] **When they asked him to stay longer, he declined; but on taking leave of them, he said, "I will return to you, if God wills." Then he set sail from Ephesus.**
> [22] **When he landed at Caesarea, he went up to Jerusalem and greeted the church, and then went down to Antioch.**

According to Luke, the trio of tentmakers made their way to Cenchreae, the eastern port of Corinth, where they would set sail for Ephesus across the Aegean Sea. Before embarking, however, Paul had his hair cut as a sign that he had taken a vow. From antiquity, the Israelites had an order of holy men called Nazirites (see Judg. 13:4–5; Amos 2:11–12) who vowed never to drink wine or cut their hair. It was also possible to take this vow as a temporary measure (Num. 6:1–21). Usually one's hair was cut at the onset of the vow, though Paul's action might also indicate the completion of time under the Nazirite vow. By this action Luke probably intended to illustrate that Paul was extraordinarily faithful to Judaism and that he was going through a process of purification in anticipation for the journey to Jerusalem.

From Cenchreae the three missionaries sailed to Ephesus where they parted company. Priscilla and Aquila remained in Ephesus while Paul went on to Jerusalem (v. 19). These travel verses are quite terse. Luke inserts parenthetically that Paul visited the synagogue at Ephesus before departing for Jerusalem, and he merely "greeted the church" in Jerusalem before returning to his mission headquarters in Antioch. Luke's record of Paul's second missionary journey has come to an abrupt ending.

9. Paul's Third Missionary Journey
Acts 18:23–21:16

APOLLOS IN EPHESUS AND CORINTH
Acts 18:23–28

18:23 **After spending some time there he departed and went from place to place through the region of Galatia and Phrygia, strengthening all the disciples.** [24] **Now there came to Ephesus a Jew named Apollos, a native of Alexandria. He was an eloquent man, well-versed in the scriptures.** [25] **He had been instructed in the Way of the Lord; and he spoke with burning enthusiasm and taught accurately the things concerning Jesus, though he knew only the baptism of John.** [26] **He began to speak boldly in the synagogue; but when Priscilla and Aquila heard him, they took him aside and explained the Way of God to him more accurately.** [27] **And when he wished to cross over to Achaia, the believers encouraged him and wrote to the disciples to welcome him. On his arrival he greatly helped those who through grace had become believers,** [28] **for he powerfully refuted the Jews in public, showing by the scriptures that the Messiah is Jesus.**

We are about to join Paul on his third missionary journey. Paul's first journey focused on the province of Galatia in Asia Minor, and the second brought Paul and his message farther westward, to Greece. The third journey will be Paul's most extensive, revisiting churches he had established, but spending the bulk of his time in Ephesus. This journey begins in Syrian Antioch.

Luke notes that after resting in Antioch, Paul revisited the churches of Galatia and Phrygia (see 16:6). At this point Luke leaves Paul to introduce the reader to another Christian missionary—Apollos. Like Paul, Apollos was a Jew and a son of high Hellenic culture. Luke indicates that Apollos was "well-versed in the scriptures." By this Luke means that Apollos not only knew biblical content, but that he was also, like Paul, a master of biblical interpretation. However, whereas Paul learned his interpretive tools

174

from the rabbis of Jerusalem, Apollos was influenced by a method of biblical interpretation associated with the Alexandrian school.

From the third century B.C.E. there had been in Alexandria, Egypt, a community of Jews vitally concerned to relate scriptures to Greek culture. Perhaps the most famous exponent of the dialogue between Greek philosophy and Jewish scriptural tradition was Philo of Alexandria, a contemporary of Apollos, Paul, and Luke. Philo developed a method of biblical interpretation that relied heavily on allegory to bridge the gap between Jewish biblical tradition and Greek philosophy. The literal words of Moses (or most any other biblical text) may be understood to have a higher (spiritual) meaning that can be discovered by use of allegory. For example, scripture often speaks of "the face of God." Philo concluded that a literal (and physiological) reading of this phrase renders a finite God who needs body parts. Therefore, it might be better to interpret "the face of God" figuratively—"the face of God" means that God is omnipresent. God has the face of the supreme monarch from whom no soul can hide.

It may be that in Apollos we have a link between Philo's famous Hellenistic Jewish school of Alexandria and the influential Christian catechetical school of Alexandria headed by Pantaenus, Clement, and Origen (second and third centuries C.E.). The latter was a particularly elegant exponent of allegorical biblical interpretation.

In keeping with this scholarly tradition, Apollos of Alexandria is described as eloquent and well-versed in scriptures. Perhaps he, too, had mastered the allegorical method. Apollos had also been "instructed [the same word used of Theophilus in Luke's introduction; Luke 1:4] in the Way of the Lord" (v. 25). Furthermore, he taught "accurately" (again, the same word Luke used in his introduction) the things concerning Jesus. Presumably, as a teacher from Alexandria his principal method of teaching about Jesus would have been through allegorical interpretation of scripture. Many commentators, including Martin Luther, have suggested that Apollos may have been the author of Hebrews, with its heavy use of allegorical-typological Christology.

As well-educated as Apollos was, however, Priscilla and Aquila (see comments on 18:1–17) found his teaching deficient. In Luke's narrative, the couple politely took Apollos aside and explained the Word of God "*more* accurately." Presumably, the deficient part of his teaching had to do with baptism, for "he knew only the baptism of John," a baptism of repentance (v. 25). The passage indicates that Apollos "spoke with burning enthusiasm," literally "a burning spirit" (the Holy Spirit?). Had he not linked Christian baptism with the Holy Spirit? Did Priscilla and Aquila inform him that Christian baptism was done in the name of Jesus (not John), and that Christian baptism was related to the Holy Spirit (not repentance)? This confusion about baptism emerges again in Acts 19, and I return to the issue there.

When Apollos finally got his theology straight, he went to Corinth with the blessing of the Ephesian church. In Corinth, he continued Paul's mission, "showing by the scriptures that the Messiah was Jesus" (see 18:5; also see 1 Corinthians 3:1–9 for Paul's own discussion of Apollos's role in the Corinthian Christian community).

PAUL'S MISSION TO EPHESUS
Acts 19:1–41

Paul and the Twelve Disciples of Ephesus (Acts 19:1–7)

> 19:1 **While Apollos was in Corinth, Paul passed through the interior regions and came to Ephesus, where he found some disciples.** [2] **He said to them, "Did you receive the Holy Spirit when you became believers?" They replied, "No, we have not even heard that there is a Holy Spirit."** [3] **Then he said, "Into what then were you baptized?" They answered, "Into John's baptism."** [4] **Paul said, "John baptized with the baptism of repentance, telling the people to believe in the one who was to come after him, that is, in Jesus."** [5] **On hearing this, they were baptized in the name of the Lord Jesus.** [6] **When Paul had laid his hands on them, the Holy Spirit came upon them, and they spoke in tongues and prophesied—** [7] **altogether there were about twelve of them.**

This is a strange story that introduces us to Paul's lengthy ministry in Ephesus (the fourth largest city in the empire and the cultural and religious center of Asia Minor). Paul had already visited this city (18:19), and Priscilla and Aquila had remained there to develop a Christian community. Upon Paul's return, he came upon some "disciples." Ordinarily, this term identifies Christians, and in this context it could refer to Christians who had been taught by Apollos during the time when "he knew only the baptism of John" (18:25). One would need to ask why they too, along with Apollos, did not come under the influence of the "more accurate" teaching of Priscilla and Aquila? These "disciples" may well have been disciples of John the Baptist, members of a movement that existed side by side with Christians during the first century; in his Gospel, Luke referred to John's followers as "disciples" (see Luke 5:33; 7:18, 29; 11:1).

Paul's instruction seems to suppose that his hearers are John's disciples: "John baptized with the baptism of repentance, telling the people to believe in the one who was to come after him, that is, in Jesus" (v. 4). This sounds like a snippet of ancient pro-Christian and/or anti-Baptist polemic (see 13:24–25; also John 1:19–34). After hearing Paul, they were baptized in the name of Jesus and received the Holy Spirit through the hands of Paul. Luke has offered a significant afterthought—there were "about twelve of them" (Luke uses the indefinite term "about" before all numbers; 2:41; 4:4; 5:7, 36; 10:3; 13:18, 20; 19:7, 34). This certainly would remind the reader of the original "twelve disciples" of Jesus (Luke 6:13). In this passage, Jesus has gained twelve new disciples—John's "twelve disciples."

Paul Separates from the Synagogue in Ephesus (Acts 19:8–10)

> **19:8 He entered the synagogue and for three months spoke out boldly, and argued persuasively about the kingdom of God. 9 When some stubbornly refused to believe and spoke evil of the Way before the congregation, he left them, taking the disciples with him, and argued daily in the lecture hall of Tyrannus. 10 This continued for two years, so that all the residents of Asia, both Jews and Greeks, heard the word of the Lord.**

Paul's mission to Ephesus follows the pattern of other cities where he worked (Pisidian Antioch, 13:13–52; Corinth, 18:1–17). After a series of discussions in the synagogue, he is met with resistance, and he leaves the synagogue taking new Christians with him. Often Paul is quickly forced to leave town. This time, however, Paul was able to pursue his missionary work for an exceptionally long time—two years and three months.

According to Luke, he spoke daily in the hall of Tyrannus. The NRSV translates "lecture hall" from the Greek *schole* (which did not mean "school" as we know that word); the term means "spare time, leisure, or rest," and those things that take place during leisure time—attending lectures and learned discussions. Some students take this word literally and snooze during classes. It is unknown whether Tyrannus was a famous lecturer, owner of the hall, or "Tyrannus Hall" was simply the name of the building. The NRSV marginal note for 19:9 points to some manuscripts which read that Paul was occupied in discussions "from eleven o'clock in the morning to four in the afternoon," in other words, during the "off hours" when most people would be eating and taking a long afternoon nap. The scribe who initiated this manuscript tradition assumed that Paul worked at his trade from sunup to eleven A.M., spoke in the (rented?) hall during the early afternoon, and then resumed making tents into the evening.

It may be that Luke has ended this scene as he has others—with a bit of exaggeration. "*All* the residents of Asia, both Jews and Greeks, heard the word of the Lord." Luke may be reflecting the fact that Ephesus was the center of trade between Asia Minor to the east and the western Roman Empire. "All Asia" did indeed come to this great city and many Asians may have heard Paul during their leisure time, some becoming believers and taking the seeds of Christianity with them to such towns as Smyrna, Pergamum, Thyatira, Sardis, Philadelphia, Laodicea where early Christian communities are known to have existed (Revelation 1—3). Churches at Colossae and Hierapolis may also have been founded during this period of time.

During this two-year period (ca. 53–55 C.E.), Paul also wrote a series of letters to the church at Corinth, and squeezed in a quick visit to that community. In that correspondence he indicates that he had suffered considerable persecution at Ephesus (1 Cor. 15:32; 2 Cor. 1:8). Some scholars have suggested that during his stay in Ephesus, Paul also wrote to the churches of Galatia and Philippi, as well as the personal letter to Philemon (perhaps Philemon's runaway slave, Onesimus, had planned to "disappear" in the city of Ephesus; eventually Onesimus found his way to Paul and the Christian message).

Miracles and Magic:
Paul and the Sons of Sceva (Acts 19:11–20)

19:11 **God did extraordinary miracles through Paul,** [12] **so that when the handkerchiefs or aprons that had touched his skin were brought back to the sick, their diseases left them, and the evil spirits came out of them.** [13] **Then some itinerant Jewish exorcists tried to use the name of the Lord Jesus over those who had evil spirits, saying, "I adjure you by the Jesus whom Paul proclaims."** [14] **Seven sons of a Jewish high priest named Sceva were doing this.** [15] **But the evil spirit said to them in reply, "Jesus I know, and Paul I know; but who are you?"** [16] **Then the man with the evil spirit leaped on them, mastered them all, and so overpowered them that they fled out of the house naked and wounded.** [17] **When this became known to all residents of Ephesus, both Jews and Greeks, everyone was awestruck; and the name of the Lord Jesus was praised.** [18] **Also many of those who became believers confessed and disclosed their practices.** [19] **A number of those who practiced magic collected their books and burned them publicly; when the value of these books was calculated, it was found to come to fifty thousand silver coins.** [20] **So the word of the Lord grew mightily and prevailed.**

Ephesus was a significant center of magical arts in the ancient world. To be called an Ephesian was synonymous with magician, and magical books were called Ephesian scriptures.

In Acts, Luke seems particularly interested in distinguishing between miracle and magic, a distinction that was not always obvious to people of antiquity. Several magical texts have survived the centuries which contain divine names, including Yahweh and Jesus, in the incantations. The question must have been raised in the early church: What about these non-Christian healers running around attempting to cure people in the name of Jesus? Who has the right to use the divine name and the power inherent in that name? For Luke (as for all early Christians), there must have been a fine line between invocation and incantation, miracle and magic.

The stories of miracles performed by Peter (his shadow heals the sick) and Paul (cloth that touches his skin has the power to effect cures) may seem fantastic; Luke has intended them to be so. One way for Luke to make the distinction between miracle and magic is by measuring divine power in comparative terms. His purpose with such stories is to show that the power of (and behind) Peter and Paul is greater than the power of ordinary magicians. The existence of other healers and wonder workers is not denied; ancient literature abounds with stories of their amazing exploits. Yet for Luke, and for the early church, they are simply not in the same league as the apostles of Jesus. Every time a follower of Jesus encounters a famous magician, the magician is bettered and humiliated: Simon, who passed himself off as a god, stood quaking before Peter (8:9ff.); Elymas was temporarily blinded by Paul (13:6ff.); and now *seven* magicians who invoked the name of Jesus are pummeled by the man from whom they tried to exorcise an evil spirit, and they run away wounded and naked (19:13ff.).

In the story of Peter and Simon Magus, the magician offered to purchase the right to use Peter's source of power. Peter bluntly refused Simon's offer and gave him a stinging rebuke instead. In the story of Paul and the sons of Sceva, the magician-sons do not even ask to purchase the source of Paul's power; they simply try to usurp it. If one cannot purchase God's gift, then why not just take it? Having observed Paul perform "extraordinary miracles," they seek to imitate him by calling on the name of Jesus during their exorcisms. Yet, even the evil spirit immediately realizes that they have no legitimate claim to Jesus' name. The spirit knows Jesus; it even knows Paul. With a touch of humor, the spirit (like the caterpillar in *Alice in Wonderland*) asks the magicians, "But *who* are *you?*" Even such self-important figures as sons of a Jewish high priest are unknown by this evil spirit. (NOTE: Sceva is not the name of any high priest in Jewish history. Luke may intend the reader to understand that these men were not just itinerant riffraff, but highly respected Jewish exorcists, sons of aristocracy, perhaps even related to a high priest.) These aristocratic magicians flee from Paul, humiliated, beaten, and stripped naked by the very spirit they tried to exorcise.

The awesome power of God cannot be purchased or usurped. It is God's gift. The Ephesians take heed and are "awestruck" by what they have just witnessed. Whereas these Ephesians might have been tempted to use the name of Jesus in incantation, now "the name of the Lord Jesus was praised"—a proper, and certainly more prudent, use of this divine name! Many who became Christians "confessed and disclosed their [former magical] practices." Those magicians who became Christian believers gathered their magic books and burned them in the town square. It must have been a brilliant bonfire of books that lit the evening sky. Books worth fifty thousand silver coins would be equivalent to fifty thousand days' wages going up in smoke (about five million dollars!). That the books of incantations were disposed of by burning is significant. One might have expected these former magicians to bury their texts. To burn such books was thought by some to release into the air the spirits and powers embedded in the text. By their action these new Christians deny that there is any power whatsoever inherent in the pages of these Ephesian scriptures.

Paul's Travel Plans (Acts 19:21–22)

> 19:21 **Now after these things had been accomplished, Paul resolved in the Spirit to go through Macedonia and Achaia, and then to go on to Jerusalem. He said, "After I have gone there, I must also see Rome."** 22 **So he sent two of his helpers, Timothy and Erastus, to Macedonia, while he himself stayed for some time longer in Asia.**

Paul would like to revisit the churches in Greece before returning to Jerusalem. The real goal of his journeys, however, is Rome. "After I have gone there, I *must* also see Rome." This is not any ordinary "must"; Paul is not saying, "I really want to make that trip to Rome!" Rather, the Greek word *dei* is a theological term that indicates a divine imperative. It is God's will that Paul must go to Rome. Luke is fond of this small but significant word. He used *dei* in his Gospel to explain why Jesus met with such great suffering (Luke 9:22; 17:25; 24:7, 26, 44–46). In the book of Acts, Luke used the term to explain that Paul came to Rome in accordance with divine necessity (Acts 19:21; 23:11; 27:24).

However, before he reaches Rome, Paul wants to pay another visit to the churches he founded in Greece. To prepare the way in Greece, Paul sent Timothy and Erastus as an advance party. We know that Timothy did sail to Corinth and returned quickly with bad news about conditions in the church there (1 Cor. 4:17). This was followed by a short trip made by Paul in a futile attempt to heal the growing rift between him and the Corinthian congregation. This quick trip is unrecorded in Acts. Nor did Luke acknowledge the real reason for the advance party to Greece: to gather from the churches of Greece and Asia Minor a monetary gift which Paul would bring to the Jerusalem community as a tangible sign of unity among all the churches of Christ (1 Cor. 16:1–9; 2 Corinthians 8—9; Rom. 15:25–29). Luke's failure to mention this collection is seen by some as a significant omission in his account of the acts of Paul, and it is one of those items that lends support to those who question the contention that the author of Acts was a close friend and companion of Paul (also see 20:1–6 and 21:1–16; however, in Acts 24:17 Luke does acknowledge that Paul "brought alms to [his] nation." Luke may have known about the collection; it was just not terribly important to his story).

The Riot in Ephesus (Acts 19:23–41)

19:23 **About that time no little disturbance broke out concerning the Way. **[24]** A man named Demetrius, a silversmith who made silver shrines of Artemis, brought no little business to the artisans. **[25]** These he gathered together, with the workers of the same trade, and said, "Men, you know that we get our wealth from our business. **[26]** You also see and hear that not only in Ephesus but in almost the whole of Asia this Paul has persuaded and drawn away a considerable number of people by saying that gods made with hands are not gods. **[27]** And there is danger not only that this trade of ours may come into disrepute but also that the temple of the great goddess Artemis will be scorned, and she will be deprived of her majesty that brought all Asia and the world to worship her."**

[28] When they heard this, they were enraged and shouted, "Great is Artemis of the Ephesians!" **[29]** The city was filled with confusion; and people rushed together to the theater, dragging with them Gaius and Aristarchus, Macedonians who were Paul's travel companions. **[30]** Paul wished to go into the crowd, but the disciples would not let him; **[31]** even some officials of the province of Asia, who were friendly to him, sent him a message urging him not to venture into the theater. **[32]** Meanwhile, some were shouting one thing, some another; for the assembly was in confusion, and most of them**

did not know why they had come together. [33] Some of the crowd gave instructions to Alexander, whom the Jews had pushed forward. And Alexander motioned for silence and tried to make a defense before the people. [34] But when they recognized that he was a Jew, for about two hours all of them shouted in unison, "Great is Artemis of the Ephesians!" [35] But when the town clerk had quieted the crowd, he said, "Citizens of Ephesus, who is there that does not know that the city of the Ephesians is the temple keeper of the great Artemis and of the statue that fell from heaven?" [36] Since these things cannot be denied, you ought to be quiet and do nothing rash. [37] You have brought these men here who are neither temple robbers nor blasphemers of our goddess. [38] If therefore Demetrius and the artisans with him have a complaint against anyone, the courts are open, and there are proconsuls; let them bring charges there against one another. [39] If there is anything further you want to know, it must be settled in the regular assembly. [40] For we are in danger of being charged with rioting today, since there is no cause that we can give to justify this commotion." [41] When he had said this, he dismissed the assembly.

Before Paul left Ephesus, a major dispute erupted between the Way and the non-Christian Greeks of the city. The dispute focused on the principal divinity in Ephesus, Artemis (Diana, in Roman mythology). In Ephesian theology, Artemis was earth mother and the goddess of fertility. It is possible that her image was first "seen" (through vivid imagination) in a meteorite ("the statue that fell from heaven"; v. 35) that was preserved in a temple constructed for the goddess. Possession of the heavenly relic put Ephesus on the religious map as the center for worship of this fertility deity. Pilgrims from all over the empire would come to worship at her shrine, praying for their own fertility and prosperity. Luke records the cry of the crowd, "Great is Artemis of the Ephesians!"—a familiar rousing ceremonial shout of praise to the goddess.

Quite naturally, businessmen and businesswomen in the city found a way to capitalize on this flow of traffic to the temple. A considerable enterprise emerged which involved manufacturing miniature temples and statuettes that were cast in precious metals, polished, and sold as souvenirs, votive offerings, and charms. An entire industry depended on a steady flow of worshipers to the shrine, eager to purchase a little silver temple to take home to show their friends or to use as a centerpiece for private worship.

Demetrius, a spokesman for the silversmiths, became alarmed because business had seriously declined since the arrival of Paul. Perhaps pilgrims visiting the shrine at Ephesus also stopped by the hall of Tyrannus to hear this interesting Jewish-Christian rabbi. According to Demetrius, part of Paul's message was that "gods made with hands are not gods" (v. 26). Demetrius concluded that this message not only cut into business so severely that the silversmith industry might collapse (why buy these useless silver souvenirs?), but the cult of Artemis itself might be jeopardized. His self-serving argument is thinly veiled: "She will be deprived of her majesty that brought all Asia and the world to worship her" (v. 27). The last part of this phrase held the real threat. If people stop coming to Ephesus to visit the shrine, they will stop buying the wares of the silversmiths. Demetrius rightly discerned that Paul's message was a threat to Ephesian theology and economy.

Realizing what was at stake, the silversmiths were whipped into a frenzy, which also infected other members of the community, until a great mob came running to the amphitheater (which could hold about twenty-five thousand people), dragging with them two of Paul's travel companions—Gaius and Aristarchus. Paul himself was warned away from the theater, even by officials of the province.

Luke offers a picture of total chaos in the amphitheater, so much so that most people had no idea why they were there. Even Demetrius, having started the mess, has disappeared from view. Apparently, the crowd sensed that the issue had something to do with the relationship between theology and economics. It also had something to do with the preaching of the Jewish-Christian rabbi, Paul. Jews probably felt threatened and wished to distance themselves from Christians in the matter. They asked Alexander to make a statement on their behalf, but he was not even allowed to speak. The devotees of Artemis would have realized that Alexander's own theology regarding the goddess would not have been much different from Paul's! And so they shouted him down.

Even two millennia later, one can still hear the echo of twenty-five thousand people shouting in unison for two hours: "Great is Artemis of the Ephesians!" It was Super Bowl Sunday for Artemis.

The town clerk finally managed to quiet the crowd and offered an elegant, cautionary little speech. His advice was simple: Since the evidence of the existence of Artemis is undeniable—after all, they had solid evidence in the form of her image from heaven—"you ought to be quiet and do nothing rash" (v. 36). He concluded that Paul's companions were neither temple robbers nor blasphemers. Paul's theological ramblings in the hall of Tyrannus could not dispute the hard evidence enshrined in the temple to Artemis. The town clerk was smart enough to realize that the real problem had to do with economics, not theology, and Demetrius apparently did not have the courage to pursue that issue. With good Roman sensibility, the clerk reminded the crowd that if Demetrius or any other artisan would like to bring suit against Paul in order to enjoin him from interfering in the local economy, "the courts are open, and there are proconsuls" (v. 38). Otherwise, there was a regular assembly of the people held three times a month for rational resolution of such matters. Finally, the clerk cautioned the crowd that they themselves were in danger of being charged under Roman law with disturbing the peace, and he strongly warned them that their riotous behavior was unwarranted. With this, the crowd was dismissed.

Once again, Luke, through his narration of Paul's mission, has raised an important ethical issue, an issue that pervades all cultures including our own. By now one should be suspicious of the connection between popular religion (in its various guises from televangelism to professional sports) and economics. Paul's message invites us to seek the God beyond the gods of religion—those "gods made with hands." This is a dangerous message because it shakes one's faith in familiar social structures.

The call to discover the God beyond the gods of religion is as old as the story of Moses leading the Children of Israel out of Egypt where the Israelites had a well-defined (and according to the Egyptian pharaoh, a divinely ordained) place in the economy—as slaves! With God's help, they escaped from Egypt and claimed their freedom. Yet they remained slaves to the religious-economic ideology which they carried into the wilderness. Feeling adrift and anxious in unfamiliar surroundings, the children of Israel constructed a golden calf. While they had escaped slavery, they were still in bondage to the power of Egypt's popular religion that promised fertility and productivity, a religion that promised economic blessing. So the Israelites made a golden calf, a symbol of the Egyptian goddess of fertility, and raised the rallying cry, "These are your gods!" (Exod. 32:4). Thirteen centuries later, the Ephesians were still shouting, "Great is Artemis!"

In his story about Paul and Demetrius, Luke has subtly revisited the connection between religion and economics. The Ephesians worshiped silver statues of Artemis, the Asian goddess of fertility and productivity. Demetrius rightly saw the connection between religion and economics, and who stands to lose if this connection is disturbed. But Paul broke the illusion that faith and fertility are linked. Demetrius correctly understood the economic-religious threat in Paul's message: "In almost the whole of Asia this Paul has persuaded and drawn away a considerable number of people by saying that gods made with hands are not gods" (v. 26). Luke encourages the reader of this story to question the alliance between economics and religion, and to seek God who transcends all religion.

PAUL VISITS CHURCHES HE HAD ESTABLISHED IN GREECE AND ASIA
Acts 20:1–6

20:1 **After the uproar had ceased, Paul sent for the disciples; and after encouraging them and saying farewell, he left for Macedonia. ² When he had gone through those regions and had given the believers much encouragement, he came to Greece, ³ where he stayed for three months. He was about to set sail for Syria when a plot was made against him by the Jews, and so he decided to return through Macedonia. ⁴ He was accompanied by Sopater son of Pyrrhus from Beroea, by Aristarchus and Secundus from Thessalonica, by Gaius from Derbe, and by Timothy, as well as Tychicus and Trophimus from Asia. ⁵ They went ahead and were waiting for us in Troas; ⁶ but we sailed from Philippi after the days of Unleavened Bread, and in five days we joined them in Troas, where we stayed for seven days.**

In these six short verses, Luke has compressed a significant journey of Paul. After the riot in Ephesus—

1. Paul sailed across the Aegean Sea from Asia to Macedonia, visiting again the cities of Philippi, Thessalonica, and Beroea. During this time Titus came to Paul with good news from the church at Corinth which prompted Paul to write a letter to that church (many scholars suggest that 2 Corinthians 1—9 comprises Paul's "letter of reconciliation").
2. Then Paul traveled south to "Greece" (synonymous with Achaia in this passage). It is likely that he spent the three months working with the Corinthian congregation to heal the wounds opened by bitter debate between the apostle and this church (see 2 Corinthians 10—13). It was from Corinth that Paul wrote his letter to the Romans (see Rom. 15:22–29).
3. Paul had planned to sail from Corinth across the Mediterranean to Syria in order to reach Jerusalem in time for Passover. But having learned of a plot against him, Paul chose to travel back to Macedonia.
4. Finally, Paul sailed from Philippi to Troas in Asia Minor. Once in Asia Minor, he traveled along the Mediterranean coast from Troas to Patara, where he set sail for Syria with the hope of being in Jerusalem in time for Pentecost (Acts 20:13–21:1).

Luke also lists members of Paul's entourage—representatives from the churches of Greece and Asia Minor who will accompany Paul back to Jerusalem. While Luke has identified each member of the party, he curiously leaves out the reason for this gathering and their purpose for traveling with Paul. They were representatives of Paul's missionary churches bringing a collection gathered from these churches for the "saints at Jerusalem" (2 Corinthians 8 and 9; also see comments on at 19:21–22, 21:1–16, and 24:17).

It may also be the case that the author of Acts is letting the reader know that he too has rejoined the entourage by resuming the first-person plural pronoun, "us . . . we" (vv. 5–6). Perhaps Luke remained in Philippi after Paul left that city at the request of the magistrates (16:39–40; the prior occurrence of the we passage narrates the mission to Philippi, 16:10–17). Now Luke rejoins Paul as a representative of the Philippian church.

PAUL'S (ALMOST) DEADLY SERMON
Acts 20:7–12

> 20:7 **On the first day of the week, when we met to break bread, Paul was holding a discussion with them; since he intended to leave the next day, he continued speaking until midnight. 8 There were many lamps in the room upstairs where we were meeting. 9 A young man named Eutychus, who was sitting in the window, began to sink off into a deep sleep while Paul talked still longer. Overcome by sleep, he fell to the ground three floors below and was picked up dead. 10 But Paul went down, and bending over him took him in his arms, and said, "Do not be alarmed, for his life is in him." 11 Then Paul went upstairs, and after he had broken bread and eaten, he continued to converse with them until dawn; then he left. 12 Meanwhile they had taken the boy away alive and were not a little comforted.**

Once again, Luke has given his reader a slice of life in the early Christian community—a description of the community gathered for worship on a Sunday evening. "The first day of the week"—Sunday, the day of Jesus' resurrection, would not have been a day free from work as it is for many people today. Therefore, Christians gathered for worship early in the morning, or in the evening, or at both times. The "breaking of bread" may indicate an ordinary meal or the Lord's Supper. Luke's combination of these two details—"the first day of the week . . . we met to break bread"—leads one to assume that the community is gathered for worship.

Luke's additional descriptive detail—"there were many lamps in the room"—is a nice touch. It was no doubt quite difficult for a young man, relaxing on a window ledge after a long day of work, to keep his eyes open in the soft glow of lamplight on this warm spring night. As the hours rolled on, sleep finally overwhelmed Eutychus and he fell out of the third-story window.

The surprised worshipers rushed downstairs to find the young man dead. Paul also hurried down and embraced him. From the text it is difficult to tell if Eutychus really was dead and Paul had performed a miracle like that of Peter raising Tabitha (9:36ff.), or if he only had the wind knocked out of him. The ambiguity may also be due to Paul's statement: "Do not be alarmed, for his life is in him" (v. 10).

When the excitement finally died down, Paul and the congregation walked back upstairs to resume their conversation. While Paul continued to speak to the gathering (until dawn five hours later!), the young man was taken home by his relieved friends.

PAUL'S JOURNEY FROM TROAS TO MILETUS
Acts 20:13–16

20:13 We went ahead to the ship and set sail for Assos, intending to take Paul on board there; for he had made this arrangement, intending to go by land himself. 14 When he met us in Assos, we took him on board and went to Mitylene. 15 We sailed from there, and on the following day we arrived opposite Chios. The next day we touched at Samos, and the day after that we came to Miletus. 16 For Paul had decided to sail past Ephesus, so that he might not have to spend time in Asia; he was eager to be in Jerusalem, if possible, on the day of Pentecost.

Once again we sense that we are reading from a travel diary. In order to keep track of Paul's route from Troas to Miletus, it will be helpful to consult a map of the Mediterranean world.

Paul made the first part of the journey by himself traveling twenty miles on foot, from Troas to Assos. At Assos, he rejoined his companions aboard ship and sailed along the coast until they reached Miletus.

Luke notes that Paul decided not to disembark at Ephesus, a port of call along the way. A visit with his friends at Ephesus would have been time-consuming and he wanted to be in Jerusalem in time to celebrate Pentecost, about five weeks away. Paul may have had another motive for declining a visit to Ephesus; he may have been afraid for his life. He had recently written to the Corinthians "of the affliction that we experienced in Asia; for we were so utterly, unbearably crushed that we despaired of life itself. Indeed, we felt that we had received the sentence of death" (2 Cor. 1:8–9). The riot in Ephesus may have been more severe than Luke acknowledged (Acts 19:23–41). Therefore, Paul chose to have the elders of the Ephesian church come to him in Miletus.

PAUL'S FAREWELL SPEECH
TO THE EPHESIAN ELDERS
Acts 20:17–38

20:17 **From Miletus he sent a message to Ephesus, asking the elders of the church to meet him.** [18] **When they came to him, he said to them:**

"You yourselves know how I lived among you the entire time from the first day that I set foot in Asia, [19] **serving the Lord with all humility and with tears, enduring the trials that came to me through the plots of the Jews.** [20] **I did not shrink from doing anything helpful, proclaiming the message to you and teaching you publicly and from house to house,** [21] **as I testified to both Jews and Greeks about repentance toward God and faith toward our Lord Jesus.** [22] **And now, as a captive to the Spirit, I am on my way to Jerusalem, not knowing what will happen to me there,** [23] **except that the Holy Spirit testifies to me in every city that imprisonment and persecutions are waiting for me.** [24] **But I do not count my life of any value to myself, if only I may finish my course and the ministry that I received from the Lord Jesus, to testify to the good news of God's grace.**

[25] **"And now I know that none of you, among whom I have gone about proclaiming the kingdom, will ever see my face again.** [26] **Therefore I declare to you this day that I am not responsible for the blood of any of you,** [27] **for I did not shrink from declaring to you the whole purpose of God.** [28] **Keep watch over yourselves and over all the flock, of which the Holy Spirit has made you overseers, to shepherd the church of God that he obtained with the blood of his own Son.** [29] **I know that after I have gone, savage wolves will come in among you, not sparing the flock.** [30] **Some even from your own group will come distorting the truth in order to entice the disciples to follow them.** [31] **Therefore be alert, remembering that for three years I did not cease night or day to warn everyone with tears.** [32] **And now I commend you to God and to the message of his grace, a message that is able to build you up and to give you the inheritance among all who are sanctified.** [33] **I coveted no one's silver or gold or clothing.** [34] **You know for yourselves that I worked with my own hands to support myself and my companions.** [35] **In all this I have given you an example that by such work we must support the weak, remembering the words of the Lord Jesus, for he himself said, 'It is more blessed to give than to receive.'"**

[36] **When he had finished speaking, he knelt down with them all and prayed.** [37] **There was much weeping among them all; they embraced Paul and**

kissed him, [38] **grieving especially because of what he had said, that they would not see him again. Then they brought him to the ship.**

Paul has sent for the leaders of the Ephesian church to meet with him in Miletus, about thirty miles away. Luke has used two terms to identify these leaders. In verse 17 they are called "elders" (*presbyteroi*); in verse 28, Luke describes them as "overseers [*episkopoi*, sometimes translated as "bishops"], to shepherd the church of God." It was not until the early second century that these offices were fixed, with presbyters subject to the authority of bishops. In Luke's time the offices were not yet distinct and the titles were used interchangeably.

Paul's speech consists of four parts. Paul begins by recalling the early days of his ministry in Ephesus (vv. 18–21). He reminds the Ephesian elders of his earnest service and of the trials which he was compelled to endure. He both preached and taught, publicly in the hall of Tyrannus and privately in house churches. Verse 21 is an extreme condensation of the content of his message: "repentance toward God and faith toward our Lord Jesus."

In the second section of the speech (vv. 22–24), Paul describes his present situation. It is his intention to travel to Jerusalem in spite of warnings given by the Holy Spirit "in every city" (actually, these are yet to happen in Tyre [21:4] and Caesarea [21:10–11]) that he faces certain danger in Jerusalem. This section closes with a foreboding note: Paul does not count his life "of any value"; his only wish is to "finish [his] course" and "testify to the good news of God's grace" (see 2 Tim. 4:6–8; in the second century the term "testify" [*martyreo*] had acquired an alternate meaning of "martyr," one who is killed because of his or her testimony as a Christian).

The third part of the speech (vv. 25–31) is an appeal for those who will take Paul's place to "keep watch," to "be alert" (vv. 28, 31). Behind this command is an ominous prediction: "I know that none of you . . . will ever see my face again" (v. 25). It is quite likely that Luke has Paul address not only the Ephesian elders, but all Christians. Luke, writing several years after Paul's death, knows that Paul is on his final journey to Jerusalem; from there he will be sent to Rome and martyrdom.

The last half of verse 28 presents the interpreter with a problem. According to the NRSV, Paul says that the church of God was "obtained with the blood of his own Son." Notice, however, the marginal note that indicates some serious problems with this passage. The better manuscripts do not contain the word "Son." What, then, is the meaning of God obtaining the church with "the blood of his own"? Who is "his own"? Readers often quite naturally assume that "his own" refers to Jesus. However, Luke may have had Paul in mind. The church of God was obtained not only through the blood of Jesus but also through the blood of Jesus' witnesses and martyrs; most notably for Luke, this means Paul. (A further consideration is the fact that Luke nowhere else describes the death of Jesus as an act of atonement. Luke considers Jesus' death to have been a miscarriage of justice. And yet, in spite of this typically human failure, God incorporated the death of Jesus into God's grand design for the salvation of the world. God had willed that Jesus, the crucified teacher from Galilee, would be God's Messiah for the world.)

Paul closes the third section of his speech with a warning to be aware of heretics who will come from without and from within the church. "Therefore be alert" (v. 31).

In the fourth and final section of this speech, Paul offers a benediction (v. 32) and a challenge to the elders (vv. 33–35). Through his work as a tentmaker, Paul has set an example for these church leaders. By working hard at their trades, they will be able to provide for themselves. More than that, they will also be able to provide for others just as Paul had been able to support his companions. Paul concludes his speech with a quote from Jesus (not found elsewhere in the New Testament): "It is more blessed to give than to receive" (v. 35).

The speech before the Ephesian elders contains numerous statements that closely resemble phrases found in Paul's letters. Though the speech is not a pastiche concocted from Pauline letters, it is the written record of one who has internalized the apostle's work and words (while Luke nowhere speaks of Paul's epistolary activity, this does not mean he was unaware of it). The speech is a summary of Paul's thinking and it is conveyed in language that is distinctly Pauline. As we noted above (Acts 16), Luke had the ability to weave Paul's theological themes into stories about Paul's mission to the Gentiles.

After Paul finished his address, he and the elders prayed together. In a poignant scene, the Ephesian elders embraced Paul and kissed him, "grieving especially because of what he had said, that they would not see him again" (v. 38).

PAUL'S JOURNEY FROM MILETUS TO JERUSALEM
Acts 21:1–16

21:1 **When we had parted from them and set sail, we came by a straight course to Cos, and the next day to Rhodes, and from there to Patara.** 2 **When** we found a ship bound for Phoenicia, we went on board and set sail. [3] We came in sight of Cyprus, and leaving it on our left, we sailed to Syria and landed at Tyre, because the ship was to unload its cargo there. [4] We looked up the disciples and stayed there for seven days. Through the Spirit they told Paul not to go on to Jerusalem. [5] When our days there were ended, we left and proceeded on our journey; and all of them, with wives and children, escorted us outside the city. There we knelt down on the beach and prayed [6] and said farewell to one another. Then we went on board the ship, and they returned home.

[7] When we had finished the voyage from Tyre, we arrived at Ptolemais; and we greeted the believers and stayed with them for one day. [8] The next day we left and came to Caesarea; and we went into the house of Philip the evangelist, one of the seven, and stayed with him. [9] He had four unmarried daughters who had the gift of prophecy. [10] While we were staying there for several days, a prophet named Agabus came down from Judea. [11] He came to us and took Paul's belt, bound his own feet and hands with it, and said, "Thus says the Holy Spirit, 'This is the way the Jews in Jerusalem will bind the man who owns this belt and will hand him over to the Gentiles.'" [12] When we heard this, we and the people there urged him not to go up to Jerusalem. [13] Then Paul answered, "What are you doing, weeping and breaking my heart? For I am ready not only to be bound but even to die in Jerusalem for the name of the Lord Jesus." [14] Since he would not be persuaded, we remained silent except to say, "The Lord's will be done."

[15] After these days we got ready and started to go up to Jerusalem. [16] Some of the disciples from Caesarea also came along and brought us to the house of Mnason of Cyprus, an early disciple, with whom we were to stay.

Again, we are privy to the travel diary that Luke had before him. In the first verse of this section Luke details the trip from Miletus to Patara, skirting the coast of Asia Minor. At Patara, Paul and his companions boarded a ship that sailed directly back to Palestine, landing at the ancient Phoenician port of Tyre where a church had been established, perhaps by refugees who fled Jerusalem during the persecution which took place after the martyrdom of Stephen (11:19). During their weeklong stay with members of this church, Paul was warned by them not to proceed to Jerusalem (see 20:23). Paul, however, chose to ignore their advice and fully intended to press on to the Holy City.

With verse 5, Luke has crafted one of the most beautiful scenes in the New Testament. A group of Christian men, women, and children of Tyre have accompanied Paul and his companions to the nearby seashore. There, in the morning sun, they knelt down on the beach, their prayers joined to the sound of waves lapping on the shore. Rising, they said farewell to one another, and the missionaries boarded a ship for Ptolemais while the Christians of Tyre returned to their homes.

The voyage along the coast from Tyre to Ptolemais was short, only about twenty-five miles. Perhaps the travelers disembarked to stay with church members for the night. The next day's trip to Caesarea was a bit longer, about forty miles, which was probably also made by ship (though Acts is not specific about this). By this time (the summer of 56 or 57 C.E.), the church in Caesarea must have become a congregation of considerable size. About two decades have rolled by since Peter first brought the gospel to the household of Cornelius (Acts 10). Luke notes that the travelers lodged with Philip the Evangelist, one of "the seven" leaders of the Hellenistic Jewish Christians (Acts 6:5). In Acts 8:40 there is a passing comment that Philip ended his travels through Samaria at this coastal city. Apparently he settled down in Caesarea and raised his family there. While Luke notes that Philip had four unmarried daughters who had a gift of prophecy, this is all he has to say about them (another interesting detail from a travel diary); one might have expected one of them to warn Paul against going to Jerusalem. Instead, this task is left to Agabus, who had recently come from Judea (see 11:28), perhaps with firsthand information about plots against Paul.

As with many of the stories in Acts, the narration of Agabus's prophetic activity draws heavily on Old Testament images. In a fashion similar to the Old Testament prophets, Agabus performs a prophetic symbolic act by tying his own hands and feet with Paul's belt (Jeremiah provides a classic example by breaking a clay pot as a symbol of the destruction of Jerusalem; Jer. 19:10–13; also see Isaiah 20; Jeremiah 13; 27; Ezekiel 4). Agabus's introduction to the interpretation of his action, "Thus says the Holy Spirit," also echoes the prophetic announcement, "Thus says the Lord." The prophetic action was not only symbolic, but it contained a divine guarantee that the event which the action portended would indeed take place. And this is the point where Agabus and the Old Testament prophets part company. Agabus's prophecy did not unfold precisely as he had predicted— that the Jews would bind Paul and hand him over to the Gentiles. In fact, events turned out to be quite the reverse. The Gentiles protected Paul from being delivered to the Jews. However, Agabus's prophecy may ultimately have been fulfilled if Paul, arrested at the instigation of the Jewish leadership in Jerusalem, eventually met his death at the hands of the imperial government in Rome.

On the heels of this prophecy, even Luke joined in the protest against Paul's plan to continue on to Jerusalem: "When we heard this, we and the people there urged him not to go up to Jerusalem" (v. 12). But Paul rejected their pleading, leaving Luke and the concerned crowd resigned to the will of God.

Finally, Paul, along with representatives from the churches of Asia and Greece and a contingent from Caesarea, left for the sixty-mile journey to Jerusalem. Since this would have been a two-day walk, scholars have conjectured that Mnason of Cyprus is mentioned because he housed the group overnight at a midpoint along the way.

Whether or not Paul made it to Jerusalem in time for Pentecost the reader is not told. Nor is the reader told the real reason for Paul's desire to get to Jerusalem—to bring a large contribution from the diaspora churches which he founded to the "saints at Jerusalem" (Rom. 15:26). This was a major project of the apostle to the Gentiles which spanned several years (Rom. 15:25–27; 1 Cor. 16:1–4; 2 Corinthians 8; 9). He had carefully orchestrated the collection and administration of this "generous undertaking for the glory of the Lord himself and to show our goodwill" (2 Cor. 8:19). It is surprising that Luke does not mention this at all! This is a significant omission that lends support to those who doubt that Luke really was a travel companion of Paul (though see comments at 19:21–22, 20:1–6, and 24:17). It has been speculated that the Jerusalem church gave Paul and his gift a cool reception, which Luke chose not to report.

With Paul's arrival in Jerusalem we come to the end of the second major block of material in the Acts of the Apostles. In the first part (Acts 1:1–12:25) Luke narrated stories about the early days of the apostolic church from Pentecost through Herod's persecution. In part two (Acts 13:1–21:16) Luke escorted the reader on Paul's three missionary journeys. In the third part (Acts 21:17–28:31), Luke will describe Paul's trials in Jerusalem which culminate in his final journey—to the heart of the empire, to Rome itself.

3. Paul's Arrest, Trial, and Journey to Rome

Acts 21:17–28:31

10. Paul on Trial (I)
Acts 21:17–23:32

PAUL'S ARRIVAL IN JERUSALEM
Acts 21:17–26

21:17 **When we arrived in Jerusalem, the brothers welcomed us warmly. 18 The next day Paul went with us to visit James; and all the elders were present. 19 After greeting them, he related one by one the things that God had done among the Gentiles through his ministry. 20 When they heard it, they praised God. Then they said to him, "You see, brother, how many thousands of believers there are among the Jews, and they are all zealous for the law. 21 They have been told about you that you teach all the Jews living among the Gentiles to forsake Moses, and that you tell them not to circumcise their children or observe the customs. 22 What then is to be done? They will certainly hear that you have come. 23 So do what we tell you. We have four men who are under a vow. 24 Join these men, go through the rite of purification with them, and pay for the shaving of their heads. Thus all will know that there is nothing in what they have been told about you, but that you yourself observe and guard the law. 25 But as for the Gentiles who have become believers, we have sent a letter with our judgment that they should abstain from what has been sacrificed to idols and from blood and from what is strangled and from fornication." 26 Then Paul took the men, and the next day, having purified himself, he entered the temple with them, making public the completion of the days of purification when the sacrifice would be made for each of them.**

With this passage, Luke begins the final section of the Acts of the Apostles (Acts 21—28). In the last eight chapters of Acts, Paul must endure trial by his own people, by his own government, and even a trial by the forces of nature as Paul makes a perilous journey to Rome. Through all of these trials God has promised protection to Paul, for it is God's will that Paul bring the good news to the center of the empire—to Rome.

Paul's trial consists of four hearings in which Paul is required to defend his calling and convictions. He is brought before

Claudius Lysias (21:40–23:30)
Antonius Felix (24:1–27)
Porcius Festus (25:6–12)
Festus, Herod Agrippa II, and Bernice (25:13–26:32).

Luke begins his narrative by bringing Paul safely back to the starting point for the mission to the Gentiles—Jerusalem. Yet, as the reader soon discovers, Jerusalem is anything but a safe city for the great Christian missionary. In short order Jesus' prophetic words will be fulfilled:

> But before [the last days], they will arrest you and persecute you; they will hand you over to synagogues and prisons, and you will be brought before kings and governors because of my name. This will give you an opportunity to testify. So make up your minds not to prepare your defense in advance; for I will give you words and a wisdom that none of your opponents will be able to withstand or contradict. (Luke 21:12–15)

On his arrival in Jerusalem, Paul was warmly greeted by members of the church. His first stop was at the home of James, the brother of Jesus and head of the Jerusalem Christian community, where he brought James and the elders up to date on the results of his missionary efforts among the Gentiles of Asia Minor and Greece. After an initial three-word positive response ("They praised God"), they relayed their deep concern about gossip being spread about Paul. Thousands of Jewish Christians, "all zealous for the law, . . . have been told about you that you teach all the Jews living among the Gentiles to forsake Moses, and that you tell them not to circumcise their children or observe the customs" (vv. 20–21).

Anyone who has been involved in any kind of organization will recognize this scenario; it is a situation that induces paranoia in most leaders and quickly puts them on the defensive. Rather than trusting and supporting Paul, the Jerusalem elders were more concerned about gossip and appearances. One can almost hear the panic in their voices as they ask, "What then is to be done? They [Jewish Christians who are zealous for the law] will certainly hear that you have come [here]." Paul the troublemaker strikes again! The warm greeting was immediately replaced by cold anxiety.

The gossip about Paul was serious indeed. He was being accused of leading fellow Jews into apostasy. And of course, as with all gossip, there was a kernel of truth to the story. From Paul's own account he did agree that it was proper for Antiochian Jewish Christians to be exempted from the food laws so that table fellowship might take place in the church (Gal. 2:12–13). But it is highly unlikely that he ever suggested to Jews, including Jewish Christians, that they not circumcise their children. The reader knows that Paul even had Timothy, who was half-Jewish, circumcised (16:3). Luke is again ready to show Paul's orthodoxy with respect to the law.

It is clear that the anxious Christian leaders in Jerusalem had given careful thought to their predicament even before Paul arrived in town. They had already hatched a plan and were ready to spring it on Paul as soon as their greeting faded. "So do what we tell you," they insisted with more than a hint of command in their voices. They had already asked four Jewish Christians to go through a rite of purification. Paul, the leaders insisted, was expected to join them in this rite. Moreover, he was asked to pay the charges related to this ritual. This would surely prove beyond doubt Paul's orthodoxy.

The reader might wonder about this portrait of Paul. Would the apostle we know from the letters have acquiesced to the suggestion of these anxious Christian elders that he prove his orthodoxy? Though he himself lived "as one under the law" (1 Cor. 9:20), he was convinced that the law was no longer binding on any Christian—Jew or Gentile (see Rom. 3:21–31; 7:4–6; Gal. 2:11–21; 3:23–29; 4:21–5:6). It seems unlikely that Paul would passively comply with commands to prove his Jewish orthodoxy, especially commands coming from those whom he says "were supposed to be acknowledged leaders (what they actually were makes no difference to me)" (Gal. 2:6). Nevertheless, Luke has given his reader a compliant and compromising Paul. It is ironic—an irony that is a common experience—that Paul's compliance and compromise did not work. In fact, the plan to prove his orthodoxy backfired!

PAUL IS ARRESTED AND BROUGHT BEFORE CLAUDIUS LYSIAS
Acts 21:27–39

21:27 **When the seven days were almost completed, the Jews from Asia, who had seen him in the temple, stirred up the whole crowd. They seized him, 28 shouting, "Fellow Israelites, help! This is the man who is teaching everyone everywhere against our people, our law, and this place; more than that, he has actually brought Greeks into the temple and has defiled this holy** place." [29] **For they had previously seen Trophimus the Ephesian with him in the city, and they supposed that Paul had brought him into the temple.** [30] **Then all the city was aroused, and the people rushed together. They seized Paul and dragged him out of the temple, and immediately the doors were shut.** [31] **While they were trying to kill him, word came to the tribune of the cohort that all Jerusalem was in an uproar.** [32] **Immediately he took soldiers and centurions and ran down to them. When they saw the tribune and the soldiers, they stopped beating Paul.** [33] **Then the tribune came, arrested him, and ordered him to be bound with two chains; he inquired who he was and what he had done.** [34] **Some in the crowd shouted one thing, some another; and as he could not learn the facts because of the uproar, he ordered him to be brought into the barracks.** [35] **When Paul came to the steps, the violence of the mob was so great that he had to be carried by the soldiers.** [36] **The crowd that followed kept shouting, "Away with him!"**

[37] **Just as Paul was about to be brought into the barracks, he said to the tribune, "May I say something to you?" The tribune replied, "Do you know Greek?** [38] **Then you are not the Egyptian who recently stirred up a revolt and led the four thousand assassins out into the wilderness?"** [39] **Paul replied, "I am a Jew, from Tarsus in Cilicia, a citizen of an important city; I beg you, let me speak to the people."**

In the midst of his attempts to complete the rites of purification, Paul was seized by a group of angry Jews from Asia. The irony mentioned at the end of the previous section—that compromise and compliance often backfire—plays out here. Paul's complete compliance with the law in undergoing a ritual of purification was not sufficient to placate the pent-up anger and jealousy of diaspora Jews whom he had offended. In spite of his obvious orthodoxy, Paul was accused of "teaching everyone everywhere against our people, our law, and this place" (v. 28). These angry Asians were not satisfied to level only these general accusations. According to them, Paul had actually defiled the temple by bringing non-Jews ("Greeks") into the temple precincts. Luke explains the basis of this specious charge: "For they had previously seen Trophimus the Ephesian with him in the city, and they supposed that Paul had brought him into the temple" (v. 29).

As we have seen on several occasions in the book of Acts, Paul generated considerable controversy and hostility. As elsewhere, the Jews from Asia were whipped into a frenzy by what they perceived as a breach of Roman and Jewish law. According to Roman law it was illegal to "introduce new religious doctrines . . . by which the minds of men are influenced." The shout of the crowd, that Paul was "teaching . . . against our people, our law, and this place [the temple]," may have been intended for the ears of Roman authorities. And bringing a non-Jew into the temple was strictly against Jewish regulations. Josephus, the first-century Jewish historian, reports that a clear warning in Greek and Latin was engraved on the balustrade of the temple which forbade the entrance of foreigners into the temple precincts. This report was confirmed in 1871 with the discovery of a stone tablet that reads:

> No man of another nation may enter within the fence and enclosure around the temple. Whoever is caught will have himself to blame for his death that ensues.

Josephus writes that the highest Roman authorities even allowed the execution of Roman citizens who had violated this prohibition.

Luke's narrative indicates that the mob intended to kill Paul outside the temple. As the reader has encountered so often in Acts, the scene depicts a mob wildly out of control, rather than a rational proceeding in which the truth of the matter might be discerned. Had the crowd been seriously concerned about a breach of Jewish law they would have gone after Trophimus. The warnings were clearly directed against non-Jews entering the temple; nothing is said about those who may have brought them inside. Nevertheless, in Luke's account the whole point is moot. Their anger was focused on Paul, and in any case, Paul had not brought Trophimus into the temple. As the reader has discovered, anger against Paul has clouded the truth. Yes, the Asian Jews had seen Trophimus in Jerusalem with Paul. However, when they later found Paul in the temple, they made the faulty deduction (intentionally or unintentionally) that Trophimus had accompanied the Christian missionary into the holy place.

This scene again puts the reader in touch with Luke's stereotyping tendencies. The mob of angry irrational Asian Jews is set in contrast to the reasoned, orderly, and compassionate approach of the Roman tribune, Lysias, who rushed to save Paul from being beaten to death. If the Jews had a law by which Paul could have been capitally sentenced, there is no evidence in Luke's narrative that they had an orderly means of reaching a decision through judicial process. Aside from Roman procedure, the accused had little chance for a reasoned defense before his or her accuser.

Lysias acted quickly to rescue Paul from the angry mob. He could have seen clearly all that was taking place from his position in a tower of the Antonia (the Roman fortress in Jerusalem) which was connected to the temple and overlooked the entire temple area. Unsure of the identity of this person at the storm center, the tribune ordered Paul to be bound with chains, and then asked the crowd "who he was and what he had done" (v. 33). The crowd was so frenzied that their response was a babble to

Lysias, and their agitation so great that the soldiers had to lift Paul from their grasp and carry him to safety inside the fortress. With familiar ominous words, the mob yelled at the soldiers, "Away with him!" (v. 36; in Luke 23:18, the same angry phrase was shouted at Jesus).

Finally, inside the relative quiet of the Roman fortress, Paul was able to catch his breath. Here he could have a calm conversation with the Roman officer in charge. He began by establishing his identity. First, Luke notes, Paul was able to speak fluent Greek, the language of the officer. The tribune was surprised by this, for he had assumed that Paul was "the Egyptian," an infamous anti-Roman revolutionary who had raised a guerrilla army of Sicarii, or "dagger-men," assassins who brutally murdered members of the pro-Roman Jewish aristocracy. This assumption—that Lysias had a major revolutionary on his hands—may explain the "two chains" which bound Paul.

Paul's response to the tribune established his credentials: "I am a Jew! a citizen of Tarsus, an important city in the Roman province of Cilicia." Paul was certainly no anti-Roman Egyptian!

Paul asked for and received the tribune's permission to address the crowd. Luke sets the scene for the reader. With the security of the Roman barracks behind him, Paul faced the crowd from the steps and with a sweeping motion of his hand silenced the noisy gathering. Paul began his speech in the vernacular of the crowd.

PAUL'S SPEECH TO THE JEWS IN JERUSALEM
Acts 21:40–22:21

> 21:40 When he had given him permission, Paul stood on the steps and motioned to the people for silence; and when there was a great hush, he addressed them in the Hebrew [i.e., Aramaic] language, saying:
> 22:1 "Brothers and fathers, listen to the defense that I now make before you."
> 2 When they heard him addressing them in Hebrew, they became even more quiet. Then he said:
> 3 "I am a Jew, born in Tarsus in Cilicia, but brought up in this city at the feet of Gamaliel, educated strictly according to our ancestral law, being zealous for God, just as all of you are today. 4 I persecuted this Way up to the point of death by binding both men and women and putting them in prison, 5 as the high priest and the whole council of elders can testify about me. From them I also received letters to the brothers in Damascus, and I

went there in order to bind those who were there and to bring them back to Jerusalem for punishment.

6 "While I was on my way and approaching Damascus, about noon a great light from heaven suddenly shone about me. 7 I fell to the ground and heard a voice saying to me, 'Saul, Saul, why are you persecuting me?' 8 I answered, 'Who are you, Lord?' Then he said to me, 'I am Jesus of Nazareth whom you are persecuting.' 9 Now those who were with me saw the light but did not hear the voice of the one who was speaking to me. 10 I asked, 'What am I to do, Lord?' The Lord said to me, 'Get up and go to Damascus; there you will be told everything that has been assigned to you to do.' 11 Since I could not see because of the brightness of that light, those who were with me took my hand and led me to Damascus.

12 "A certain Ananias, who was a devout man according to the law and well spoken of by all the Jews living there, 13 came to me; and standing beside me, he said, 'Brother Saul, regain your sight!' In that very hour I regained my sight and saw him. 14 Then he said, 'The God of our ancestors has chosen you to know his will, to see the Righteous One and to hear his own voice; 15 for you will be his witness to all the world of what you have seen and heard. 16 And now why do you delay? Get up, be baptized, and have your sins washed away, calling on his name.'

17 "After I had returned to Jerusalem and while I was praying in the temple, I fell into a trance 18 and saw Jesus saying to me, 'Hurry and get out of Jerusalem quickly, because they will not accept your testimony about me.' 19 And I said, 'Lord, they themselves know that in every synagogue I imprisoned and beat those who believed in you. 20 And while the blood of your witness Stephen was shed, I myself was standing by, approving and keeping the coats of those who killed him.' 21 Then he said to me, 'Go, for I will send you far away to the Gentiles.'"

This is the first of four trial scenes. Paul is in the protective custody of Claudius Lysias, commander of the Roman army stationed in Jerusalem. An outline of this episode (Acts 22:1–23:32) may be helpful:

Paul's speech to the Jews in Jerusalem (22:1–21)
    The response of the crowd (22:22–23)
    The response of the tribune, Lysias (22:24–30)
Paul's defense before the Sanhedrin (23:1–6)
    The response of the Pharisees and Sadducees (23:7–9)
    The response of the tribune (23:10)
Paul's vision (23:11)
The plot against Paul (23:12–22)
Paul is sent to the procurator, Felix (23:23–32)

The opening line of Paul's speech establishes the theme for the final segment of Luke's writings. "Listen to the defense that I now make before you." The Greek term for "defense," *apologia*, is a courtroom word referring to the argument of a defendant for his or her innocence. In the case of Paul, and in subsequent early Christian literature, the meaning of the term expands to include a defense of the faith, often an argument for the truth of Christianity—Christian apologetics. Here, Luke applies this double meaning of the term to Paul who defends both his legal innocence and argues for the truth of the gospel which he has preached.

Paul began his defense with an appeal to his credentials. He repeated publicly what he had told Lysias in private. "I am a Jew, born in Tarsus in Cilicia." Paul then moved to establish both his civic credentials and, more important for this crowd, his religious credentials. He grew up as a young man of Jerusalem, taught by one of the great teachers in Israel, Gamaliel. He was educated in the Pharisaic tradition. Luke's phrases—"educated strictly according to our ancestral law" and "being zealous for God"—are clear echoes of Paul's self-description in Galatians 2:14. So zealous was he for God that he persecuted the Jewish sect known as the Way, imprisoning men and women of the sect.

Paul then repeated the story of his life-changing experience on the Damascus road (22:6–16), which the reader has already encountered in Acts 9. The careful reader will note a few variations from the earlier version of Paul's experience. In this account we learn that Paul saw the bright light at about noon (v. 6), that Paul's companions did not hear the voice (v. 9, unlike 9:7), and that Ananias had given a commission to Paul (vv. 14–15; not found in Acts 9). Furthermore, the vision recorded in verses 17–21 is an addition to the narrative in Acts 9. In this vision Jesus appeared to Paul in order to warn him to leave Jerusalem. This conversation between Paul and Jesus also allows Luke to remind the reader of Paul's complicity in the martyrdom of Stephen (Acts 8:1). Jesus' final word to Paul was a commission to be his witness among the Gentiles. As we shall see in the next section, this commission was the straw that broke the collective back of the mob in Jerusalem.

THE RESPONSE OF THE CROWD AND LYSIAS
Acts 22:22–30

> 22:22 Up to this point they listened to him, but then they shouted, "Away with such a fellow from the earth! For he should not be allowed to live." 23 And while

they were shouting, throwing off their cloaks, and tossing dust into the air, 24 the tribune directed that he was to be brought into the barracks, and ordered him to be examined by flogging, to find out the reason for this outcry against him. 25 But when they had tied him up with thongs, Paul said to the centurion who was standing by, "Is it legal for you to flog a Roman citizen who is uncondemned?" 26 When the centurion heard that, he went to the tribune and said to him, "What are you about to do? This man is a Roman citizen." 27 The tribune came and asked Paul, "Tell me, are you a Roman citizen?" And he said, "Yes." 28 The tribune answered, "It cost me a large sum of money to get my citizenship." Paul said, "But I was born a citizen." 29 Immediately those who were about to examine him drew back from him; and the tribune also was afraid, for he realized that Paul was a Roman citizen and that he had bound him.

30 Since he wanted to find out what Paul was being accused of by the Jews, the next day he released him and ordered the chief priests and the entire council to meet. He brought Paul down and had him stand before them.

Perhaps it was Paul's reminder that Jesus had commissioned him to work among the Gentiles (v. 21) that brought the crowd back to its rancorous state. The crowd went wild, "shouting, throwing off their cloaks, and tossing dust into the air" (v. 23). They were furious with Paul, declaring that "he should not be allowed to live" (v. 22).

The tribune was impressed by the crowd's strong negative response and decided to extract a confession of wrongdoing from Paul by means of flogging. While he probably did not understand a word of the Aramaic exchange between Paul and the mob, their charged response indicated that this Jew from Tarsus must be responsible for some kind of malfeasance. Therefore, he commanded that Paul be bound and beaten.

Luke, in his typically dramatic fashion, has Paul wait until the last possible moment to speak the word that will liberate him from a dangerous situation. Stretched out and tied with leather thongs to a flogging bench, Paul looked up at the centurion in charge and asked, "Is it legal for you to flog a Roman citizen who is uncondemned?" (see 16:37ff.). The centurion wisely decided to check this out with Lysias, his superior. The tribune rushed to Paul to ask about his citizenship. Paul had earlier declared that he was a citizen of Tarsus (21:39). Roman citizenship was quite another matter, however, placing Paul under the full legal protection of the Roman Empire. Moreover, the conversation between Paul and Lysias reveals that Paul was "one up" by comparison. Lysias had purchased his citizenship "with a large sum of money." Paul, on the other hand, "was born a citizen." Luke notes that "immediately" those who were about to flog Paul jumped back, and the tribune "also was afraid."

It is often asked how Paul would be able to prove his citizenship. Did he have identification papers? Did he carry a passport? If he had purchased his citizenship he may have carried a receipt (which may be behind the tribune's statement about the "large sum of money" [v. 28]; otherwise, the declaration of the tribune makes little sense in this scene). Perhaps people with Paul's status—birthright citizens—simply had to state as such. Family records could confirm this claim, and the penalty for falsely claiming Roman citizenship was death, a sufficient deterrent for most people.

Lysias kept Paul in protective custody for the night and then released him, ordering the Sanhedrin to make an assessment of the mob's accusations against Paul.

PAUL BEFORE THE SANHEDRIN
Acts 23:1–11

23:1 **While Paul was looking intently at the council he said, "Brothers, up to this day I have lived my life with a clear conscience before God." 2 Then the high priest Ananias ordered those standing near him to strike him on the mouth. 3 At this Paul said to him, "God will strike you, you whitewashed wall! Are you sitting there to judge me according to the law, and yet in violation of the law you order me to be struck?" 4 Those standing nearby said, "Do you dare to insult God's high priest?" 5 And Paul said, "I did not realize, brothers, that he was high priest; for it is written, 'You shall not speak evil of a leader of your people.'"**

6 When Paul noticed that some were Sadducees and others were Pharisees, he called out in the council, "Brothers, I am a Pharisee, a son of Pharisees. I am on trial concerning the hope of the resurrection of the dead." 7 When he said this, a dissension began between the Pharisees and the Sadducees, and the assembly was divided. 8 (The Sadducees say that there is no resurrection, or angel, or spirit; but the Pharisees acknowledge all three.) 9 Then a great clamor arose, and certain scribes of the Pharisees' group stood up and contended, "We find nothing wrong with this man. What if a spirit or an angel has spoken to him?" 10 When the dissension became violent, the tribune, fearing that they would tear Paul to pieces, ordered the soldiers to go down, take him by force, and bring him into the barracks.

11 That night the Lord stood near him and said, "Keep up your courage! For just as you have testified for me in Jerusalem, so you must bear witness also in Rome."

A number of strange features appear in this scene. The hearing before the Sanhedrin was arranged by the tribune in order to understand more clearly the nature of the charges against Paul made by the Jews of Jerusalem. Yet, the tribune is none the wiser at the conclusion of this hearing. An opportunity to illumine the facts becomes lost in the fire of intemperate and irrational exchanges.

Paul began with a declaration of his overall innocence. The record of his past action is a clean one (this is the meaning of the term translated as "clear conscience"; the concept of conscience as a moral faculty that guides personal conduct is a modern one and would have been foreign to Paul). In response to this declaration, the high priest Ananias (this is the third Ananias reported by Luke [see 5:1–5 and 9:10–17]) ordered Paul to be struck on the mouth. The tribune must have found this an exceedingly strange way to begin a fact-finding session. But the strangeness continues.

Paul responded to the high priest's physical abuse with a verbal broadside of his own. "God will strike you!" Paul shouted at the high priest (v. 3). Perhaps Luke was aware that Paul's predictive curse came true, for Ananias was assassinated in C.E. 66. Paul adds insult to future injury, calling the high priest a "whitewashed wall." While the point of this comparison is uncertain, the reader might be reminded of an insult that Jesus heaped on the scribes and Pharisees whom he called

> whitewashed tombs, which on the outside look beautiful, but inside they are full of the bones of the dead and of all kinds of filth. So you also on the outside look righteous to others, but inside you are full of hypocrisy and lawlessness. (Matt. 23:27–28)

The context in which Paul uses the metaphor of a whitewashed wall certainly fits Jesus' description. This man, the high priest, was a public symbol of righteousness before the law. Yet, inside the walls of the Sanhedrin he has defiled the council (turning it into a "tomb") by violating the law. The person most responsible for upholding the law summarily violated the law by prematurely rendering a judgment in what is only a hearing to ascertain the nature of the charges against the accused (see Lev. 19:15). Paul's metaphor—a whitewashed wall—was certainly heard as an insult (v. 4).

A further strange response strikes the reader in Paul's confession that he was not aware that the high priest was recipient of his curse and insult (v. 5). A number of curious rationalizations have been posited for this lapse: perhaps Paul did not recognize the high priest because Ananias was new to the position, or because Paul had poor eyesight; or perhaps Paul had intended searing irony—he had not expected such unworthy conduct from "God's high priest." In the end, Paul appears to apologize with a quote from the law (Exod. 22:28; "You shall not . . . curse a leader of your people").

By this time, the tribune must have been truly mystified. Furthermore, remember that this exchange is taking place in Aramaic, which can only have deepened Lysias's mystification.

According to Luke, Paul wisely took note of the sectarian split in the Sanhedrin between the Pharisees and the Sadducees. As a point of information for the Gentile reader, Luke describes the difference between these two groups: the Pharisees believe in the resurrection, angels, and spirits; the Sadducees do not. Paul declared himself to be a member of the Pharisaic party, and this wing of the Sanhedrin decided to protect one of its own. In a judgment reminiscent of Pilate's declaration about Jesus, the Pharisees contend, "We find nothing wrong with this man" (see Luke 23:4, 14, 22). At this statement, a violent discussion ensues forcing the tribune once again to rescue Paul from this body which had been convened to seek the truth and offer sound advice. The scene continues Luke's stereotypical presentation of the Sanhedrin as an irrational and violence-prone deliberative assembly which violates the very principles it claims to uphold (carefully compare the accounts of Jesus before the Sanhedrin in Mark 14:53–65 and in Luke 22:54–23:2).

This hearing was quite out of keeping with the kind of jurisprudence a Roman official would have expected. Lysias was forced to intervene—without receiving a shred of additional evidence about the case against this Jew from Tarsus. Therefore, the tribune took Paul back into the protective custody of Rome.

That night in the shelter of the Antonia, Paul received a vision of Jesus who offered encouragement and a divine promise. "For just as you have testified for me in Jerusalem, so you must [*dei*, see the comments on Acts 19:21–22] bear witness also in Rome" (v. 11). Paul has been divinely ordained to fulfill the promise Jesus made to the apostles: "You will be my witnesses in Jerusalem, in all Judea and Samaria, and to the ends of the earth" (Acts 1:8).

THE PLOT AGAINST PAUL
Acts 23:12–22

23:12 **In the morning the Jews joined in a conspiracy and bound themselves by an oath neither to eat nor drink until they had killed Paul. 13 There were more than forty who joined in this conspiracy. 14 They went to the chief** priests and elders and said, "We have strictly bound ourselves by an oath to taste no food until we have killed Paul. [15] Now then, you and the council must notify the tribune to bring him down to you, on the pretext that you want to make a more thorough examination of his case. And we are ready to do away with him before he arrives."

[16] Now the son of Paul's sister heard about the ambush; so he went and gained entrance to the barracks and told Paul. [17] Paul called one of the centurions and said, "Take this young man to the tribune, for he has something to report to him." [18] So he took him, brought him to the tribune, and said, "The prisoner Paul called me and asked me to bring this young man to you; he has something to tell you." [19] The tribune took him by the hand, drew him aside privately, and asked, "What is it that you have to report to me?" [20] He answered, "The Jews have agreed to ask you to bring Paul down to the council tomorrow, as though they were going to inquire more thoroughly into his case. [21] But do not be persuaded by them, for more than forty of their men are lying in ambush for him. They have bound themselves by an oath neither to eat nor drink until they kill him. They are ready now and are waiting for your consent." [22] So the tribune dismissed the young man, ordering him, "Tell no one that you have informed me of this."

This scene offers the occasion that transfers Paul from the protection of Lysias in Jerusalem to that of Antonius Felix, the Roman governor of Judea stationed in Caesarea. A group of Jews (the reader is left in the dark as to which Jews—Asians? Sadducees?) hatch a plot to lynch Paul. The reader also learns that Paul had a married sister living in Jerusalem, and that her son "heard about the ambush." Luke does not tell the reader *how* Paul's nephew heard about the plot. One would think that such a plan would be a tightly held secret; perhaps Paul's nephew was an "insider," with access to the conspirators. He quickly gained entrance to the barracks and reported the scheme to Paul. Paul then asked his nephew to tell Lysias about plans for the ambush.

In this passage, Luke again makes clear how much the authorities hated Paul. This Pharisaic rabbi turned Jewish-Christian missionary to the Gentiles must have been seen as a serious threat to them in a number of ways:

Theologically: Paul's conviction that God has chosen to make God's grace available for all people through Jesus the Messiah calls into question their own theological convictions regarding God's sovereignty and God's election of Israel.

Personally: Paul's congregations, independent of the synagogue, threaten their traditional positions of leadership and power within the Jewish community.

Institutionally: Paul's mission calls into question the identity of "the people of God"—God has chosen the church, made up of Jews and Gentiles, to be part of "Israel."

For all these reasons, the authorities in Jerusalem hated Paul with a passion. They wanted him dead!

LYSIAS SENDS PAUL TO ANTONIUS FELIX
Acts 23:23–32

23:23 **Then he summoned two of the centurions and said, "Get ready to leave by nine o'clock tonight for Caesarea with two hundred soldiers, seventy horsemen, and two hundred spearmen.** [24] **Also provide mounts for Paul to ride, and take him safely to Felix the governor."** [25] **He wrote a letter to this effect:**
   [26] **"Claudius Lysias to his Excellency the governor Felix, greetings.** [27] **This man was seized by the Jews and was about to be killed by them, but when I had learned that he was a Roman citizen, I came with the guard and rescued him.** [28] **Since I wanted to know the charge for which they accused him, I had him brought to their council.** [29] **I found that he was accused concerning questions of their law, but was charged with nothing deserving death or imprisonment.** [30] **When I was informed that there would be a plot against the man, I sent him to you at once, ordering his accusers also to state before you what they have against him."**
   [31] **So the soldiers, according to their instructions, took Paul and brought him during the night to Antipatris.** [32] **The next day they let the horsemen go on with him, while they returned to the barracks.**

Once the tribune was informed by Paul's nephew of the plot against Paul, he determined to have this Roman citizen protected at all costs. An exceptionally large convoy of 470 troops (about half of the army stationed in Jerusalem and an overwhelming force against forty would-be assassins) would leave as soon as darkness descended on Jerusalem. Paul's nephew reported that the council would ask to see Paul the next morning, therefore Lysias spirited Paul out of Jerusalem by nine o'clock that night. The entire company made an all-night journey to Antipatris, about forty miles northwest of Jerusalem. Here the foot soldiers left the company to return to Jerusalem (it must have been an exhausting and difficult march) while the horsemen and Paul continued the remaining twenty-five miles to the governor's headquarters in the coastal city of Caesarea. With his arrival at the palace, the level of Paul's protection has moved up a significant notch.

The letter the tribune sent along with Paul is typical of letters from an officer to his commander; it attempts to show his own behavior in the best possible light. He was a dutiful son of Rome, who pursued judicial truth by sending a difficult case to a higher authority. In light of the chaotic Sanhedrin hearing conducted in Aramaic, it is difficult to know how the tribune deduced that Paul "was accused concerning questions of their law, but was charged with nothing deserving death or imprisonment." In the end, perhaps he relied on Paul's own version of the discussion.

The reader begins to perceive the will of God being carried forward by the Roman authorities. Just as centuries before the prophet Isaiah hailed Cyrus of Persia as savior of Israel and her mission to the nations (Isaiah 45), so now Luke identifies Caesar (and his appointees) as savior of Paul and his mission to the Gentiles.

11. Paul on Trial (II)
Acts 23:33–24:27

PAUL IS BROUGHT BEFORE FELIX
Acts 23:33–35

23:33 **When they came to Caesarea and delivered the letter to the governor, they presented Paul also before him.** [34] **On reading the letter, he asked what province he belonged to, and when he learned that he was from Cilicia,** [35] **he said, "I will give you a hearing when your accusers arrive." Then he ordered that he be kept under guard in Herod's headquarters.**

Paul and the letter from Lysias have been delivered to Felix. Felix's question of Paul about his place of origin reminds the reader of the question Pilate asked Jesus, "whether [Jesus] was a Galilean" (Luke 23:6). In discovering that Jesus was from Galilee, Pilate attempted to rid himself of a difficult case. In this passage, however, it is unclear *why* Felix asks about Paul's home province. In Jesus' case, the location of Jesus' arrest (Judea) and the location of his home (Galilee) were distinct jurisdictions, under Pontius Pilate and Herod Antipas respectively. By the time Paul was arrested, Cilicia had been merged into the province of Syria (which included Judea). Perhaps Felix was just checking to be sure that he did have complete authority in this case; the place of Paul's birth and his arrest were indeed within Felix's jurisdiction.

Felix was a well-known political figure in antiquity, and was appointed Procurator of Judea in the early 50s (it is difficult to pinpoint the exact date of his rule in Palestine). The assessment of him offered by several first-century writers is quite negative. Josephus, the Jewish historian, remembers him as a severe and repressive ruler over Judea. This seems ironic, for Felix himself had been a slave set free by the emperor Claudius. Tacitus, a Roman historian and contemporary of Luke, offers this pungent description of Felix: "with all manner of cruelty and lust, he exercised the power of a king with the mind of a slave" (*The Histories* 5.9). The contemporary

212

reader might conclude that Felix's behavior exhibited repressed anger about the years he spent in slavery.

Felix agreed to give Paul a hearing as soon as his accusers arrived. In the meantime, Paul was to be kept under house arrest in "Herod's headquarters"—a palace built by Herod the Great at Caesarea, and now under Roman administration.

THE CHARGE AGAINST PAUL
Acts 24:1–9

24:1 **Five days later the high priest Ananias came down with some elders and an attorney, a certain Tertullus, and they reported their case against Paul to the governor.** [2] **When Paul had been summoned, Tertullus began to accuse him, saying:**

"Your Excellency, because of you we have long enjoyed peace, and reforms have been made for this people because of your foresight. [3] **We welcome this in every way and everywhere with utmost gratitude.** [4] **But, to detain you no further, I beg you to hear us briefly with your customary graciousness.** [5] **We have, in fact, found this man a pestilent fellow, an agitator among all the Jews throughout the world, and a ringleader of the sect of the Nazarenes.** [6] **He even tried to profane the temple, and so we seized him.** [8] **By examining him yourself you will be able to learn from him concerning everything of which we accuse him."**

[9] **The Jews also joined in the charge by asserting that all this was true.**

Paul's case has moved up a rung in the ladder of Roman authority. Recognizing this, the high priest Ananias and some of the Sanhedrin rulers have personally come to Caesarea to pursue the case against Paul. Not only that, they have hired an attorney, Tertullus, well-versed in Jewish and Roman law, to present their case against Paul. Tertullus appears to have been either a Hellenistic Jew (his Greek is impeccable) or a Gentile; the latter seems most likely. When the Jewish authorities realized that the hearing would be held in a high Roman (Gentile) court, they chose a Gentile lawyer to present their case (note that Tertullus refers to the Jews somewhat distantly as "this people" [v. 2]; and after his speech, Luke notes that "the Jews *also* joined in the charge" [v. 9]).

Their money appears to have been well spent. Tertullus has carefully crafted his speech which expresses the gratitude of the Jewish authorities to Felix, and implicates Paul under Roman law. It was certainly true that because of Felix the Jews had "long enjoyed peace"; but this "peace" was purchased with the price of Felix's fierce oppression. And since the Jewish authorities had recently lent their support to the Romans in crushing the insurrection led by "the Egyptian" (Acts 21:38; Josephus, *The Jewish War* 2.13.5), Tertullus's comment about peace is well-timed. However, it is difficult to identify just what "reforms" had been "made for this people." Luke presents Tertullus as a shameless flatterer—to describe Felix as having "customary graciousness" seems excessive (v. 4). Possibly this was Luke's tongue-in-cheek description, an inside joke for his Roman readers. Only a Gentile attorney would have uttered such outrageously ingratiating fiction to this petty tyrant who ruled "with the mind of a slave."

Finally, Tertullus comes to the heart of the matter. "We have, in fact, found this man

> a pestilent fellow,
> an agitator among all the Jews throughout the world,
> and a ringleader of the sect of the Nazarenes.
> He even tried to profane the temple. . . . " (Vv. 5–6)

The first and third charges against Paul were not serious. Being called "a perfect pest," as Moffatt delightfully translates, or a "ringleader" of a Jewish sect were not criminal activities, unless, of course, that sect was seditious. The second and fourth charges, however, were serious and had to be dealt with carefully. If conviction resulted from these charges, punishment was severe.

These two charges—being an "agitator among all the Jews" and attempting to "profane the temple"—are an elaboration of the charges leveled against Paul by the angry Jews who had followed Paul from Asia to Jerusalem. In that earlier scene, Paul was accused of "teaching everyone everywhere against our people, our law, and this place; more than that, he has actually brought Greeks into the temple and has defiled this holy place" (21:28).

Tertullus, a clever lawyer, has made two important changes to the earlier charges. First, Tertullus charged not only that Paul taught Jews throughout the empire but that his teaching was seditious. The NRSV offers a weak translation of this serious charge. According to Tertullus, Paul was not just a teacher, and he was more than an "agitator." The King James Version of this passage hits closer to the mark. In this translation, Paul was "a mover of sedition among all the Jews throughout the world" (v. 5). Paul was not just a teacher; he was a revolutionary. The charge was treason!

The second subtle change crafted by Tertullus has to do with the charge that Paul brought Gentiles into the temple. Tertullus has chosen his words carefully. The Asian Jews complained that Paul "defiled" the temple by bringing Gentiles into it. Tertullus used a different Greek word which we translate as "profane" to describe the consequence of Paul's action. The choice of this word broadened the charge to facilitate the Roman procurator's understanding and to gain a Roman conviction. It was against Roman law to profane a shrine or temple, and punishment was harsh—death.

Finally, Tertullus advised Felix to take it upon himself to examine Paul in order to discover the truth of these charges. The Jewish leaders standing near Tertullus heartily affirmed that the charges against Paul were true.

PAUL'S DEFENSE BEFORE FELIX
Acts 24:10–21

24:10 **When the governor motioned to him to speak, Paul replied:**
"I cheerfully make my defense, knowing that for many years you have been a judge over this nation. ** 11 **As you can find out, it is not more than twelve days since I went up to worship in Jerusalem. ** 12 **They did not find me disputing with anyone in the temple or stirring up a crowd either in the synagogues or throughout the city. ** 13 **Neither can they prove to you the charge that they now bring against me. ** 14 **But this I admit to you, that according to the Way, which they call a sect, I worship the God of our ancestors, believing everything laid down according to the law or written in the prophets. ** 15 **I have a hope in God—a hope that they themselves also accept—that there will be a resurrection of both the righteous and the unrighteous. ** 16 **Therefore I do my best always to have a clear conscience toward God and all people. ** 17 **Now after some years I came to bring alms to my nation and to offer sacrifices. ** 18 **While I was doing this, they found me in the temple, completing the rite of purification, without any crowd or disturbance. ** 19 **But there were some Jews from Asia—they ought to be here before you to make an accusation, if they have anything against me. ** 20 **Or let these men here tell what crime they had found when I stood before the council, ** 21 **unless it was this one sentence that I called out while standing before them, 'It is about the resurrection of the dead that I am on trial before you today.'"

While Tertullus was a fine attorney with excellent rhetorical skills, Paul the Christian rabbi was not to be outdone. Luke presents Paul as a superb orator. Paul is also gracious in his introduction, but far less obsequious than the attorney. Paul's observation about Felix is an honest one. "For many years you have been a judge over this nation." This is neither flattery nor fiction, but simply a statement of fact. Knowing that Felix is a seasoned jurist, he can make his defense in confidence. Paul expects that he will receive a fair hearing.

Paul reminds the governor that since the event in question had occurred only twelve days in the past, he could call on other witnesses (presumably Jewish Christians who could vouch for Paul) to testify. Paul flatly denies that he was disturbing anyone (let alone fomenting revolution) in the temple, the synagogues, or anywhere else in the city of Jerusalem.

"Neither can they prove to you the charge that they *now* bring against me." With this statement, Paul recognizes that Tertullus has modified the charges against him to fit the Roman context.

Paul is willing to admit that he was in the temple, but it was for the purpose of worship. He had certainly not profaned the temple, but, in fact, was "completing the rite of purification." Paul is also proud to admit that he belongs to a group called "the Way"—which his accusers identified as a "sect of Judaism," "the Nazarenes." Far from being a seditious group, they "worship the God of our ancestors, [and believe] everything laid down according to the law or written in the prophets." Furthermore, this group, like the Pharisees, believes in the resurrection. Again, Paul's mention of the resurrection must have rankled the Sadducees present at this hearing.

Rather than engaging in criminal activity, Paul brought a large monetary gift ("alms") from the churches of Asia and Europe to "my nation," that is, Israel (see comments on 19:21–22; 20:1–6; and 21:1–16—passages that ignore Paul's collection for the Jerusalem church, an omission that for some calls into question Luke's close relationship with Paul. Apparently, however, Luke *did know* about the collection; it seems not to have been as important to Luke when he crafted his story as it was to Paul when he wrote his letters thirty years earlier).

Paul informs Felix that a group of Jews from Asia brought the original charges against him, but where are they now? Since his original accusers are absent, Paul asks Felix to limit the discussion to his present accusers, members of the Sanhedrin, and their firsthand information about Paul. Paul tells Felix that in his hearing before the Sanhedrin he had offered a one-sentence defense: "It is about the resurrection of the dead that I am on trial before you today" (v. 21; 23:6).

Paul was nobody's fool, and could mount a strong defense. According to him, the charges are specious, without evidence and without witnesses to support them. Rather than being a threat to society, Paul supported his nation and its religious customs by word, deed, and money. The real rub for his Sadducaic accusers is Paul's preaching about the resurrection, a religious doctrine held sacred by the school of religious scholars to which he belonged, the Pharisees.

FELIX'S RESPONSE TO PAUL
Acts 24:22–27

24:22 But Felix, who was rather well informed about the Way, adjourned the hearing with the comment, "When Lysias the tribune comes down, I will decide your case." 23 Then he ordered the centurion to keep him in custody, but to let him have some liberty and not to prevent any of his friends from taking care of his needs.
24 Some days later when Felix came with his wife Drusilla, who was Jewish, he sent for Paul and heard him speak concerning faith in Christ Jesus. 25 And as he discussed justice, self-control, and the coming judgment, Felix became frightened and said, "Go away for the present; when I have an opportunity, I will send for you." 26 At the same time he hoped that money would be given him by Paul, and for that reason he used to send for him very often and converse with him.
27 After two years had passed, Felix was succeeded by Porcius Festus; and since he wanted to grant the Jews a favor, Felix left Paul in prison.

The picture Luke paints of Felix has essentially the same features as portraits rendered by other first-century historians, though Luke's colors are a bit more muted. Felix, well known to his contemporaries as a self-serving administrator, manipulates the situation by cutting a little slack for everyone, and in the process helps himself most of all. The Sanhedrin could still try to pursue a case against Paul. Paul remained under arrest, though he was allowed some freedom of movement in the palace and the privilege of visits from his friends. And Felix could simply wait until he could slough off this case to his successor.

Also, Luke's note—that Paul spent "two years" under arrest until Felix was released from his duties in Palestine—may indicate that Paul might have hoped for release from custody at the end of Felix's term. The statute of limitations for a litigant to pursue a case in a Roman court was usually two years. It was also the case that the procurator had considerable freedom in the granting of clemency for minor offenses (particularly in the early years of Nero's reign [54–68 C.E.] as emperor; see comments on 28:30–31). Indeed, it is not clear that the procurator had ever officially accepted the charges brought against Paul. Paul was still under "protective" custody. Finally, Paul and Felix appear to have had reasonably good rapport. Therefore, Paul might have had every expectation that Felix would release him before he left office. But this was not to be. Felix left Paul to the custody of his successor, Festus, as a favor to the Jews.

This passage also notes that Felix often sent for Paul with the pretense of enlightening conversation, while his real motive was greed. Here Luke describes the procurator whom we recognize from other first-century historians. Luke often reports little details that seem insignificant to us, yet to first-century readers they contained important reminders of the larger social-political context. Luke notes that Felix was married to Drusilla, "who was Jewish" (v. 24). Felix, ever looking for an opportunity for advancement, even married well. Drusilla, Felix's third wife, was the youngest daughter of Herod Agrippa I (see Acts 12), and the sister of Herod Agrippa II and Bernice (who appear Acts 25).

We do not know much about the frequent conversations between Paul and Felix. According to Luke, Felix was already well informed about the Way. One might have expected Luke to say that Paul elaborated on the teachings of the Way. Instead, Paul lectured Felix on "justice, self-control, and the coming judgment" (v. 25)—high virtues endemic in good Roman administration—teachings probably wasted on Felix. With echoes of the Roman philosopher Seneca, Paul challenged Felix to be just in his judgments, to exercise self-restraint, and to remember that he himself must someday be judged.

According to Luke, Paul's message made an impact on Felix, for the governor became frightened. Self-reflection was (and still is) a dangerous thing for self-righteous tyrants. Pulling back from Paul's message of justice and judgment, Felix cut off this line of conversation, perhaps hoping for more superficially pleasant philosophical chats. From this point forward, Felix would indulge Paul's presence only in the hope of a bribe, and when he was recalled to Rome, he thought he could placate the Jews by leaving Paul in prison. However, a delegation of Jewish leaders followed Felix to Rome bringing serious complaints to the emperor about the governor's excessive cruelties, abuses, and mismanagement. Felix was only saved from punishment by the intervention of his influential brother Pallas.

12. Paul on Trial (III)
Acts 25:1–12

PORCIUS FESTUS
REPLACES FELIX AS PROCURATOR
Acts 25:1–5

25:1 **Three days after Festus had arrived in the province, he went up from Caesarea to Jerusalem** [2] **where the chief priests and the leaders of the Jews gave him a report against Paul. They appealed to him** [3] **and requested, as a favor to them against Paul, to have him transferred to Jerusalem. They were, in fact, planning an ambush to kill him along the way.** [4] **Festus replied that Paul was being kept at Caesarea, and that he himself intended to go there shortly.** [5] **"So," he said, "let those of you who have the authority come down with me, and if there is anything wrong about the man, let them accuse him."**

In about 56 C.E. (the exact date is unknown), Nero appointed Porcius Festus as procurator of Judea. His administration was reasonable and fair, especially compared with that of his predecessor, Felix. An astute politician, Festus wasted no time in making contact with a significant center of power in Palestine. Three days after his arrival in the province he went to Jerusalem to visit with the Jewish leadership.

Just as the Jewish leaders had requested that Paul remain under arrest, so they now ask the new procurator for a favor. They wanted Paul transferred back to Jerusalem. Luke indicates that the old plan to ambush and kill Paul was revived (see 23:12–15). While it might have been good politics for Festus to grant their request, Festus chose to keep Paul the Roman citizen under Roman custody. However, as a good politician, Festus also invited those in authority in Jerusalem to come with him to Caesarea and to present their charges against Paul in court.

PAUL APPEALS TO CAESAR
Acts 25:6–12

25:6 **After he had stayed with them not more than eight or ten days, he went down to Caesarea; the next day he took his seat on the tribunal and ordered Paul to be brought. [7] When he arrived, the Jews who had gone down from Jerusalem surrounded him, bringing many serious charges against him, which they could not prove. [8] Paul said in his defense, "I have in no way committed an offense against the law of the Jews, or against the temple, or against the emperor." [9] But Festus, wishing to do the Jews a favor, asked Paul, "Do you wish to go up to Jerusalem and be tried there before me on these charges?" [10] Paul said, "I am appealing to the emperor's tribunal; this is where I should be tried. I have done no wrong to the Jews, as you very well know. [11] Now if I am in the wrong and have committed something for which I deserve to die, I am not trying to escape death; but if there is nothing to their charges against me, no one can turn me over to them. I appeal to the emperor." [12] Then Festus, after he had conferred with his council, replied, "You have appealed to the emperor; to the emperor you will go."**

Immediately upon his return to Caesarea, Festus brought Paul before him for a hearing. The Jews from Jerusalem were also present to reassert their charges against the Jewish-Christian missionary. Luke does not tell the reader details of the charges which they brought against Paul. He only suggests that they were several, serious, and not provable. Luke does imply, in Paul's response, that the charges were similar to those which Tertullus had earlier presented to Felix (24:5–6). At this third hearing, Paul did what his accusers had so far failed to do. He succinctly and explicitly laid out all the possible charges against him. Paul declared,

I have in no way committed an offense
  against the law of the Jews [with regard to bringing Gentiles into the temple], or
  against the temple [with regard to Roman prohibitions about temple desecration], or
  against the emperor [with regard to sedition]. (Acts 25:8)

As a favor to the Jews, Festus offered Paul a change in venue for the judicial hearing. The favor, however, was a hollow one. Paul would certainly decline the offer. Understandably, Paul was uneasy about returning to Jerusalem for trial. Perhaps he had again been informed about the plot to ambush and kill him (v. 3). Paul also may have felt that if his case were transferred back to Jerusalem, Festus would come under increased pressure from leaders of the Jerusalem Sanhedrin to support their cause against him. Paul was clearly afraid that he might be "turn[ed] . . . over to them" (v. 11).

Therefore, in order to hold fast the safety of a Roman court in a Gentile city, Paul makes the ultimate appeal as a Roman citizen. "I am appealing to the emperor's tribunal; this is where I should be tried" (v. 10). The last phrase indicates that Paul wanted to remain in Caesarea for his trial. It also indicates that Paul had placed himself firmly under the rules of Roman jurisprudence.

Much has been made of Paul's declaration, "I appeal to the emperor," and Festus's response, "You have appealed to the emperor; to the emperor you will go" (vv. 11–12). This appeal raises a host of questions. Did a Roman citizen have the right to be heard by the emperor's court simply by making such a declaration? Are we to take Paul's declaration and Festus's response literally—that Paul would be heard by the emperor himself? Would Paul be heard by one of Nero's personally appointed judges? Did Paul's appeal obligate Festus to send the apostle to Rome? Unfortunately, Roman law is unclear about these matters.

In whatever ways this appeal was intended by Paul and heard by Festus, it was an appeal that, for the moment, seemed to help Paul out of a difficult situation. In the long run, however, Paul's appeal appears to have backfired. After the end of his hearing in Caesarea, Herod Agrippa will say to Festus, "This man could have been set free if he had not appealed to the emperor" (26:32).

13. Paul on Trial (IV)
Acts 25:13–26:32

A CONVERSATION
BETWEEN FESTUS AND AGRIPPA
Acts 25:13–22

25:13 **After several days had passed, King Agrippa and Bernice arrived in Caesarea to welcome Festus.** [14] **Since they were staying there several days, Festus laid Paul's case before the king, saying, "There is a man here who was left in prison by Felix.** [15] **When I was in Jerusalem, the chief priests and the elders of the Jews informed me about him and asked for a sentence against him.** [16] **I told them that it was not the custom of the Romans to hand over anyone before the accused had met the accusers face to face and had been given an opportunity to make a defense against the charge.** [17] **So when they met here, I lost no time, but on the next day took my seat on the tribunal and ordered the man to be brought.** [18] **When the accusers stood up, they did not charge him with any of the crimes that I was expecting.** [19] **Instead they had certain points of disagreement with him about their own religion and about a certain Jesus, who had died, but whom Paul asserted to be alive.** [20] **Since I was at a loss how to investigate these questions, I asked whether he wished to go to Jerusalem and be tried there on these charges.** [21] **But when Paul had appealed to be kept in custody for the decision of his Imperial Majesty, I ordered him to be held until I could send him to the emperor."** [22] **Agrippa said to Festus, "I would like to hear the man myself." "Tomorrow," he said, "you will hear him."**

At this point, Luke introduces the reader to two notorious characters—King Agrippa and his sister Bernice. The Agrippa of this scene, Herod Agrippa II, was (1) great-grandson of Herod the Great (the murderous Herod of Jesus' birth [Matthew 2]); (2) grandnephew of Herod Antipas ("that fox" who beheaded John the Baptist [Mark 6:17–29] and later took part in the trial of Jesus [Luke 23:6–12]); and (3) the son of Herod Agrippa I (the Herod who martyred James the disciple and persecuted the early church [Acts 12]). This is a family with a bloody history with respect to the Christian community.

Herod Agrippa II was seventeen when his father died (44 C.E.; Acts 12:20–23) and was considered too young to assume his father's dominion. By the time Agrippa appears in this passage, fifteen years have passed and the emperor Claudius has granted him sovereignty over the territory once held by his great-uncle Philip (Luke 3:1).

It is worth noting that Luke introduces a Herodian at this point in Paul's trial. The reader of Luke's two volumes may recall that Jesus also was brought before a ruler of the Herodian dynasty during his trial (an episode found only in Luke's Gospel). The Roman procurator Pilate, discovering that Jesus was from Galilee, sent Jesus to Herod Antipas, the tetrarch of Galilee (Luke 23:6–7). Now, in Acts, Paul is brought before Herod Antipas's grandnephew, Herod Agrippa II.

Luke also introduces us to Bernice, sister of Agrippa II (and Drusilla, Felix's wife; 24:24); the web of family and politics in the Roman Empire becomes increasingly apparent. After the death of Bernice's husband, Herod of Chalcis (who was also her uncle, her father's brother), she came to live with her brother Agrippa. In short order, rumors began to circulate about an incestuous relationship between the two. Neither Agrippa nor Bernice did much to dispel the rumors, and their relationship apparently continued in spite of Bernice's short marriage to King Polemon of Cilicia. When Titus (Emperor Vespasian's son and himself a future emperor) came to Palestine to put down the Jewish rebellion, she became his mistress and later followed him to Rome expecting to become his wife. This was not to be, for the bloody Jewish-Roman War whipped up so much anti-Jewish sentiment in Rome that Titus felt compelled to separate from Bernice and expel her from the city.

Luke reports that shortly after the new imperial procurator arrived at his post in Palestine, Bernice and Agrippa came to Caesarea to welcome him. In short order, Festus raised the topic of Paul and the case against him, hoping for some enlightenment from the Herodians. Luke has probably constructed this conversation out of his own well-honed political imagination. Festus's description of the case of the man left in prison by Felix is an opportunity for Luke to recap Paul's case for the Herodians and for his readers. Luke also adds Festus's own interpretation of the case—a typical non-Christian, non-Jewish understanding of Paul's message.

According to Festus, Paul's accusers "did not charge him with any of the crimes that I was expecting" (v. 18). It appears that Festus expected that the charges against Paul would be serious offenses against the state which could be adjudicated in a Roman court. "Instead," Festus concluded, "they had certain points of disagreement with him about their own religion and about a certain Jesus, who had died, but whom Paul asserted to be alive" (v. 19).

An interesting shift in the case against Paul has taken place. The charges the leaders of the Sanhedrin brought against Paul in Felix's court were serious infractions of Roman law: fomenting sedition among Jews all over the world and attempting to profane the temple (24:5–6). The two-year period of Paul's imprisonment seems to have dampened the enthusiasm of the Jewish leaders for these charges. Luke reports only the vague observation that they brought "many serious charges against him, which they could not prove" (25:7).

Because these charges seem to be related to Judaism, Festus offered to transfer the case to Jerusalem. But Paul, in a self-protective move, appealed to Rome. If the case were to be transferred anywhere, let it be the imperial capital. Perhaps Paul was right in appealing to Rome. He was right in suspecting that a trial in Jerusalem would not be held before Festus (25:9). Festus would, no doubt, turn the adjudication of these religious matters over to the Sanhedrin. Festus (and Luke) understands that the appeal to Caesar not only protected Paul by keeping him in Roman custody, but also guaranteed the right of a hearing before "his Imperial Majesty."

Festus talked at length about this case with Agrippa because he hoped to gain some insight about the issues involved. Agrippa, after all, was Jewish (though Jews might not easily accept him as one of their own). Furthermore, Herod came from a long line of rulers that had crossed paths with Jesus and his followers. Perhaps Festus, like Pilate, wanted an "objective" Jewish perspective on the case (see Luke 23:6–15).

PAUL IS BROUGHT BEFORE
FESTUS, AGRIPPA, AND BERNICE
Acts 25:23–27

> 25:23 **So on the next day Agrippa and Bernice came with great pomp, and they entered the audience hall with the military tribunes and the prominent men of the city. Then Festus gave the order and Paul was brought in.** 24 **And**

Festus said, "King Agrippa and all here present with us, you see this man about whom the whole Jewish community petitioned me, both in Jerusalem and here, shouting that he ought not to live any longer. 25 But I found that he had done nothing deserving death; and when he appealed to his Imperial Majesty, I decided to send him. 26 But I have nothing definite to write to our sovereign about him. Therefore I have brought him before all of you, and especially you, King Agrippa, so that, after we have examined him, I may have something to write— 27 for it seems to me unreasonable to send a prisoner without indicating the charges against him."

Luke has taken exquisite care in setting the scene for the greatest of Paul's speeches recorded in Acts. Luke's description was intended to impress the reader. The long procession into the great audience hall of Herod's praetorium was led by King Agrippa and his sister Bernice, followed by officers of the Roman army stationed in Caesarea and important citizens of the city. Once they were all inside and seated, Festus ordered Paul to be brought before the assembled dignitaries.

Festus began the proceedings by briefly reviewing Paul's case. Luke must have considerably shortened Festus's remarks; he presumed that the reader was by now familiar with specifics of the case. Much like Pilate during Jesus' trial, Festus concluded: "I found that he had done nothing deserving death" (v. 25; Pilate said of Jesus: "He has done nothing to deserve death"; Luke 23:15; also 23:4, 22). Both procurators found their prisoners innocent. However, Pilate yielded to the pressure of the crowd, while Festus must honor the dignity of Roman law and grant Paul's appeal to Rome. Jesus, the non-Roman peasant, had been dealt with arbitrarily, while Paul, the Roman citizen, was accorded the full measure of protection under the law.

But now Festus has another problem. Paul's appeal to Rome has caught his Roman protector off guard. When the procurator accepted Paul's appeal, he also accepted responsibility for sending a reasonable case to the courts in Rome. What is the basis for remitting this case to the imperial court? What specific charges shall Festus record regarding Paul's case? He admits that he has "nothing definite to write to our sovereign," and that it would be extremely embarrassing to send a Roman citizen to the emperor for trial without specific and serious charges. One would not risk offending Caesar by wasting his time with a trivial case. Therefore, Festus solicits King Agrippa's help. Agrippa must have some knowledge of things Jewish, and he might be able to help translate the concerns of the Jewish leaders into Roman legal language.

PAUL'S FINAL SPEECH
Acts 26:1–23

26:1 Agrippa said to Paul, "You have permission to speak for yourself." Then Paul stretched out his hand and began to defend himself:

2 "I consider myself fortunate that it is before you, King Agrippa, I am to make my defense today against all the accusations of the Jews, 3 because you are especially familiar with all the customs and controversies of the Jews; therefore I beg of you to listen to me patiently.

4 "All the Jews know my way of life from my youth, a life spent from the beginning among my own people and in Jerusalem. 5 They have known for a long time, if they are willing to testify, that I have belonged to the strictest sect of our religion and lived as a Pharisee. 6 And now I stand here on trial on account of my hope in the promise made by God to our ancestors, 7 a promise that our twelve tribes hope to attain, as they earnestly worship day and night. It is for this hope, your Excellency, that I am accused by Jews! 8 Why is it thought incredible by any of you that God raises the dead?

9 "Indeed, I myself was convinced that I ought to do many things against the name of Jesus of Nazareth. 10 And that is what I did in Jerusalem; with authority received from the chief priests, I not only locked up many of the saints in prison, but I also cast my vote against them when they were being condemned to death. 11 By punishing them often in all the synagogues I tried to force them to blaspheme; and since I was so furiously enraged at them, I pursued them even to foreign cities.

12 "With this in mind, I was traveling to Damascus with the authority and commission of the chief priests, 13 when at midday along the road, your Excellency, I saw a light from heaven, brighter than the sun, shining around me and my companions. 14 When we had all fallen to the ground, I heard a voice saying to me in the Hebrew language, 'Saul, Saul, why are you persecuting me? It hurts you to kick against the goads.' 15 I asked, 'Who are you, Lord?' The Lord answered, 'I am Jesus whom you are persecuting. 16 But get up and stand on your feet; for I have appeared to you for this purpose, to appoint you to serve and testify to the things in which you have seen me and to those in which I will appear to you. 17 I will rescue you from your people and from the Gentiles—to whom I am sending you 18 to open their eyes so that they may turn from darkness to light and from the power of Satan to God, so that they may receive forgiveness of sins and a place among those who are sanctified by faith in me.'

19 "After that, King Agrippa, I was not disobedient to the heavenly vision, 20 but declared first to those in Damascus, then in Jerusalem and throughout the countryside of Judea, and also to the Gentiles, that they should repent and turn to God and do deeds consistent with repentance. 21 For this reason the Jews seized me in the temple and tried to kill me. 22 To this day I have

had help from God, and so I stand here, testifying to both small and great, saying nothing but what the prophets and Moses said would take place: 23 that the Messiah must suffer, and that, by being the first to rise from the dead, he would proclaim light both to our people and to the Gentiles."

It is significant that the last speech recorded by Luke comes from his hero, Paul. The setting for this speech is the great audience hall of the praetorium in Caesarea. One has the feeling that everything written in Acts points to this moment, a moment in which our narrator lets out all the stops. Luke even describes Paul's gesture (he "stretched out his hand") as he begins his speech. Scholars have also noted the sophisticated language Paul uses. Paul (and Luke) is at his rhetorical best, choosing words carefully and phrasing them well.

In the best oratorical style of the day, Paul begins by ingratiating himself with his hearers. Paul acknowledges that Agrippa is on hand to help Festus make sense of the charges the Jews have leveled against him.

Paul begins his defense proper by pointing out that he was a Jew from birth and that as a young man he joined the "strictest sect" of Judaism and "lived as a Pharisee." Keeping his defense within a Jewish framework, Paul indicates that he is "on trial on account of my hope in the promise made by God to our ancestors, a promise that our twelve tribes hope to attain, as they earnestly worship day and night" (vv. 6–7). This hope—"that God raises the dead"—Paul shares with his Pharisaic brothers (v. 8). So far Paul has mentioned nothing about Jesus. He has simply established his connection with the Pharisaic school of Judaism and his hope of a general resurrection of the dead—a hope instilled in him by his Pharisaic teachers. It is surprising, therefore, that Jewish leadership in Jerusalem should pursue a case against one who holds a hope in common with other well-known Jewish leaders (an inference that Festus and the others might have made).

Paul's question—"Why is it thought incredible by any of you that God raises the dead?"—seems rhetorical. A good number of his hearers probably neither believed nor understood the notion of resurrection. Certainly the skeptics in the audience included the Sadducees (the high-priestly party) as well as non-Jews.

So far, Paul has been arguing that he had lived as an orthodox Jew, believing what Pharisees believe. He goes on to argue that in his orthodoxy, he came to see the Christian branch of Judaism as standing outside the limits of acceptable faith. They were Jews who had strayed beyond the bounds of usual Jewish belief and practice. In his zeal to stamp out this radical movement, he confesses that he—under the authority of the chief priests—

locked many Christians in prison, and voted the death penalty for those who were condemned. More clearly here than in any of his other autobiographical accounts, we feel Paul's intense anger against this aberrant Jewish sect. Modern readers might conclude that it was overdetermined anger. Paul says, "I was so furiously enraged at them" (v. 11). He even tried to get Christians to blaspheme, to curse Christ.

Paul next recounts the familiar story of his conversion on the road to Damascus. However, this version of the story includes words of Jesus that are missing from the other two accounts (Acts 9 and 22). While traveling to Damascus, Paul was confronted by a bright heavenly light. Paul adds the detail that the voice which came to him from that light spoke Aramaic (the NRSV reads "Hebrew," though see marginal note at 26:14). After the greeting, "Saul, Saul, why are you persecuting me?" the voice added a Greek proverb (presumably translated into Aramaic): "It hurts you to kick against the goads." The goad was a sharp pointed stick used to prod an ox while plowing a field. Paul's activity against Christians was beginning to hurt not just them, but himself as well. Paul must have felt the pain that comes from a growing awareness of being in the wrong as he harassed and arrested these brother and sister Jews. Like the ox implied in the goad metaphor, Paul had been moving against the direction of God's will.

Paul addressed the voice as "Lord," acknowledging the divine power that was grasping him. One has the image of Jacob wrestling with the angel of God, perhaps a parallel Paul (or Luke) may have intended (Gen. 32:22–32). In the Genesis story, there is likewise an emphasis on names and identity. There, Jacob the trickster became Israel the father of a nation. Here, Saul the persecutor becomes Paul the light to the nations. There, Jacob asked the name of the one who prevailed against him, but the name was not revealed—only that he has indeed "seen God face to face" and lived. Here, Paul asks the name of the voice, and the voice answers, "I am Jesus whom you are persecuting." There, Jacob was sent away limping because he was wounded by God. Here, Paul is led away blinded by the divine light (though Paul omits this detail in this account).

Not only does Paul omit any mention of blindness in this speech, but Ananias completely drops out of the story. In this shortened version, Paul receives his commission directly from Jesus (which corresponds with Paul's account in Galatians 1). Paul was appointed by Jesus "to serve and testify to the things in which you have seen me and to those in which I will appear to you" (v. 16). Jesus will send Paul to the Gentiles so that they may "receive forgiveness of sins and a place among those who are sanctified by faith in me" (v. 18). This, for Paul the Pharisee, must have been a very difficult command to hear. How could he, an orthodox Jew committed to maintaining a purity of faith that excluded the messianic sect, now reach out, through preaching and teaching in the name of Jesus, to non-Jews?

The next sentence is decisive: "I was not disobedient to the heavenly vision." Paul brought the Christian message of repentance to Damascus, Jerusalem, and "also to the Gentiles." It is because of his missionary activity that his adversaries are trying to kill him.

Paul concludes his defense by harking back to his Jewish identity. He had preached only "what the prophets and Moses said would take place" (v. 22). However, Paul's very last sentence contains the essence of the problem that he had with his fellow theologians. "That the Messiah must suffer" *was* a radically new concept (see comment on 3:18; 5:30–31). Furthermore, to declare that the resurrection had begun in the person of Jesus ("the first to rise from the dead"), and to suggest that Jesus, a crucified criminal, was raised by God to reveal God's light to both Jews and Gentiles would only compound the theological offense felt by Jewish leaders. Here is where he parts company with both Sadducees and Pharisees. Paul's trial is not simply about the resurrection, as he often claims. It is about *whose* resurrection! And it is about *what* that resurrection means for Israel's mission to the Gentiles!

These items *are* theological issues. Festus had rightly asserted at the outset that this intense debate revolved around "certain points of disagreement . . . about their own religion and about a certain Jesus, who had died, but whom Paul asserted to be alive" (25:19). If Festus had expected legal clarity through Paul's defense, he would have been sorely disappointed. In fact, Festus is left completely baffled, if not frustrated. He must still have wondered what he should write to the emperor about Paul's case. What legal issues make this case worth sending to Rome? How does this case merit the emperor's time? He would certainly want to avoid sending foward a frivolous case that makes him look foolish in the eyes of his superiors in Rome.

THE RESPONSE OF FESTUS AND AGRIPPA
Acts 26:24–32

26:24 **While he was making this defense, Festus exclaimed, "You are out of your mind, Paul! Too much learning is driving you insane!"** 25 **But Paul said, "I am not out of my mind, most excellent Festus, but I am speaking the sober truth.** 26 **Indeed the king knows about these things, and to him I speak freely; for I am certain that none of these things has escaped his notice, for this was not done in a corner.** 27 **King Agrippa, do you believe the prophets? I know** that you believe." [28] Agrippa said to Paul, "Are you so quickly persuading me to become a Christian?" [29] Paul replied, "Whether quickly or not, I pray to God that not only you but also all who are listening to me today might become such as I am—except for these chains."

[30] Then the king got up, and with him the governor and Bernice and those who had been seated with them; [31] and as they were leaving, they said to one another, "This man is doing nothing to deserve death or imprisonment." [32] Agrippa said to Festus, "This man could have been set free if he had not appealed to the emperor."

According to Luke, Festus could not take any more of Paul's defense. Out of frustration, he interrupts Paul with a curt response, "You're crazy, Paul!" Festus follows this outburst with a phrase many students love to hear. "Too much learning is driving you insane!" While this looks like an interruption of Paul's speech, it also underscores the decisive point Paul was trying to make—that he is on trial because of the resurrection.

In declaring Paul mad, perhaps Festus was also trying to find a way of freeing Paul. According to ancient Roman law, "the personal character of the accused should be taken into account, whether he could have committed the offense, . . . and also if he was of sane mind . . . , for although the rash person ought to be punished, still they should be excused just as insane persons are" (Digest 48.4.7).

Paul declares that he is indeed in his right mind and turns to King Agrippa for support, reminding the king of his own Jewish heritage. The verbal exchange between Paul and Agrippa is fascinating. The one being questioned now becomes the questioner. "Do you believe the prophets?" asks Paul. "I know that you believe." One might expect Paul to continue to argue from the prophets that the Messiah was Jesus. Apparently this is what Agrippa anticipated, for he responds, "Are you so quickly persuading me to become a Christian?" One can almost hear the laughter in his voice. If sarcasm was intended, Paul ignored it with his response. He hopes that "all who are listening"—and this includes all who read Luke's trial transcript—"might become such as I am"—a believer.

Without further response, the king, his sister, and the procurator get up to leave the great hall of the palace. In the silence of his cell, Paul must have pondered often what he overheard as they were leaving. "This man is doing nothing to deserve death or imprisonment. . . . This man could have been set free if he had not appealed to the emperor" (vv. 31–32). One might conclude that Paul made a poor decision in appealing to Rome. In the end, however, that appeal guaranteed that he would bring the gospel to the heart of the empire.

14. Paul's Odyssey to Rome
Acts 27:1–28:31

THE VOYAGE FROM PALESTINE TO CRETE
Acts 27:1–12

27:1 When it was decided that we were to sail for Italy, they transferred Paul and some other prisoners to a centurion of the Augustan Cohort, named Julius. ² Embarking on a ship of Adramyttium that was about to set sail to the ports along the coast of Asia, we put to sea, accompanied by Aristarchus, a Macedonian from Thessalonica. ³ The next day we put in at Sidon; and Julius treated Paul kindly, and allowed him to go to his friends to be cared for. ⁴ Putting to sea from there, we sailed under the lee of Cyprus, because the winds were against us. ⁵ After we sailed across the sea that is off Cilicia and Pamphylia, we came to Myra in Lycia. ⁶ There the centurion found an Alexandrian ship bound for Italy and put us on board. ⁷ We sailed slowly for a number of days and arrived with difficulty off Cnidus, and as the wind was against us, we sailed under the lee of Crete off Salmone. ⁸ Sailing past it with difficulty, we came to a place called Fair Havens, near the city of Lasea.

⁹ Since much time had been lost and sailing was now dangerous, because even the Fast had already gone by, Paul advised them, ¹⁰ saying, "Sirs, I can see that the voyage will be with danger and much heavy loss, not only of the cargo and the ship, but also of our lives." ¹¹ But the centurion paid more attention to the pilot and to the owner of the ship than to what Paul said. ¹² Since the harbor was not suitable for spending the winter, the majority was in favor of putting to sea from there, on the chance that somehow they could reach Phoenix, where they could spend the winter. It was a harbor of Crete, facing southwest and northwest.

Agrippa's statement at the end of Paul's hearing—"This man could have been set free if he had not appealed to the emperor" (26:32)—guarantees that Paul and the gospel will reach Rome under the aegis of Roman law. An unnecessary, and perhaps mistaken, appeal by Paul became the vehicle for carrying out the will of God. Paul will arrive safely in Rome because

God's will was at work through the protection of Roman judicial process and the Roman army.

The reader will notice in the first sentence of this section that Luke has inserted himself back into the narrative as the we passages return. As I noted in the Introduction, it is difficult to say with certainty whether Luke is reporting his own eyewitness account, incorporating someone else's travel diary, or using his considerable literary skill to heighten the exciting effect of the odyssey by bringing the "writer" (and reader—"we") into the action.

It is also worth remembering that the we passages occur only in the travel sections. Luke discontinued his first-person narrative as soon as Paul arrived in Jerusalem (Acts 21:17). The episodes that took place in Jerusalem and Caesarea are described from a third-person perspective. Now that the trials are behind Paul and he is on the way to Rome, Luke returns to telling the story as an eyewitness: "We put to sea" (v. 2).

We are reminded that Paul is still a prisoner. "Paul and some other prisoners" were transferred to a centurion of the Augustan Cohort (an honorary title often used of auxiliary troops consisting of non-Roman soldiers drawn from the local population; this unit was probably from Syria). The reader is told that Julius was the name of the officer in charge of transporting Paul from Caesarea to Rome and that "Julius treated Paul kindly, and allowed him to go to his friends to be cared for" (v. 3). Apparently, the author of this account and Aristarchus (also an earlier "travel companion" of Paul, 19:29; 20:4) were two of those friends who paid for their own passage and for Paul's needs along the way.

Chapter 27 is full of details about the voyage: nautical terms and practices, ports of call, ancient meteorology, information about Rome's merchant marine. Luke offers us one of the better-documented first-century travel narratives. The reader will be aided by consulting a map of the region in charting Paul's voyage to Rome.

Luke begins the sea voyage by noting that the entourage boarded a ship that was about to return to its home port of Adramyttium (located on the west coast of ancient Asia). From Caesarea they sailed northward along the coast to Sidon, then out into the Mediterranean Sea, around Cyprus and along southern Galatia to Myra in Lycia. Here the centurion and his charges disembarked, and transferred to another vessel (from the north Egyptian city of Alexandria) sailing for Italy. Luke tells the reader that it was slow going between Lycia and Crete, where they finally put in at Fair Havens.

In light of the slow journey, Paul must have anticipated that the ship's owner would be anxious to push on. Luke notes that the Fast, that is, the

Day of Atonement which occurs in September or October, had already passed. Navigation was precarious after September 15 and ceased altogether on November 15. Therefore, at very best, there were about six more weeks of safe sailing weather. Paul's words to those in charge of the ship proved to be prophetic. In Crete, he told the centurion, the captain, and the owner that "the voyage will be with danger and much heavy loss, not only of the cargo and the ship, but also of our lives" (v. 10). Later on, Paul will remind them, "I told you so!" (27:21).

It looks as if those in charge of the ship simply wanted to sail a few miles along the coast of Crete to a better harbor, Phoenix, where they would tie up for the winter.

THE SHIP RUNS INTO A STORM
Acts 27:13–32

27:13 **When a moderate south wind began to blow, they thought they could achieve their purpose; so they weighed anchor and began to sail past Crete, close to the shore. ** [14] **But soon a violent wind, called the northeaster, rushed down from Crete. ** [15] **Since the ship was caught and could not be turned head-on into the wind, we gave way to it and were driven. ** [16] **By running under the lee of a small island called Cauda we were scarcely able to get the ship's boat under control. ** [17] **After hoisting it up they took measures to undergird the ship; then, fearing that they would run on the Syrtis, they lowered the sea anchor and so were driven. ** [18] **We were being pounded by the storm so violently that on the next day they began to throw the cargo overboard, ** [19] **and on the third day with their own hands they threw the ship's tackle overboard. ** [20] **When neither sun nor stars appeared for many days, and no small tempest raged, all hope of our being saved was at last abandoned.**
[21] **Since they had been without food for a long time, Paul then stood up among them and said, "Men, you should have listened to me and not have set sail from Crete and thereby avoided this damage and loss. ** [22] **I urge you now to keep up your courage, for there will be no loss of life among you, but only of the ship. ** [23] **For last night there stood by me an angel of the God to whom I belong and whom I worship, ** [24] **and he said, 'Do not be afraid, Paul; you must stand before the emperor; and indeed, God has granted safety to all those who are sailing with you.' ** [25] **So keep up your courage, men, for I have faith in God that it will be exactly as I have been told. ** [26] **But we will have to run aground on some island."**
[27] **When the fourteenth night had come, as we were drifting across the sea of Adria, about midnight the sailors suspected that they were nearing land. ** [28] **So they took soundings and found twenty fathoms; a little farther on they**

took soundings again and found fifteen fathoms. [29] Fearing that we might run on the rocks, they let down four anchors from the stern and prayed for day to come. [30] But when the sailors tried to escape from the ship and had lowered the boat into the sea, on the pretext of putting out anchors from the bow, [31] Paul said to the centurion and the soldiers, "Unless these men stay in the ship, you cannot be saved." [32] Then the soldiers cut away the ropes of the boat and set it adrift.

Luke has given us a truly classic odyssey. The first-time reader does not know the outcome of this dangerous voyage, and must trust that the angelic promise is true. The sea is a frightening place where human control of the environment is quickly challenged and lost. It is clear that the ship carrying Paul, Julius, and the others is out of control, nearly running aground on the island of Cauda (just south of Crete), then surging into the open angry sea, then almost grounding again on the Syrtis, a shoal west of Cyrene (about one hundred miles south of Crete). Luke provides an eyewitness description: "We were being pounded by the storm . . . violently" (v. 18).

In the midst of all this chaos, Paul shouts out, "Men, you should have listened to me." The crew who had been forced to throw the ship's cargo and tackle overboard may have been seriously tempted to pitch Paul as well. No wonder prophets have not been popular. Fortunately, Paul had received an additional message from an angel of God. "God has granted safety to all those who are sailing with you" (v. 24). But first, according to Paul, the ship will run aground on some island. While this message from God may have brought comfort to the ship's passengers, it would not have pleased the ship's owner.

The angelic message also reaffirmed the divine imperative. Paul "must" stand before the emperor (see comments on 19:21–22). This is God's will and nothing—not even the chaos of nature—can stop it from happening.

As they drifted out of control in the pitch dark of their fourteenth night at sea, the sailors suspected that they were nearing land. Soundings confirmed this and raised fear among the crew that the ship might finally break apart on the rocks.

Some of the sailors, pretending to let out the anchors, attempted to escape in the ship's dinghy, but Paul foiled their plan. He declared to the centurion and the soldiers, "Unless these men stay in the ship, you cannot be saved" (v. 31). One can only imagine the look on the faces of these sailors as they saw their means of escape cut loose by the soldiers and set adrift. Paul now had more to fear than shipwreck.

The entire scene may have reminded the reader of two other biblical stories: Jonah sailing a stormy sea and Jesus calming the sea (Matt. 8:23–27; Mark 4:35–41; Luke 8:22–25). In the story of Jonah, this ancient prophet of Israel was trying to escape God's commission to travel to Nineveh (Israel's hated enemy) to preach to the Ninevites, offering them an opportunity for repentance and divine forgiveness. Unlike Paul, Jonah tried to duck his missionary calling. After Jonah embarked in a ship that would take him in the opposite direction, a great storm forced the sailors to throw the cargo overboard and then to draw lots in order to identify the culprit responsible for this disaster. The lot fell on Jonah who had been fast asleep in the hold of the ship, and he too was cast overboard. With that, "the sea ceased from its raging" (Jonah 1:15). The reader is invited to read the rest of this Hebrew short story to discover how, as with the story of Paul's journey to Rome, God's will prevails. Jonah did eventually reach Nineveh, and even though he detested his commission to preach the gospel of repentance to the Ninevites, he carried out the will of God.

In the second story, Jesus, like Jonah, was asleep in a boat in the midst of a stormy sea. His disciples feared for their lives and wondered if Jesus even cared for their safety (Mark 4:38). The frightened disciples woke Jesus and asked, "Do you not care?" Then, after Jesus calmed the sea with those famous words—"Peace! Be still!"—Jesus asked his disciples a question of his own: "Have you still no faith?"

Luke's narrative of Paul in the midst of a stormy sea seems to combine elements of these biblical stories. Paul, like Jonah, is being sent by God to a center of political and military power. He is going to preach a message of repentence. But unlike Jonah, Paul's message is intended for the Jews of Rome (they will be asked to repent, to change their minds about Jesus), and not for the foreign overlords. Paul appears to have been, like Jonah, the cause of the sailors' plight. The reader might surmise that Paul's presence on board the ship brought on a storm that provided God an opportunity to show that the divine will is stronger than the ravages of nature.

And as in the story of Jesus, Paul offers a way of salvation to the anxious sailors. Jesus asked his storm-tossed disciples, "Why are you afraid?" Likewise, Paul exhorts his companions: "Keep up your courage, men, for I have faith in God" (v. 25); "Unless [you] stay in the ship, you cannot be saved" (v. 32). That salvation, as we shall see in the next section, is presented to these frightened passengers in the form of a meal.

PAUL AND THE PASSENGERS SHARE A MEAL
Acts 27:33–38

27:33 **Just before daybreak, Paul urged all of them to take some food, saying, "Today is the fourteenth day that you have been in suspense and remaining without food, having eaten nothing.** [34] **Therefore I urge you to take some food, for it will help you survive; for none of you will lose a hair from your heads."** [35] **After he had said this, he took bread; and giving thanks to God in the presence of all, he broke it and began to eat.** [36] **Then all of them were encouraged and took food for themselves.** [37] **(We were in all two hundred seventy-six persons in the ship.)** [38] **After they had satisfied their hunger, they lightened the ship by throwing the wheat into the sea.**

In the midst of the stormy sea, when "no small tempest raged, and all hope of our being saved was at last abandoned" (v. 20), Paul sealed the divine promise of salvation for the ship's passengers with a meal. It is neither by accident nor by unconscious habit that Luke combines the giving thanks to God, the breaking of bread aboard a doomed ship, and the promise of salvation to the passengers. It has been suggested that this passage describes a celebration of the Lord's Supper (or Eucharist, meaning "thanksgiving"). However, six objections have been raised against such an interpretation of this passage.

1. No cup is mentioned.
2. It was not unusual for Jews to render thanks before a meal.
3. This looks like an ordinary meal in which "they had satisfied their hunger."
4. The term "salvation" (obscured by the word translated as "survive," v. 34) has no cosmic connotations here.
5. Paul would not have shared the Lord's Supper with non-Christians.
6. The words of institution are not mentioned.

Yet, none of these arguments singly or together destroy the possibility that Luke has described a eucharistic scene. First, the words and practice related to the Lord's Supper remained in a state of flux during the first century C.E. Luke's own account of the Lord's Supper is considerably different from that presented in the Gospels of Matthew and Mark (compare Luke 22:17–20 with Matt. 26:26–28 and Mark 14:22–23). Certainly if wine was unavailable on a half-wrecked ship (probably pitched overboard), it is not inconceivable that the Lord's Supper would have been carried out with bread alone. We should also note that in Luke 24:30 the risen Christ was made known to two disciples in the "breaking of bread," and in Acts 20:7 Luke uses the phrase "breaking of bread" as a description of the Lord's Supper. Furthermore, it was still the practice of the church to link the Lord's Supper with a common meal. Paul had already offered the Corinthians advice on how the Lord's Supper, eaten in the context of a common meal, may be celebrated without abuse (1 Cor. 11:17–34).

Second, Luke and Aristarchus were traveling with Paul so that at least these three Christians could share the sacred meal. And what more appropriate time? The meal was also offered to the others on board ship and presented as "a meal for your salvation" (an alternate translation of v. 34, "food . . . [which] will help you survive"). But does the saving of life and limb have anything to do with the Lord's Supper? It is clear that the early church had already made this connection. Paul himself declared that those who abuse the Lord's Supper risk bodily ills and death (1 Cor. 11:30). The converse, that the Lord's Supper offers the promise of physical salvation, may also have been claimed by the apostle (a few years later, Ignatius, Bishop of Antioch, described the Lord's Supper as "the medicine of immortality, and the antidote which wards off death" [*Ephesians* 20:2]).

Finally, this scene has been carefully crafted by Luke. He has deliberately presented Paul taking the initiative in gathering the ship's crew, the soldiers, and the prisoners for a meal in the most unlikely place of all—in the midst of a disastrous storm. One might have expected to read about a thanksgiving meal after Paul and the others had reached the safety of land. But it is in the midst of chaos—such themes as darkness and the depths of the sea (Genesis 1) would not be wasted on the ancient reader—that Paul brings the word and the meal of salvation. Luke's first-century reader would not have glossed this over, nor should we.

"A meal for your salvation"—not merely survival—is what gives the entire sea voyage its poignancy and theological punch. Otherwise, one wonders why Luke included this scene, and why he nuanced it in the way he did. Luke writes on two levels at the same time. At the level of ordinary experience, he records a meal of sustenance which the passengers share. At the level of the extraordinary, he has nuanced his language to suggest that they shared a meal of salvation that had positive consequences for those aboard this sinking ship.

This was the *last supper* for these folks, for "after they satisfied their hunger, they lightened the ship by throwing the wheat into the sea." This act of casting grain on the sea brings to mind an ancient metaphor for missionary activity—disseminating (literally, scattering seeds of grain) the gospel. An ancient church manual, *The Teaching of the Twelve Apostles* (also called *The Didache*), records a very early eucharistic prayer that contains this phrase: "As this bread was scattered over the hills and then was brought together and made one, so let your church be brought together from the ends of the earth into your Kingdom" (*Didache* 9:4; see also Jesus' parable of the sower, Matt. 13:1–23; Mark 4:1–20; Luke 8:4–15). Even in the midst of a stormy sea, Paul was involved in scattering the seeds of gospel truth, and will shortly bring this truth to Rome.

SHIPWRECK!
Acts 27:39–44

> 27:39 **In the morning they did not recognize the land, but they noticed a bay with a beach, on which they planned to run the ship ashore, if they could. ⁴⁰ So they cast off the anchors and left them in the sea. At the same time they loosened the ropes that tied the steering-oars; then hoisting the foresail to the wind, they made for the beach. ⁴¹ But striking a reef, they ran the ship aground; the bow stuck and remained immovable, but the stern was broken up by the force of the waves. ⁴² The soldiers' plan was to kill the prisoners, so that none might swim away and escape; ⁴³ but the centurion, wishing to save Paul, kept them from carrying out their plan. He ordered those who could swim to jump overboard first and make for the land, ⁴⁴ and the rest to follow, some on planks and others on pieces of the ship. And so it was that all were brought safely to land.**

In exciting detail, Luke describes the wreck of the ship carrying Paul toward Rome. Ordinarily, the guards would have killed their prisoners, rather than take the chance that they might escape. God, however, had plans for Paul. Luke writes that Julius, the Roman centurion, had a part to play in God's saving activity. He, too, was guided by a commission—to bring Paul safely to Rome. It may be that Julius went well beyond the requirements of his orders. Once the ship began to break up, the soldiers were quite correct in wanting to kill the prisoners. The centurion, however, "wishing to save Paul," overruled the plan of his men, unshackled the prisoners, and ordered them to swim for safety. Just as Julius and his men had been saved by the commission which the angel of God gave to Paul, so Paul was "saved" by Julius's order to his soldiers.

PAUL ON MALTA
Acts 28:1–10

28:1 **After we had reached safety, we then learned that the island was
called Malta.** [2] **The natives showed us unusual kindness. Since it had begun
to rain and was cold, they kindled a fire and welcomed all of us around it.**
[3] **Paul had gathered a bundle of brushwood and was putting it on the fire,
when a viper, driven out by the heat, fastened itself on his hand.** [4] **When the
natives saw the creature hanging from his hand, they said to one another,
"This man must be a murderer; though he has escaped from the sea, justice
has not allowed him to live."** [5] **He, however, shook off the creature into the
fire and suffered no harm.** [6] **They were expecting him to swell up or drop
dead, but after they had waited a long time and saw that nothing unusual
had happened to him, they changed their minds and began to say that he
was a god.**

[7] **Now in the neighborhood of that place were lands belonging to the leading man of the island, named Publius, who received us and entertained us
hospitably for three days.** [8] **It so happened that the father of Publius lay sick
in bed with fever and dysentery. Paul visited him and cured him by praying
and putting his hands on him.** [9] **After this happened, the rest of the people
on the island who had diseases also came and were cured.** [10] **They bestowed
many honors on us, and when we were about to sail, they put on board all
the provisions we needed.**

After floating awhile on debris from the broken ship, Paul and the others finally washed ashore on the small island of Melita (modern Malta, just
south of Sicily). Luke reports that the "natives" (literally, "barbarians"—
those who do not speak Greek) who met them on the beach were unusu-
ally hospitable. The survivors of the shipwreck, cold and wet from the sea
and rain, found relief from a huge bonfire kindled by their Maltese hosts.
Paul, attempting to be helpful by putting more wood on the fire, was bit-
ten by a poisonous viper hidden in the woodpile. Aware that Paul was a
prisoner, the Maltese concluded that Paul's guilt was self-evident. "This
man must be a murderer." The gods have allowed him to escape the sea,
but not the serpent. "Justice [a Greek goddess] has not allowed him to live"
(v. 4). Yet Paul simply shakes the snake from his hand into the fire.

Luke, ever the master storyteller, paints a vivid picture of quaint islanders circling around Paul, waiting for him to swell up or drop dead. The
Greek text gives the sense that they waited expectantly for a long period
of time. Slowly they began to change their minds about Paul, coming to
the opposite conclusion. Paul is no criminal. He is a god! No matter what

judgment is rendered in Rome, the gods have spoken regarding Paul's character. He is one of theirs.

Luke adds a second story about Paul's Maltese adventure. A "leading man" (probably a Roman official) named Publius befriended Paul and his companions and entertained them. In the course of events Paul discovered that Publius's father was sick with dysentery. Paul prayed for the man and he was healed. For the next three months, according to Luke, Paul cured the rest of the islanders who had diseases. Luke, again with a double meaning in mind, says that Paul and his companions received many "honors," a term that can also describe the physician's fee.

With the coming of early spring, Julius was ready to leave this small island to take his prisoners to their final destination—Rome.

"AND SO WE CAME TO ROME"
Acts 28:11–16

> 28:11 **Three months later we set sail on a ship that had wintered at the island, an Alexandrian ship with the Twin Brothers as its figurehead.** [12] **We put in at Syracuse and stayed there for three days;** [13] **then we weighed anchor and came to Rhegium. After one day there a south wind sprang up, and on the second day we came to Puteoli.** [14] **There we found believers and were invited to stay with them for seven days. And so we came to Rome.** [15] **The believers from there, when they heard of us, came as far as the Forum of Appius and Three Taverns to meet us. On seeing them, Paul thanked God and took courage.**
> [16] **When we came into Rome, Paul was allowed to live by himself, with the soldier who was guarding him.**

Paul and those with him spent the winter months on Malta. When shipping safely resumed in February, Julius negotiated with the owner of a grain ship from Alexandria to transport his entourage to Italy. Luke includes the detail that the Twin Brothers were carved as the ship's figurehead, representing the patron gods of sailors, Castor and Pollux.

Their first port of call was Syracuse on the island of Sicily. After three days, Luke notes that they caught a favorable south wind that whisked them up to Puteoli, Italy, in just two days. Puteoli served as both the port city for Naples and was the normal port of entry for travelers to Rome from the east. Here a group of Christians met Paul and invited him to stay with them for a week. Presumably, they played host to other members of the entourage as well. After the week of Christian hospitality, the group headed for Rome, following the famous Appian Way.

In one terse sentence, Luke reports one of the most significant events in the life of the early church: "And so we came to Rome." God has brought Paul and his gospel message to the capital of the empire. Christians from Rome, hearing that Paul was on his way, rushed out to meet him, walking "as far as the Forum of Appius [43 miles] and the Three Taverns [33 miles]" (v. 15).

The existence of Christians in Italy prior to Paul's visit indicates that considerable missionary work had already been done there. We know of two very likely candidates for this work: Priscilla and Aquila. According to Acts 18, while visiting Corinth, Paul "found a Jew named Aquila . . . who had recently come from Italy with his wife Priscilla, because Claudius had ordered all Jews to leave Rome" (49 C.E.). Claudius issued the expulsion edict because "the Jews at Rome caused continuous disturbances at the instigation of Chrestus [Christ?]" (Suetonius, *Lives of the Caesars*, Claudius 25). It could well be that at this early date serious—and heated—discussions were taking place within the Jewish community about the new messianic movement which was spreading from Palestine into Asia, Africa, and Europe.

Claudius's ban was lifted in 54 C.E., and the Jews who had been expelled were allowed to return to Rome. Apparently Priscilla and Aquila were among the Jewish Christians who chose to return, for Paul greets them in his letter to the church at Rome (Rom. 16:3). This hardworking missionary couple would have had ample time to develop a strong Christian mission in Italy.

Upon hearing news of Paul's arrival in Italy, a group of these zealous Christians rushed out of Rome to meet the great missionary to the Gentiles. Paul was buoyed by their presence, and the knowledge that he would have a basis of support in the capital city.

Verse 16 concludes the "we" narration of Acts. Luke has achieved his geographic goal: "We came into Rome." Here Paul was permitted to live by himself, with only one soldier guarding him. He was held in light custody, under house arrest.

PAUL IN ROME
Acts 28:17–28

28:17 **Three days later he called together the local leaders of the Jews. When they had assembled, he said to them, "Brothers, though I had done nothing against our people or the customs of our ancestors, yet I was**

arrested in Jerusalem and handed over to the Romans. [18] When they had examined me, the Romans wanted to release me, because there was no reason
for the death penalty in my case. [19] But when the Jews objected, I was compelled to appeal to the emperor—even though I had no charge to bring
against my nation. [20] For this reason therefore I have asked to see you and
speak with you, since it is for the sake of the hope of Israel that I am bound
with this chain." [21] They replied, "We have received no letters from Judea
about you, and none of the brothers coming here has reported or spoken
anything evil about you. [22] But we would like to hear from you what you
think, for with regard to this sect we know that everywhere it is spoken
against."

[23] After they had set a day to meet with him, they came to him at his lodg-
ings in great numbers. From morning until evening he explained the matter
to them, testifying to the kingdom of God and trying to convince them about
Jesus both from the law of Moses and from the prophets. [24] Some were convinced by what he had said, while others refused to believe. [25] So they disagreed with each other; and as they were leaving, Paul made one further
statement: "The Holy Spirit was right in saying to your ancestors through the
prophet Isaiah,

[26] 'Go to this people and say,
    You will indeed listen, but never understand,
        and you will indeed look, but never perceive.
[27] For this people's heart has grown dull,
        and their ears are hard of hearing,
            and they have shut their eyes;
            so that they might not look with their eyes,
        and listen with their ears,
        and understand with their heart and turn—
        and I would heal them.'
[28] Let it be known to you then that this salvation of God has been sent to the
Gentiles; they will listen."

True to his missionary program, Paul spoke first with the Jews of Rome.
It is clear, however, that Paul wished to do more than proclaim the gospel.
He was curious to know if the Sanhedrin in Jerusalem had contacted the
Roman Jewish community in order to pursue the case against him. It
would have been unlikely that the high priest and his staff would have personally pursued their case against Paul in Rome, but they might have en-
listed the Jewish leaders at Rome to further their cause.

Rather than proclaiming his gospel message to the Roman Jewish leaders, Paul presented an exceedingly defensive statement. In stating that
he had done "nothing against our people or the customs of our ancestors,"

he identified with the Jewish community (v. 17). The Roman governor had been prepared to release him, but because the Jewish leadership in Jerusalem insisted on pursuing the case, he was forced to appeal to Caesar.

Paul's next statement is a bit strange. What does he mean by, "I was compelled to appeal to the emperor—even though I had no charge to bring against my nation" (v. 19)? According to Luke's narrative, the complaint had been the other way around—the leaders of Paul's nation were bringing charges against him. In this meeting with the Roman Jewish leaders Paul wants to be very clear that he is in Rome *not* to bring charges against the Jerusalem Jewish leaders. It would have been the experience of the Roman Jewish community that embassies of Jews from Jerusalem had on several occasions brought charges to the imperial courts against both Roman and Jewish rulers in Jerusalem.

Paul's defensive stance proved unnecessary, for the Jews of Rome knew nothing about his troubles with the Jerusalem authorities. They had received no letters of condemnation from Jerusalem. They were not aware of any expectation that they should pursue the case against Paul on behalf of the Sanhedrin. Furthermore, those in the Jewish community who knew of Paul had nothing bad to report about him. The Roman Jewish community has maintained a respectful distance from the Jerusalem Jewish community. It is also clear that the leaders of the Roman synagogues have kept their distance from the Roman Christian community as well, for they want to hear from Paul firsthand his opinions about the messianists, a branch of Judaism "that everywhere . . . is spoken against" (v. 22).

Paul and the Jewish leaders scheduled a meeting to talk about the Christian movement. On the appointed day a large group of people gathered in the house where Paul was staying. Paul spent a full day trying to help them understand the Christian message about Jesus. In his discussion Paul interpreted scriptural texts ("the law of Moses and . . . the prophets") that pertain to the reign of God and God's work through Jesus (those two items are parallel concerns for Paul). As usual, wherever Paul presented his message, some were convinced and some were not. Luke puts the matter simply: "So they disagreed with each other." Luke adds, however, a final bitter note from Paul as he quotes the prophet Isaiah (6:9–10), who also had been exasperated with his own people eight centuries earlier. They have eyes, yet do not see; they have ears, but do not hear; they have faculties for understanding, and comprehend nothing.

Paul put his own twist on Isaiah's summation. The ancient prophet asked, "How long, O Lord?" and the Lord answered:

> Until cities lie waste without inhabitant,
>   and houses without people,
>   and the land is utterly desolate;
>   until the LORD sends everyone far away,
>   and vast is the emptiness in the midst of the land.
>   (Isa. 6:11–12)

For Paul, like Isaiah, there had been a depressing emptiness in the land of Israel, an emptiness that he felt deeply as he left Jerusalem on a mission to persecute those beyond the boundaries of Israel. Yet, on the road to those faraway lands, God intervened with a mission of God's own. The voice of Jesus redirected Paul's energies—not for more death and desolation, but for life—among the Gentiles. Paul came to discover that the good news gives life and salvation to the Gentiles—"they will listen" (v. 28).

THE END
Acts 28:30–31

28:30 **He lived there two whole years at his own expense and welcomed all who came to him,** 31 **proclaiming the kingdom of God and teaching about the Lord Jesus Christ with all boldness and without hindrance.**

With these words Luke brings his two volumes to a close. What began as a tiny fellowship of Jesus' closest followers has grown into scores of communities embracing thousands of Christian believers. What began as a small sect of Judaism has become an independent religious movement with a growing majority of non-Jews. What began in the distant province of Judea has reached Rome, the cultural and political center of the empire. Luke has finally reached the goal of his literary work. He has completed his narrative of "all the events that have been fulfilled among us" (Luke 1:1), from the life and ministry of Jesus in Luke's Gospel to the life and ministry of the church in his Acts of the Apostles.

According to Luke, Paul spent two full years in Rome, where he lived "at his own expense and welcomed all who came to him" (v. 30). If Paul is still in the custody of Rome (see 28:20), then he is under the lightest possible house arrest, with considerable freedom of movement. The freedom he experienced reflected the prevailing political climate in Rome. It is entirely possible that Paul was expecting complete vindication by the emperor's court. Paul's arrival in Rome in about 57 C.E. coincided with the early years of the reign of Emperor Nero (54–68 C.E.). While Nero is infamous for his violent persecution of Roman Christians (and other "enemies") in 65 C.E., the early years of his reign were radically different. He began his imperial rule by establishing an enlightened and tolerant administration. He was hailed as the "New Augustus," bringer of the "Golden Age" to Rome, and promising *clementia* (clemency), even to those among the lower social classes who had been previously judged as enemies of the empire. Paul's appeal to Caesar was not ill-placed. He had every reason to hope for vindication and freedom.

Luke's final statement summarizes Paul's two years in Rome. The great missionary filled his days teaching anyone who came to him. His message was the same one he had taught the Jewish leaders of Rome—about the kingdom of God and the Lord Jesus Christ. In these few words Luke has compacted the preaching and teaching of Paul. He *preached* about the reign of God and he *taught* about the Lord Jesus Christ. The subject of Paul's *preaching*—the coming reign of God—may have been problematic for some in Rome, where the emperor was the reigning monarch.

It was the subject of Paul's *teaching*, however, that contained seeds of serious consequence. Note the words used to describe Jesus: Lord and Messiah (Christ). They seem ordinary to our ears and not terribly threatening. Yet, in first-century Rome, such terms were loaded with political significance. The three titles Nero preferred were Augustus, Caesar, and Lord. To claim that Jesus is Lord might have been considered an act of treason. The further claim, that Jesus is Messiah, increases political suspicions about Christians living in Rome. Remember the accusation against Jesus which the leaders of the Sanhedrin brought to Pilate. "We found this man . . . saying that he himself is the Messiah, *a king*" (Luke 23:2, and only found in Luke's Gospel). Paul's teaching about Jesus was certainly politically suspect, especially for Jews of Rome who wished to maintain peace with the imperial powers. They would not have wanted another banishment as had occurred under Claudius in 49 C.E.

Nevertheless, the Roman authorities tolerated Paul's proclamation; he was able to preach and teach "with all boldness and without hindrance" (v. 31).

Luke brings his story to an end much too suddenly. As with every good story, we are left wanting more. What happened to Paul? Did his case ever come to trial? Did he receive clemency? Was he released from house arrest? Did he go on to Spain as he planned (Rom. 15:22–29)? Luke's detail that Paul had been held for "two whole years" may indicate that the statute of limitations ran out. Ordinarily, if a complainant did not pursue a case within two years, the matter was dropped. Perhaps the Jerusalem Jews who had been upset with Paul found other things to absorb their energy (at this same time in Judea, a serious revolution against Rome was on the rise which not only challenged Roman rule but also threatened positions of power held by those in charge of the Sanhedrin—the Sadducees). Perhaps the leaders of the Sanhedrin chose not to pursue the matter, the case was dropped, and Paul was freed.

Or was Paul compelled to stand trial before the emperor? Was he executed as later tradition suggests? While it is true that Nero tolerated a wide variety of religious movements during the first decade of his reign, we also know that this toleration came to a bloody end as the emperor became increasingly paranoid and ruthless. Within a few years of Paul's arrest, Christians in Rome became politically suspect (falsely charged with setting Rome on fire in 65 C.E.) and their leaders were violently persecuted and martyred.

It may be that Paul was released from custody after "two whole years," continued with his missionary work (in Spain?) for a while, and then returned to Rome where he was again arrested, tried, and executed. Clement, a bishop of Rome writing to the Corinthian church at the end of the first century, is the first Christian writer to imply that Paul was martyred in Rome (*1 Clement* 5:5–7).

And what of Peter and the other apostles? They have not been heard from since the middle of Acts. Surely Luke must have known something about the continuing ministry of Peter, James, and other early Christian leaders. Why did he not continue the story?

Perhaps, like a good storyteller, Luke concluded the story knowing that all of these questions, and more, would be left unresolved. If he has drawn us in and piqued our interest about the Christian church, he has done his job. And yet, how unusual for such an excellent writer to close his book so abruptly.

Some have suggested that Luke did have more to say. Perhaps he intended to write a third volume which would narrate the work of Peter and the other apostles, but was unable to do so. Perhaps he did write a third volume and it is now lost to us (one scholar has made the clever suggestion that we do indeed possess Luke's third volume—an imitation of Paul's letters known as the Pastoral Epistles—1 and 2 Timothy and Titus). Or perhaps Luke's original manuscript once had a longer ending, which was lost or left off by early scribes. Or perhaps Luke died before he could finish his work.

Perhaps . . . Perhaps . . . One could continue to speculate, but little is gained by it. We have Luke's story. It is a superb story that has become scripture. If Luke has drawn us in so that we continue the story of God's marvelous work in the world, he has accomplished his task. He has left us an orderly account "of the events that have been fulfilled among us . . . so that you may know the truth concerning the things about which you have been instructed" (Luke 1:1–4). Thanks to Luke, we are well instructed.

POSTSCRIPT

The ending of the Acts of the Apostles, viewed in light of Luke's two volumes (the Gospel and Acts), might not be so odd after all. As I noted in the Introduction, Luke's narration continues the magnificent journey of God with God's people,

> from Abraham and Sarah, who left the comfort of family and friends to claim God's gift of a distant promised land;
> to Moses and Miriam, who led a band of Hebrew slaves to reclaim the promised land under the leadership of God;
> to Isaiah the prophet, who called the people of God to announce God's sovereignty over all lands.

In Luke's narrative, Jesus traveled from Nazareth to Jerusalem proclaiming the coming reign of God, and Paul traveled from Jerusalem to Rome affirming that God indeed reigns over all lands through God's servant, Jesus the Messiah.

Luke might have imagined that those who read his history would be traveling their own segment of the sacred journey, and that they would write their own continuation of his story. In leaving his story up in the air, Luke has encouraged the reader to continue the story by appending his or her personal journey of faith. Luke would also have known that no mortal is able to write an ending to this story. The sacred journey is God's story, and God will write the final lines when we reach our journey's goal in God's eternal love.

Works Cited

The Apostolic Fathers. 2 vols. Trans. Kirsopp Lake. Loeb Classical Library. Cambridge, Mass.: Harvard University Press, 1924–25. (For *Clement to the Corinthians; Didache; Ignatius to the Ephesians.*)

Cadbury, Henry J. *The Style and Literary Method of Luke.* Cambridge, Mass.: Harvard University Press, 1920.

Hobart, W. K. *The Medical Language of St. Luke.* Dublin: Hodges, Figgis, 1882. Reprint, Grand Rapids: Baker Book House, 1954.

Irenaeus. *Against Heresies.* In *Early Christian Fathers.* Edited by Cyril C. Richardson. Philadelphia: Westminster Press, 1953.

Josephus. *Works.* 9 vols. Trans. H. St. J. Thackeray et al. Loeb Classical Library. Cambridge, Mass.: Harvard University Press, 1926–65.

The Mishnah. Trans. Herbert Danby. Oxford: Clarendon Press, 1933. (For translation of the tractate *Pirke Aboth.*)

Schneemelcher, Wilhelm, ed. *Acts of Paul and Thecla* and *The Infancy Story of Thomas.* In *New Testament Apocrypha.* 2 vols. Trans. R. M. Wilson. Philadelphia: Westminster Press, 1959, 1964.

Suetonius. "Claudius." In *Lives of the Caesars.* 2 vols. Trans. J. C. Rolfe. Loeb Classical Library. Cambridge, Mass.: Harvard University Press, 1914.

Tacitus. *Histories.* 2 vols. Trans. C. H. Moore. Loeb Classical Library. Cambridge, Mass.: Harvard University Press, 1925, 1931.

The hymn "Blest Be the Tie That Binds" is by John Fawcett, 1782, and is found in *The Presbyterian Hymnal,* 438. Louisville, Ky.: Westminster/John Knox Press, 1990.

For Further Reading

Barrett, C. K. *A Critical and Exegetical Commentary on the Acts of the Apostles.* 2 vols. Edinburgh: T. & T. Clark, 1994.

Cadbury, Henry J. *The Book of Acts in History.* London: A. & C. Black, 1955.

————. *The Making of Luke-Acts*. New York: Macmillan Co., 1927.

Conzelmann, Hans. *The Theology of St. Luke*. New York: Harper & Row, 1960.

Haenchen, Ernst. *The Acts of the Apostles, A Commentary*. Philadelphia: Westminster Press, 1971.

Harper's Dictionary of the Bible. Paul J. Achtemeier, general editor. San Francisco: Harper & Row, 1985.

Lake, Kirsopp, and Henry J. Cadbury. *The Beginnings of Christianity*, part I: *The Acts of the Apostles*. Vol. 4: *English Translation and Commentary*. 1932. Reprint, Grand Rapids: Baker Book House, 1979.

Powell, Mark Allan. *What Are They Saying about Acts?* New York: Paulist Press, 1991.

Willimon, William H. *Acts*. Interpretation: A Bible Commentary for Teaching and Preaching. Atlanta: John Knox Press, 1988.